NO SURRENDER

NO SURRENDER

*Reflections of a Happy Warrior
in the Tory Crusade*

Hugh Segal

HarperCollins*Publishers*Ltd

http://www.harpercollins.com

First Edition

Canadian Cataloguing in Publication Data

Segal, Hugh
No surrender : reflections of a happy warrior in the Tory crusade

ISBN 0-00-255321-X

1. Conservative Party of Canada. 2. Segal, Hugh.
3. Canada - Politics and government - 1963-1984.*
4. Canada - Politics and government - 1984-1993.*
5. Canada - Politics and government - 1993-   .*
I. Title.

FC635.S4 1996   971.064   C95-932440-2
F1034.2.S4 1996

96 97 98 99 ❖ RRD 10 9 8 7 6 5 4 3 2 1

Printed and bound in the United States

To the Segals, Armstrongs, Dankners, Cossettes, Kaufmans, and Langlois, whose faith, heritage, and hard work helped build their parts of Canada in Quebec, New Brunswick, and Ontario in times of peace and times of war.

But for them, my wife, Donna, my daughter, Jacqueline, and I would not be here, nor would we share the Canada that the dreams of these families helped build and that has in turn given life to the dreams of millions.

It is with those great-grandfathers and great-grandmothers and with those who have come since that we must not break faith. Regardless of geography, language, or culture, we owe each other at least that much.

CONTENTS

ACKNOWLEDGEMENTS

THE IDEA OF MY WRITING A BOOK that reflects on my thirty years in the Conservative cause emanated, if in somewhat different form, from a lunch with editor Iris Tupholme of HarperCollins and an old friend and inscrutable literary agent and publisher, Nancy Colbert. At their invitation, we lunched in May 1993 to discuss a very different kind of book. As I had little interest in a kiss-and-tell tome—that would offend my senses of loyalty and confidentiality—Nancy and Iris suggested the "Mr. Smith Goes to Washington" genre. That would allow me to reflect, in a light way, on the astonishing insularities and peculiarities of a city and federal system that had long ago lost contact with much of the world most Canadians inhabited.

This, then, is a personal history, the party, its struggles, triumphs, and prospects amplified through the limited, sometimes narrow, and always personal prism of my own experiences in many varied roles. As such, the imperfections or inaccuracies reflect flaws in my own perception, recollection, or interpretation of what went on at any point in my partisan activities. None whose assistance or advice I acknowledge here bears any burden for my mistakes or misapprehensions.

Iris Tupholme, publisher and editor-in-chief at HarperCollins, was an endless source of advice, encouragement, and constructive criticism without which I could not have progressed. My editor, Greg Cable, an accomplished and often-published writer in his own right, was far more than an editor. The many long discussions we had on both content and form, the myriad of questions he forced me to address, the amazing editorial creativity he brought to restructuring and editing the often pedantic prose of a speechwriter and speech-maker (with all the foibles and weaknesses I brought to both those historical burdens) are utterly immeasurable.

At Gluskin Sheff and Associates, the investment counsel and portfolio firm with which I have been associated since August 1994, Ira Gluskin and Gerry Sheff have been more than encouraging about this effort and understanding about the time demands involved. At Queen's University, Keith Banting, director of the School of Policy Studies, was a constant source of encouragement and perspective. At various stages of the manuscript, Angie VanPeppen, Eva Ivanov, and Veronica (Vicki) Ryce worked long hours to assemble revisions and various drafts. Mark McQueen, now of the Bank of Montreal, and Katheryn MacDonald, now taking her MBA at the University of Toronto, both helped me remember and replenish experiences we had shared when in the service of Her Majesty and the prime minister between the fall of 1991 and the end of April 1993.

To the Hon. David MacDonald, United Church minister, a minister in the Clark government, and an MP from 1965 to 1980 for Egmont, P.E.I., I owe the gratitude one can never overestimate, that of having been given one's first chance.

To the Rt. Hon. Robert L. Stanfield, I owe the debt I can only describe as that owed a mentor whose intrinsic decency and moderation provided a rare glimpse of the leadership only wisdom can illicit.

To the Hon. William G. Davis, my debt is best described as that a young medical student might owe the seasoned practitioner who taught, through his own deeds, the true differences between theory and day-to-day medical practice; in other words, the difference between opposition and government.

To the Rt. Hon. Brian Mulroney, I owe the debt that a freshly minted junior officer owes a hardened field commander who, despite huge casualties and overwhelming odds, battled through to an honourable peace, defending his nation's basic battlefield interests and prepared to sacrifice even his own career in the larger cause. The battlefield was that of massive global economic change, liberalized trade flows, and the very unity of the country.

There are people who encouraged me in many different ways:

my brother Brian, whose common-sense support and unfailing encouragement saw me through the frequent dry writing spots; Stuart Fyffe of the Department of Political Studies at Queen's, who ran the Skelton Clarke Fellowship program; John Meisel, professor emeritus in that same department; Prof. George Perlin, who heads the Centre for Public Opinion Studies and who is surely among the finest political scientists anywhere; Dr. Tom Courchene, the John J. Deutsch professor of economics at Queen's and one of the brightest, most creative, down-to-earth and utterly unpredictable academics and policy analysts in the world; Shelley Pilon, who as a research assistant helped in many ways; David Warren, the bright, unfailingly decent, and most literate High Church Tory who, as a former editor-in-chief of *The Idler* magazine, offered good-humoured and inspired counsel about facing one's own intellectual demons head on.

And, of course, the most longsuffering of all, my wife, Donna, and my daughter, Jacqueline, who displayed the patience, good humour, and tolerance vital when a husband and father is obsessed with a manuscript when family activities should have priority. Jacqueline never failed to have a view: "I'll bet, if it's about the Tories, Dad, it's a real page-turner!" Sweet-spirited sarcasm runs in the family.

And I will mention my old friend Angel, the seven-year-old mildly arthritic Bouvier who never failed to tiptoe downstairs early in the morning or hang in loyally late at night when the manuscript made sleeping in or early to bed unfathomable luxuries. Her relaxed, if somewhat disengaged, company made it possible to read out entire chapters time and time again to a seemingly appreciative and attentive, if subdued, audience of one. In and of itself, not bad preparation these days for a Tory who still believes.

MAY 1991

MY THOUGHTS AS THE FAMILY DROVE home from the cottage the
third weekend in May were distinctly troubled. With Donna
at the wheel, and our daughter, Jacqueline, and Angel, the singing
Bouvier, fast asleep in the back of the van, I was left to ponder what
the next few hours might be like.

Earlier in the morning, I had received a call from Rick Morgan,
executive assistant to Prime Minister Brian Mulroney, to confirm that
I should arrive on a flight landing in Ottawa at seven that evening to
meet with the prime minister. It was a trip and an event to which I
was not looking forward.

As the terrain and the fast-food service centres of westbound
Highway 401 rolled past, I wondered how I had let myself get into this
situation. I reflected on how, no matter what transpired over the next
few hours, my relationship with the Conservative Party and the politics
of the country, and my view of my own strengths and weaknesses,
would never be the same. I thought about my family and how easily
good people become innocent hostages to events beyond their control
when the exigencies of public life invade and take up residence.

It occurred to me, as I free-ranged inside my head in search of
some obvious choices, that when parents die relatively early in one's
life, what a son or daughter misses most is not only sharing the grandchildren and the joys of the journey through life but also the good
old-fashioned, down-to-earth, uncontaminated parental advice and
wisdom that come from them knowing what they know of the

world and, more important, what they know of you. I missed that advice often, at no time more than right now.

My thought processes as we barrelled down the highway towards Toronto were similar to those I'd had almost exactly one year earlier. The summer of 1990 had begun with a call in June from Stanley Hartt, then Mulroney's chief of staff. He said I had better drop in to see him on my next trip to Ottawa, and I did. He then told me that I was the clear choice to be his successor. This was not something I wanted to hear. It had all kinds of implications for my family. My company had just made a major investment in the publishing and broadcasting field, which was taking more and more of my time, and it was an area I was very much enjoying. The last thing I needed was this kind of interruption.

I asked Stanley for time. Two weeks later, we met at the Le Cercle Universitaire and tried over dinner to discuss some of the requirements of the task. He was called away to the phone at least eight times. Despite this omen, I began to weaken to the notion of going to Ottawa. I found Stanley between the G7 summit in Houston and his brief holiday to inform him that if I were asked, I would not refuse the prime minister. I also said I'd be untroubled if I were not asked. He said he would pass that on.

When *The Globe and Mail* published a piece speculating on potential chiefs of staff and included my name, I heard through the grapevine that some people within the party who were troubled by my populism and Ontario-Quebec roots launched an intense campaign to scuttle the appointment. I also heard from ministers eager to campaign in support of my joining up. I encouraged them to disengage. The last thing anyone who got the job would want was a perception that he had campaigned for it. If someone else was chosen, I would have simply dodged the bullet, and that would not be a bad thing.

By August of 1990, the matter was becoming disruptive at home. We had decisions to make about school and the fall. At the end of the month, Stanley called. I don't know what he said to the prime minister, but to me he said, "I've got good news and better news for you. The good news is that the prime minister is very grateful for the fact you're prepared to serve. The better news is that he's chosen Norman Spector, who'll do a superb job."

I was delighted. I called Norman to wish him well, then took Donna out to dinner at a little place by our cottage and celebrated with a bottle of wine. I had, thank God, dodged the bullet.

I tried to recreate that year-old sense of relief as I focused on this latest bullet approaching fast with exactly the same trajectory. I talked with Donna about where this was all headed. We understood that where I come from, when a prime minister asks you to take on a responsibility, agreeing to meet for a discussion is tantamount to an agreement in principle. I was being approached to serve because Premier Robert Bourassa had, after Newfoundland Premier Clyde Wells quashed Meech Lake, decreed that in 1992, Quebec would hold a referndum solely on sovereignty. We understood I could never live with myself if the referendum came and went and Quebec and the country were lost, not if I had declined the chance to help in however insignificant a way. I would always hold myself unreasonably responsible for the failure to prevent a mortal wound to the country. I have, after all, always been pretty good at carrying around guilt for all sorts of the world's sins of omission and commission.

"Adding that guilt could cause you to gain another twenty or thirty pounds," Donna said.

After arriving back at our Toronto home and getting changed, I gave Donna and Jacqueline a kiss and Angel a scratch and headed for the airport. Donna, whose openness to the idea was tinged with the resignation of someone who reads tea leaves well enough but prefers coffee, said what she often says: "Listen with your head and let's see where that leads us before you let your heart occupy all the decision-making space." I am always struck by how right she always is.

On a Sunday-night plane from Toronto to Ottawa, it is inevitable that you bump into MPs and senators wending their way back to the nation's capital, and this flight was no different. I watched MPs going through their clipping files, correspondence, and papers utterly absorbed. I thought of the civil servants and their memos and briefing books, the interdepartmental committees, the special task forces, the parliamentary committees, the caucus subcommittees, and all the other spokes of inertia separating the outer rim of reality from the centre.

I thought of the intrigues at play in Ottawa—ministers jockeying for position in preparation for when and if Mulroney chose to step down, civil servants seeking one more appointment or career change for them or their colleagues during the pre-election period, extreme nationalists like Marcel Masse destabilizing the government every chance they could, moderate and decent nationalists who had become federalists, like Benoît Bouchard, trying to hang in. I thought of the burden of a collapsed ratification process around Meech Lake and the long tentacles of Trudeauist orthodoxy using Clyde Wells and Sharon Carstairs to destroy Meech, with Jean Chrétien's help, precipitating the present crisis and the government's problems. I thought of the sheer stupidity around the design of the GST, ensuring that no one could transact any business anywhere in this country without finding a reason to dislike the Tory government.

Flying over eastern Ontario, I looked down at the limestone, rivers, and canals, the bedrock farms, and the towns and villages where people had become alienated from a Conservative government they had supported in 1984, in part because Liberals had skilfully frightened seniors over the effect of free trade on pensions and had scared dairy farmers over its effect on milk prices. I thought of how Ontario Premier Bill Davis had said I had a duty at this moment in the history of the country and the party to be helpful. I thought of how long-time friend, decorated war hero, and Titan of Ontario Tory politics Eddie Goodman had argued that to think I could make a difference was the ultimate conceit.

I was met at Uplands Airport by a junior member of the Prime Minister's Office tour staff and driven to 24 Sussex Drive. I was informed the Mulroneys were in the process of moving to Harrington Lake for the summer and that he would be perhaps a little rushed, which didn't surprise me much.

When I got to 24, I waited in the back den, just beyond the main vestibule. The first time I had stood in that den overlooking Hull and the Ottawa River was on the eve of the final 1981 constitutional session, when Pierre Trudeau met first with Bill Davis and then subsequently with Richard Hatfield, premier of New Brunswick, to sort out the joint federalist strategy for the conference. I had been at 24 Sussex most recently at a dinner in honour of Davis. While Davis tickled the ivories, the prime minister sang, although he did not join in when Davis played his version of "What a Friend We Have in Jesus." The version was boogie-woogie, but still far too Methodist for an Irish-Catholic like Mulroney.

After about twenty minutes, the prime minister, wearing a sweater, came around the corner and said, "Hi, my friend, it's good to see you. Let's step out back here for a moment and look around."

It was a glorious evening. The sun was setting and the house provides a compelling view of the capital, with the French embassy, the British high commissioner's (John A.'s former residence, Earnscliffe, which if the British had any decency they would return), the inter-provincial bridge, and Parliament Hill itself all in view.

He said, "We don't get out here in the back as much as we'd like, you know. It's not really all that private."

It isn't private at all. Everyone from pleasure-boaters on the river to folks driving down the Rockcliffe Parkway to snooping photographers who park their cars at turns in the road just beyond the house can pretty well see into the backyard. Few homes in prime residential districts across the country have such little privacy.

Mulroney was relaxed, outgoing, and expansive, although he was feeling his way. We had not had a substantive discussion since the outbreak of the Gulf War. Then, he had called me and many others for opinions on how Canadian participation was being perceived and what anxieties were circulating on the street. His was a consultative skill unparalleled in Canadian history. Rather than be advised by a small, self-contained group, whether as a kitchen cabinet, a senior staff of officials, or a coterie of cronies, he would reach out by telephone to a broad range of Canadians, within the party and without, with all kinds of experience and backgrounds, seeking their independent views.

This was a great source of discomfort in the public service. The notion that a prime minister's information base about the country could be much broader and diversified than that which the public service could offer, with loyalty and determination, did not sit well with the Ottawa crowd.

As we moved in to dinner, I wasn't sure what I would hear and find. Would I see the self-aggrandizing, hyperbolic, vainglorious excess the media had led me to believe was at the core of this man? Would I see a self-centred politician too caught up in his own day-to-day problems to understand how difficult and treacherous the situation out in the country truly was? Would I meet someone who, when seeking an adviser, didn't have the ability to take any advice, a shibboleth the national media had created and which, after you had read it frequently enough, you were disposed to believe?

What I experienced was the frankest, most bare-knuckle self-assessment, assessment of the country, and assessment of the party, the opposition, the Bloc Québécois, and Reform I had ever heard from any source, all presented in a fashion so humble and direct as to make me wonder whether or not he was too down on himself to help. He understood why he was where he was in the polls. He did not try to diminish whatever personal responsibility he had for that circumstance, which included some elements of his style, things he had said, the unpopular decisions he had made on serious matters, and the way those decisions had been made. He had no illusions about the party's ability to descend into factiousness or about the battle necessary to keep the caucus and cabinet together. He had no illusions about what would befall the country if the referendum transpired in October of 1992 as Quebec's legislated plans provided for.

Over dinner, he said that from where he stood, his order of priority was, first, the country, then the party. When those matters had been addressed, he would reflect upon his own future. He made it clear that his priority for the country was to get beyond the Quebec referendum with either the bullet being taken out of the gun or the separation option being clearly trounced. As far as the party was concerned, he wanted to see it increase its standing in the polls, continue to raise money, reinvigorate itself through a policy process, and be in fighting trim for the next election.

He was not even responding to a question of mine when he spoke to the curiosity everyone felt about how long he could sustain the party leadership at 9 percent in the polls. He simply paused, looked at me directly, and said, "And look, my friend, I'm no John Diefenbaker. I'm a child of this party and I won't wait for anybody to ask the question or make the suggestion. When the time comes, what is in the party's interest will be what's in my interest. I will not superimpose my interest over that of the party."

A decade older than me, Mulroney had lived through the Diefenbaker–Camp battles, seeing them divide the party and create blood feuds that went on for decades. Living through them, largely on the side of Camp and those who wanted more democracy and accountability, he understood their corrosive effects.

What became apparent to me was that the easiest and most selfish thing he could do at that point in the party's history was to step aside, go back to the private sector, increase his income and privacy, and reduce his aggravation immensely. He would still be the only Conservative leader to have won back-to-back majorities since John A. Macdonald and would still be the only elected Conservative leader to hand over a government while in office. But that would have left the country's problem unaddressed. The country's problem was the 1992 Quebec referendum set after Meech by Robert Bourassa.

I didn't say much during dinner. As we came to the end, he offered me the position of Senior Policy Advisor and said, "Your help on the Constitution—your help on bringing the party into the policy process—would make a difference. I hope I can count on your help."

I told him I would, with his permission, meet with Chief of Staff Norman Spector in the morning, speak to Donna, and reflect on what taking the position would mean before coming to a decision.

He agreed, took me to the door, and asked Joe, one of the domestic staff, to drive me to the Château Laurier. Joe took the opportunity of the ride to tell me that Marshal Tito, who had died seven years previously, was a Russian plant, because otherwise he would have spoken Croatian more often and he never did, which meant that the real Tito was abducted when he went to Russia for surgery some years earlier. I thanked Joe for that information, went up to my room, called Donna to report in, and went to bed.

The next morning, I met with Spector, who was welcoming and friendly about the modalities, and I caught a plane home that afternoon.

In flight, I began to do the calculus in my head. The party was dismally low in the polls and likely doomed in the next election. The economy was in clear and determined recession. High unemployment was tearing the national fabric. The prime minister was singularly unpopular and unlikely to be able to run again, although in a strange way I felt he would be the most likely to hold the electoral coalition together as much as it could be held. Ministers were jockeying for position. The caucus was under attack from the Bloc in Quebec and Reform in the west.

The normal Ottawa antibody reaction to someone who was not of the civil service and who had not supported Mulroney in either of two leadership conventions would likely, at best, diminish any contribution I could make. I would hate being away from my family; I could not move them to Ottawa, crushing Donna's career and taking my daughter Jacqueline out of a school and a milieu she dearly loved.

My business interests were doing well and were just beginning to generate some leverage in shareholder value for the long haul. Clearly, I would have to sell all my commercial interests during a recession and reduce my family's net worth considerably. I would be joining the *Titanic* after it had hit several icebergs, and my family would certainly pay a price. I would be working in a hostile Ottawa completely disengaged from day-to-day reality.

My thoughts took shape, and as I took a cab from Toronto's airport the conclusion was inescapable. The personal costs would be too great and the financial cost enormous. The separation from my family would be far too painful. The cause was far too gone, as Eddie Goodman had wisely offered, and it would be a major conceit to think I could make a difference. The prime minister, while the most successful prime minister to lead our party since John A., was clearly facing overwhelming political obstacles that defied rational solution. I disliked Ottawa and the juggernaut nature of a civil service focused largely on its own needs.

As a Red Tory, I would not be comfortable with all of the government's policies and certainly not with some of the more extreme right-wing types in the caucus. All I could possibly achieve by joining up was to join those who would be blamed when the inevitable search for those who should be blamed began.

I had a happy family life, lived in a great neighbourhood, got a few holidays every year, and was enjoying my work as a Skelton Clarke fellow at Queen's University.

There could be only one answer.

I opened the front door to smell stir-fry for dinner. I found Jacqueline in the family room reading *Moby Dick* and Donna uncharacteristically home early from work.

"We held dinner, sweetie," she said. "How did the day go?"

"It was okay. I've thought about all the dislocation we'd go through and, frankly, how hopeless it all seems."

"And?" she said, betraying no emotion.

"On balance, I guess there are other ways to help."

"I understand that."

This all seemed so comfortable, reassuring, and balanced. It was so wonderfully reasonable and sane. We ate dinner and spoke of other things.

"Donna?"

"Yup?"

"It's the only country we have."

"Aren't you really saying that you think you should go? I really don't know how the Hugh Segal I know could live with himself if he put business first."

"This will cost us a lot, Donna. We will probably never, ever be rich, or even close to it."

She smiled that thousand-watt smile that has kept me alive, motivated, and hopelessly in love since the day we met. "And why would that matter more than doing what's right?"

I called the prime minister after dinner.

NO SURRENDER

1

FIRE IN THE BELLY

JOHN DIEFENBAKER CAME TO MY SCHOOL in 1962. I was a twelve-year-old student in grade seven, and his message, quite frankly, grabbed me by the throat.

Many people join political parties because of family tradition or deeply held convictions. Many are drawn to a party because of an issue that grinds their axe in a compelling way. My Tory credentials can claim no such noble parentage. I am a Tory because of John Diefenbaker.

When you grow up in a home where your father is a cab driver and many a month the decision was whether to pay the rent or pay the butcher or the druggist, because, God knows, there was no chance we were ever going to pay all three, you live with the perception that many opportunities in this world are closed to you. You live with the expectation that, for people who are poor, there are severe limitations in life.

My grandfather was a Menshavik in Russia before he emigrated to Canada. He supported Kerensky and the social democrats, who had a very short time in office and were not well liked by either the czar or the Bolsheviks. When the Bolsheviks took power in 1917, my grandfather put his finger to the wind and figured it was time to go. His home town, in the region between Odessa and Moscow, changed hands many times. Finally, he stole through Romania to Canada and, a few years later, sent for his wife and children, one of whom was my father. My father arrived in this country around 1920 or 1921, right in the middle of the Russian civil war.

A tailor by trade, Zaida (Grandpa) had a strong commitment to

Canadian democracy and to the freedom he had to earn a living, feed his family, be of a minority faith, and accomplish many other things, large and small, that he could never hope to accomplish in Russia. He became an organizer for the International Ladies' Garment Workers Union, leading strikes on the streets of Montreal, and was a strong supporter of the CCF and the NDP through all his sixty-two years in Canada. As an AFL-CIO kind of leftist, he hated the communists intensely. He saw them as people who would try to break up the Garment Workers' meetings with baseball bats because they knew that the success of free social-democratic trade unions would mean the end of the Communist Party as a meaningful force in post-depression Canada, which, in fact, is what transpired.

My father was a Liberal because the Liberals were in power when his wave of immigration came ashore and because the power structure in the Jewish community had strong links to the Liberal Party. Primarily because of the ethnic connection, my father had been a sectoral campaign manager for Milty Klein, a prominent MP in the downtown Montreal riding of Cartier.

Even members of the board of my parochial school, United Talmud Torah (or United Bible Study Academy), were heavily involved in the politics of the federal Liberal Party and the Quebec Liberal Party, although some had ties to the Union Nationale.

United Talmud Torah had two major purposes. It ensured that students had, beyond the general curriculum of the Protestant school board of Montreal, a full religious and linguistic curriculum focused on the Bible, commentaries on the Old Testament, and Hebrew language, literature, and history. Second, it would attract only people of one community of faith, which was an added benefit to parents who, in the tradition of first-generation minority groups all over North America, feared nothing more than the marriage of their children out of their faith.

UTT was a bit more worldly than other parochial schools, having many of its non-religious lecturers, English and French, coming in from McGill and Sir George Williams University. Talks by outside visitors were always a special event, and on the eve of the 1962 general election, Prime Minister John G. Diefenbaker came to address the student body and present a copy of his Bill of Rights, a beacon of decency, fairness, tolerance, and opportunity that was particularly well received in a school peopled largely by the children of immigrants.

Diefenbaker's speech that afternoon was the most compelling non-family event in my life to that point. At parochial school, you spend a good part of your time learning the history of the Jews as, rightly or wrongly, an oppressed people everywhere in the world. And here was Diefenbaker saying that he could have used his mother's maiden name of Bannerman to avoid discrimination on the Prairies and in law school and politics, but he hung in with Diefenbaker because that was the kind of Canada he wanted. He wanted a country where citizens didn't have to have a "Mac" or a "Mc" before their name to build some place for themselves in society. He spoke about a Canada that was open to all, a place of opportunity and freedom for people of all ethnic and religious backgrounds.

Dief's message portrayed the Conservative Party as a populist instrument for all those folks who fell outside the mainstream to find a way into the mainstream, whether they were fishers in the maritimes, small family farmers in eastern Ontario or the prairies, or small businesspeople struggling against the elites. Where they lived and what they did was irrelevant. Dief spoke for the people outside the system.

It was a fascinating message and it struck a chord that has made me embrace the more populist side of the party and of domestic politics ever since.

There was often a fair amount of political discussion around the dinner table at my home. I knew that my grandfather, especially, had no time whatever for the Conservative Party, seen at best as a bastion of the wealthy and those who oppressed others and at worst as an anti-Catholic, anti-Semitic, anti-French WASP enclave within Canada's political framework. That Friday night at the Sabbath dinner table, I told my family what Diefenbaker had said and how impressed I was both by the prime minister and with his message. I also said that I would support his local candidate in the riding of Mount Royal, a gentleman by the name of Stan Shenkman. Mount Royal had been Liberal forever. Alan Macnaughton, who had been a speaker of the House of Commons, was the incumbent Liberal candidate, had served in Parliament for some time, was quite prominent, and, all in all, was not a bad person.

My grandfather Benjamin Segal, who was a women's tailor in a factory in the garment business owned by someone in the community who would have been Liberal (they all were), said, "You can't do that. That's the bosses' party."

I said, "No, Zaida. The Liberals are the bosses' party. They're *your* boss's party."

To my proposal to work for Stan Shenkman, my father said, "Over my dead body." When you're twelve and your father speaks like that, you know you're on to something. That Friday night dinner began a long march under circumstances that served me extremely well in the future, namely enjoying the role of the underdog and standing up for the minority in a sea of hostility.

My mother, who simply wanted peace in the family, waded in. "Now look, Hughie. Let's be frank. What you should do is, you should write Mr. Diefenbaker and Mr. Pearson and Mr. Douglas and Mr. Thomson and ask them all to tell you why you should join their party." As always, hers was good advice, which I followed to the letter.

It was indicative of how badly organized Diefenbaker's office was that I received form letters and pamphlets from the NDP, Socreds, and Liberals. From the prime minister, I received a personally signed three-paragraph letter with a long list of reasons why I should join the Conservatives, along with old speeches of his about Quebec, with passages underlined.

My first thought was, "Is this real?" I smudged the signature. It was. All I could think was, "I come from a family of no political consequence. He has no idea who I am. But he actually found time to sign a letter like this to a kid."

During that period in history, Dief faced a fiscal crisis and a battle with the governor of the Bank of Canada, James Coyne, over who had the final say in monetary policy. History might say he should have spent much more time running the country and straightening out the economy, rather than writing to young people, and that misallocation of time may, in fact, have been one of his great weaknesses as a prime minister. But it was no weakness in the soul he brought to the political process.

Once the letter arrived, neither hypnosis nor sodium pentothal could have changed my fundamental position. I became a Conservative.

In the 1962 campaign, I went door to door campaigning with and for Stan Shenkman, whose slogan was "Stan's the Man." We wore bakers' hats and travelled about in a truck from neighbourhood to neighbourhood handing out free hotdogs. But the anti-Tory parents of Quebec had done their work. We would go into a park full of kids and no one would come near us. You know you're in deep doo-doo when you give away hotdogs and no one comes.

In that election the Conservative slogan was "Il n'y a pas d'erreur: Diefenbaker / You can't go wrong with Diefenbaker." I plastered my school books with these stickers, including the five Books of Moses, which we studied regularly. This was like sticking slogans on a hymnal, which was not considered a good thing to do. I was soon thrown out of class. For me, the incident became a substantial cause célèbre. My parents quickly sided with the teacher and the issue got wrapped up by a brown and broad apology on my part, but it became a very significant part of my self-definition.

Those were the days of the Diefenbuck and the Diefendollar, pegged at ninety-two cents American, which seemed then to be a huge collapse. The Grits gave out Diefenbucks every chance they could to underline what had happened to the economy, which stung Conservatives deeply. On Bay Street and places where Wallace McCutcheon and Donald Fleming had stood for integrity and fiscal probity, the notion that a Conservative government would have played a part in a currency crisis and a run on the dollar did more to affect the standing of the party within the business constituency than any other flaws, creating the kinds of wounds that fester, rarely heal, and, even after decades, can produce a faintly uncomfortable itch.

Diefenbaker argued for the notion that, in the end, it should be the democratically elected prime minister and cabinet who had the final authority over the economy. James Coyne took the contrary view, which has prevailed to this day. To me, at the age of thirteen, the Coyne affair became a symbol of the bureaucratic business complex shutting out people like Diefenbaker even when they were elected, because such people represented the riffraff, all those people who didn't work on Bay Street or St. James.

In the 1962 campaign, Dief just hung on with a minority. I watched him on TV as he came out of his railway car in Prince Albert with his sleeves rolled up to address the nation. I became intently focused on this one individual as the reflection of all the values that were meaningful to me. My young, idealised views of Diefenbaker have changed over the years, but in those days I was emotionally fixated on his message. Over time, the facts don't matter. The emotional commitment is fundamental.

I have measured every Conservative leader I have had a relationship with since against the fundamental Diefenbaker mould. They may not have advanced the policy in precisely the way Diefenbaker did or in similar terms, but they were always breaking the establishment hold on the country to bring about greater opportunity and empowerment for people who were left out. That has always been the emotional test: is this leader attempting to open up the mainstream for people who cannot now play for reasons that are not their fault? If the answer is "Maybe" or "I'm not sure," then I stand back and may not get terribly involved. If the answer is "Yes, that is what this candidate is about," that's a strong motivation for me to enlist in the cause, whatever the candidate's weaknesses or prospects might be.

The identification with Diefenbaker and his message became a means of self-realization, an opportunity for saying when I looked in the mirror, "His beliefs are part of who I am," which is important for a young person to do. Some people do it through sports, some through rock music, some through academic activity. For me, the path of self-definition became the Conservative Party, a blessing and a debt I can never repay.

I began to see the hold that the Liberal Party had on the establishment in the country and the extent to which people who aspired to the establishment felt they had to be Liberals. It became a self-fulfilling prophecy. It was not hard to build a strong sense of the Liberal Party as always being the party of the established view and of the wealthy or those on the make, while the Conservative Party spoke for everyone else. I saw Diefenbaker and the Conservatives as the voice of a fundamental truth, speaking of a more open society where the old strictures of class, bigotry, and intolerance did not apply.

The most prominent person my family seemed to know was an accountant who had been a Liberal bagman of some sort. My parents asked him to be the toastmaster for the luncheon following my bar mitzvah. Having had a little too much to drink, he stood up and declared, "Before we begin this wonderful repast, I have a few words I'd like to say."

An hour and ten minutes later in the hot October synagogue basement, my father, who suffered from high blood pressure, was fast asleep at the head table. The rest of the crowd was more than a little fidgety, interested only in getting on to lunch. I knew that when—if—I ever delivered my bar mitzvah speech, no one would care to hear even one-tenth of it. This helped my understanding of what Liberals were about: occupy all the territory and leave no room for the common folk, even if you're an invited guest yourself. The experience fed into my general view of Liberals as pompous, self-centred people without substance.

I soon began to write long pieces for local community newspapers, attacking those in the community who become "cap in hand" Liberals manipulated by the old Liberal ward heelers and unable to think for themselves. Every attack on Diefenbaker and every instance when the Montreal establishment supported the Liberals, which was always, fed my view of why he was right. The newspapers in Montreal were horrifically Liberal. I wrote letters to the Montreal *Star*, a terribly Grit paper, defending Diefenbaker and attacking its pro-Pearson and pro-establishment editorials.

All teenagers attempt to establish some measure of individuality and set themselves apart from their parents, older people generally, and from the establishment. It may not strike many people today that being a Conservative is an anti-establishment thing to do, but in Montreal in the early sixties, it was about the most anti-establishment thing anyone could do. To be English-speaking and a Conservative in Montreal was to be a member of the smallest minority conceivable, save one, which was to be English-speaking and a Conservative in the Montreal Jewish community. It was difficult to know which group was smaller, Jews in the Conservative Party or Conservatives in the Jewish community.

The party and the importance of politics generally became a badge of honour. I played hockey for the Ponsard Hockey League in the west end of Montreal. As I skated around in my number 9 Chicago Blackhawks sweater with Conservative stickers on it, other kids would say, "Who cares? This is hockey. It doesn't matter." But it does matter. It may be a conceit to think that it matters and it may be a worse conceit to think that your own involvement can make a difference. But if you begin to take the position that your involvement should be determined by what is convenient, you begin to lose some of yourself.

The emotional commitment and my belief in the party were fleshed out by Diefenbaker's nationalism, which became stunningly apparent around issues like the Bomarc missile question in 1963, when Dief defended Canadian sovereignty and stood up against those who said we had to have American nuclear warheads on our missiles in North Bay and elsewhere.

This was the time of Castro, the October Cuban crisis, Khrushchev, bomb shelters, and people keeping canned food in the basement. Diefenbaker appeared on TV to speak about "these dangerous and serious times." One Saturday morning, I heard my first air-raid alert, the siren screeching from the roof of a school across a park at the end of our street.

Diefenbaker tried to find a Canadian point of purchase on the issue. Subsequently, it emerged that there was a great debate around the cabinet table as to whether our troops should be put on alert and whether Americans could fly over our territory. Like most Canadians, I was hopeful that Mr. Kennedy would prevail on the missile question, even though it began a policy of paranoia towards Cuba that has survived nine presidents since. Fidel is still in charge and Dief, having tried to find some other kind of policy, is still considered essentially cracked.

History has proved Diefenbaker correct, but his was not the establishment view. The establishment view was that the American military complex had some requirement of us and it was our job to agree. Many people, like the minister of national defence, Doug Harkness, took it as a matter of personal honour that since we had a defence-sharing agreement with the Americans, we should pull together when the time came. Others around the table, notably Howard Green, the minister of external affairs from British Columbia, took a different view. I would have been very much of the Diefenbaker-Green view. In the end, world problems are rarely solved through a testosterone-charged confrontational approach.

The Kennedy administration decided that any Canadian government unprepared to put its military sovereignty at the disposal of General Norstad, engage in high-crisis games of diplomatic and military chicken with the U.S.S.R., or reserve to itself the decision about whether Canada would be a nuclear nation simply had to go.

Short of stuffing ballot boxes themselves, Kennedy's people did everything else to bring the Diefenbaker administration down. Lou Harris, the Democratic Party's pollster, was lent to a grateful Liberal Party. The American military held briefings in the basement of the Ottawa embassy for Canadian journalists. Key U.S. publications with broad distribution in Canada savaged Diefenbaker, with a photograph of him on the cover of *Newsweek* that made him look crazy, which, given his jowly shakiness and piercing eyes, wasn't too difficult to do. Corporate U.S. defence-industry financial support flowed to the Liberal campaign.

Yet despite all that, the Diefenbaker populist link was so deep that even with high unemployment, currency problems, and massive internal dissension, Liberals could only squeeze out a minority in 1963. The Liberal leader and American choice, Mike Pearson, took two elections to even get into power.

In my youthful exhuberance I could easily believe that the Bomarc missile controversy was a CIA-driven campaign to destroy the Conservative campaign and the party. The Conservatives' nationalist stand garnered precious little support from the cultural community and the media, aside from the distinguished writing of George Grant. His *Lament for a Nation* had an indelible effect on me, encapsulating the difference between the Tory vision for Canada and the continentalist, mechanistic, commercialist view.

All this became part of a piece. Given the crisis and the good relationship between Kennedy and Pearson, Liberals were lackeys to American foreign policy. The animosity between the establishment and Diefenbaker and the quiet brokerage routine that served as an excuse for not standing up and being counted all fit neatly. I didn't have to be a wild-eyed conspiracy theorist to come away with the conclusion that Dief was all that stood between some measure of Canadian identity and the absorption of the country by Yankee commercial and defence interests.

The more Diefenbaker was ridiculed, the more he was attacked, the more passionate I became. I developed a youthful and intense distrust of Peter C. Newman because of his book *Renegade in Power*, which I saw as the simple hand of Yankee imperialism operating through Newman to destroy the Conservatives by courting the feelings of Liberal Bay Street and the Liberal business, academic, and intellectual elites. We were the only ones defending Canada's genuine national interests, just as John A. Macdonald had done. The Americans, and their media, aided and abetted by sometime nationalists like Newman, became agents of a broad, unspoken conspiracy to pillory and destroy John Diefenbaker.

This fire in the belly gave me a hyperactive interest in public affairs. I subscribed to *Hansard*, which might be considered slightly perverse for a fourteen-year-old, and read it avidly. Thank goodness Parliament wasn't televised then; I would have watched so much of it I would never have made it out of high school. I had to be satisfied with *Quentin Durgens MP*, a popular CBC show in which Gordon Pinsent played a great crusader out to break the grip of the powerful on behalf of the little guy. The program never made clear what his politics were—I always thought he was a Maritime Conservative or perhaps a Tory from Ontario—but his crusading passion seemed to correspond with Diefenbaker's populism. Thankfully, he lacked Diefenbaker's capriciousness, insensitivity to the collective process of governing, and erratic nature.

As 1963 bled into 1965, there was a notion in the air of the Grits trying to downplay the monarch, remove the Union Jack from the flag, and even remove the royal escutcheon from mailboxes across Canada. I was appalled. In my parochial school, the Queen's picture always held a place of honour at the front of the class and I always took to heart the words of my grades five, six, and seven teacher, Mrs. Adesky, that the monarchy meant we were all equal under the Crown and before the law.

I was a tremendous nationalist, and my room was festooned with flags. In the Great Flag Debate of 1965, everyone in Quebec, by and large, was for the new flag the Liberals proposed. Every car and cab sported on its bumper and aerial either the Pearson pennant (a sprig of three maple leaves between two blue bars) or the red and white single maple leaf design. I rode to school on my brother Brian's hand-me-down bike with Red Ensigns fastened to the handlebars, which was an act of some courage in those days.

The Conservative identification played a big part in selecting the courses I took in my high school—Herzliah, a secondary extension of UTT—and in the extracurricular activities I engaged in. I entered speaking contests and often won, speaking out for what I saw as a Conservative struggle against a Liberal establishment.

It became quite a joy to be a Conservative in Quebec because our fortunes had gone in the tank by Diefenbaker's second election go-round with Pearson and headed straight downhill from that moment on. The loneliness of isolated righteousness and decency is an incomparable comfort when the establishment mob sleeps soundly elsewhere. Aided by the perception that Liberals were perpetually in power, I found it easy to assimilate the notion of a Liberal establishment awash in its own corrupt juices. I could dine out on it with some easiness.

Herzliah had a model parliament, in which I led the Conservative charge, although the party that ran for office was called the Independent Conservative Party. At the age of fifteen, I was convinced that the Conservatives nationally were far too left-wing. (I went through my neo-conservative period, but I improved once I passed puberty.)

The party ran third out of three in the first election, second out of three in the second, and won in the third election, which was good because that was my year to graduate.

The notion of running against the mainstream for a political party with no roots in the community but one that was clearly right on all the issues that mattered was compelling. I campaigned amongst the students, putting forth the view that the party was attractive not because it reflected old wealth or was an instrument of grand historic tradition but rather because it represented the bravado of Macdonald building the country, taking on the powerful interests, building the railway, confronting the Americans, and shaping half a continent. It represented the bravado of Diefenbaker having the temerity to stand up to the Americans in 1962–63. (Many have since written that his temerity was really designed to cover cabinet divisions and his own incompetence as prime minister, but I had no such perspectives as a teenager and am relatively unprepared to accept such notions now.)

To me, the party was the instrument of freedom and justice. This view was immensely helped when, after 1963, we entered a period of perpetual opposition. There is nothing that deepens the sense of sanctimony, self-righteousness, determination, and nobility than the absolute knowledge that the risk of forming a government may never befall you.

In Quebec politics, I had a strong view that the Union Nationale was trying to embody some kind of fundamental economic expansionism while trying to find a balance between legitimate Quebec powers under the constitution, where the province had every right to be sovereign, and legitimate French-Canadian aspirations for some fairness and decency in their own province, where they frankly weren't treated terribly well.

I could identify comfortably with Daniel Johnson Sr. and Jean-Jacques Bertrand, who first spoke of free trade between the provinces and with the United States. I became *un jeune Unioniste*, among whom there were few in English Montreal, except for Peter White, Conrad Black, and one or two others. Being much younger than they were, I wasn't as heavily involved or significant, but I knocked on doors in the Montreal riding of D'Arcy-McGee for the Union Nationale candidate, another decent soul who lost his deposit. Many people—sometimes Jews, sometimes Greeks, sometimes Italians—slammed doors in my face because they didn't have the time or tolerance for the same nationalism they would have thought quite appropriate if their own heritage were concerned.

The upset victory for the forces of light represented by Johnson and the Union Nationale in 1966 and the speed with which the new government moved to provide full funding for all religious schools constituted a historic coming together of events that could not but deepen my sense of moral superiority and political determination. In all this non-conformity I was encouraged by my headmaster, Arthur Candib, whose bemused chuckle betrayed a healthy disdain for all things political.

I took that sense of superiority to the 1967 federal party convention as a "Youth for Dief," consumed by a paramount hatred for people like Dalton Camp and his henchmen, among them MP David MacDonald from Prince Edward Island, who identified with Camp on the other side of the question. There weren't many youths supporting the Chief, and I was so overwhelmed that I moved with deft acuity from supporting Diefenbaker in the early going, to, after Diefenbaker withdrew, siding with Duff Roblin on the last ballot. Zero for two became a predictable convention result for me.

Running for high-school parliament, knocking on doors, and carrying the message to the unconverted were thrilling, but the part of the process I found most compelling was that you had to stand and be counted. A young person looks at adults—parents, relatives, teachers—and sees them making compromises all the time. They compromise about family relationships, they compromise at work, in their personal relationships, and on the plans they would like to execute but can't. But once you stood up and said you were a Conservative, there were no compromises. Once you knocked on doors, helped someone run for office, served in a committee room as youth canvass chairman, or ran for office yourself, you were being counted. The great thing about that was that you could say to yourself, "I may be defeated. The party and the cause may be defeated. But taking a stand is better than trying to avoid an issue or shilly-shally your way through it."

The great thing about being a Conservative at that time, and indeed right up to 1984, was that it was very character-building. The notion of caring, trying, and then losing was the fundamental experience. There were no moral victories. There was just regular defeat.

Through the Diefenbaker years and into the first year of the Stanfield leadership, the Conservative allegiance became not only an emotional attachment of substance but also a means of defining myself as part of a group in society. Conservatives were in short supply not only in Montreal's ethnic communities but in ethnic communities across the country, although Conservatives had been in power for such a long time in Ontario, with such people as Allan Grossman, Eddie Goodman, John Yaremko, Lincoln Alexander, and others involved in the process, that I could actually go to meetings in Ontario and meet people of diverse cultural backgrounds who were Conservatives. There wouldn't be lots, but there would be some.

All through high school and university, I went to Young Conservative meetings across the country, meeting wonderful people from every kind of religious and economic background. Some were Conservatives for the same reasons I was; some had other reasons. But I began to get a strong sense of family across the country. Over time, the party became another family and the connection became part of growing up. The Conservative Party seemed one of those instruments by which you could become part of the broader world because it couldn't care less about your religion or background. All it cared about was whether you had something to offer and whether you were prepared to put your shoulder to the wheel and make a contribution.

While at high school in February of 1965, my father, Morris Jack Segal, passed away at the age of fifty-four. He had been a caring and wonderful father, making up for his lack of education, financial acumen, or success with a warmth and wrap-around affection that I've never forgotten. His world had been one of uphill battles, financial setbacks, and absolutely no breaks at all. His struggle against unemployment and ill health in the days before medicare and UIC remind me always of what too many face day to day. When my father passed away, our financial situation at home became more stable (he was a great success as a father but a disaster as a businessman). And the Conservative Party became an endearing and enduring part of my life.

As I finished high school, what I wanted to do most was be the candidate in the riding of Mount Royal, where I lived, against Pierre Trudeau. I had no illusions of winning, nor did I believe my candidacy would bring any measure of fame or fortune. But boy, could I stand up for the Conservatives against him. Boy, could I articulate all that was wrong about the Liberals' overly centralist, bureaucratized, insensitive, top-down approach to public policy and the contempt people like Trudeau had for honourable and average people, soon to be revealed in "Why should I sell your wheat?" and other *bon mots*. Boy, could I speak for the outsider. That I was many years his junior and that many would question my bona fides because in 1968 I was only eighteen years old and just able to vote would have been perfect. I spent much time visiting with Barney London, the president of the riding's PC Association, arguing my case. In the end, they ran a local TV actress, Huguette Marleau, who, all things considered, was probably a better candidate.

But even being able to contemplate that kind of prospect kept my fire going during high school. That I could not only lose but maybe lose my deposit made the prospect even better, because I would be doing it for the absolutely right reasons. I would be running for Parliament to make a case about what was wrong and what could be fixed and about how the government was insensitive to people like the unemployed and how the regions were being disenfranchised at the centre by Liberal bureaucratic policies and their "father knows best" approach. The race struck me as a wonderful opportunity. It would have been a battle of no significance to Mr. Trudeau—contemptuous would have been his response—but of great significance to me.

People tend now to look at political parties in terms of what they see on television: the leader, the spokesperson, the conflict, the parliamentary debate. All that is just the thin shell around the outside of the egg. Inside, there are relationships between people who are volunteers in a common cause, who have put their shoulders to the wheel and lost, who have made foolish mistakes in public, and who have seen their reputations trashed or enhanced. That bond becomes very strong. It can lift you out of a sense of defeat after you suffer a tremendous political setback. You can share a gallows humour with each other in the face of setbacks because you've been through them so often before. Those experiences give you the ability to do battle for causes that, by all apparent evidence, look overwhelmingly lost.

But the warrior doesn't think about winning or losing, only about whether the battle is right and whether there is any other place he would rather be or should be. Accountants and bank managers don't jump for joy at that kind of impractical assessment, but it sure helps when you put your head on the pillow at night. You can say to yourself, "That is where I should have been. I would have liked to have won. I didn't. But better to have done that than to have said it's just kind of inconvenient."

As a young person, that's a wonderful torch to carry. Young Conservatives meeting in Ottawa. Policy discussions. Political debate. It was all great stuff, not better than sex but, on occasion, comparable.

2

LOSS OF INNOCENCE

HAVING GROWN UP AS A YOUNG Conservative not part of Montreal's anglophone Liberal establishment, I knew there was a fundamental reality called French Canada I would not come into contact with in the anglophone ghettos. In Quebec in those days, anglophones could proceed through the better part of their professional lives almost completely in English. I knew viscerally that this was unconstructive, so I looked carefully at my post-secondary options with a view to establishing contact with the "other" reality.

I chose to attend the University of Ottawa. Among its many benefits, it offered courses in English and French, and you could write papers in your mother tongue until your proficiency in the other language increased. It also had one of the most renowned French-language history faculties in the country. Its English-language faculty was pretty good too. They offered entirely different views of Canadian history, but one of the great attractions of the place was that students had the opportunity to live both views on campus.

The late sixties was a fascinating time, and Ottawa U. was very much a microcosm of the country. Among the student body were English and French, people from east and west, people from small towns and large cities, students of the social sciences and of the heavy sciences, medicine, and law. The campus was essentially divided politically, with a hard-line sovereigntist, hard-left crowd having a dominant voice in the student government. In 1968, universities around the world were in turmoil. In this country, the Canadian Union of

Students was increasingly radical, and Ottawa was in the vanguard of the CUS movement.

When I arrived in Ottawa, driven down by my oldest brother Seymour, who, along with my brother Brian, lent me the money for my first term's tuition and rooming house, I knew no one. I had no family in the city to offer support or a friendly hand as I faced this new experience. But it helped my confidence to know I could join the Conservative Club and within three or four days have two or three friends I would not otherwise have. The small Conservative Club at Ottawa U. consisted of Jim Harbick, John Hoyles, Maureen McTeer, Bill Webb, and me. We all became involved in the Debating Society and became active in federal and provincial politics.

I became involved with Conservative federal politics in late 1968 and early 1969, after the Nigerian civil war broke out. Two MPs, the Reverend David MacDonald, a Conservative from Egmont riding in P.E.I. and minister of the United Church, and Andrew Brewin, a New Democrat from Toronto, travelled to Africa to draw attention to what the Nigerian administration was doing to the Ibos, the Christian community in the breakaway state of Biafra. The Commonwealth generally supported the Nigerian central government. Pierre Trudeau, when asked about the serious humanitarian issue, said, in classic Trudeau fashion, "Where's Biafra?"

When David came back from Biafra, he spoke on campus at a meeting sponsored by the Young Conservatives. He spoke about the larger responsibility we have to not sit silently when these sorts of things take place, tying Biafra's experience to the Holocaust and other horrific travesties. This was a critical moment for me, in that I began to see the other side of the Conservative Party. Yes, there was the populist, fiery Diefenbaker side I had been reared on, but there was also a Red Tory side, which was compassionate, worldly, and humane. I began to get the sense of how broad the party was and how different the views were within it, all of which made it much more interesting.

In my first year on campus, students began talking about how many of the people in the student government were consumed with left-wing ideology. They regularly read literature coming out of Cuba and engaged in every kind of anti-imperialist activity. But, meanwhile, the student government wasn't doing much with the students' money that was actually for the students. So in the spring of 1969, a group of independents ran for student government to offer a clear alternative. A Liberal law student, Allan Rock, who had been a "Youth for Hellyer" activist in 1968 and was active on campus in the Law Society, ran for president.

Three English-speaking candidates, including me, ran for the vice-presidency, along with one francophone candidate, Denis Monière, now a prominent sovereigntist academic. On a campus that was essentially half francophone, half anglophone, the francophone should have won. But my group put together an interesting campaign around fundamental and deadly serious academic issues, and I soon found myself on the student union executive with president Allan Rock.

We set to work redressing the distorted priorities of the previous council, focusing intently on student needs, with the odd nod to the cultural imperatives of the day. During our time in office, Allan went down to Montreal to coax John Lennon out of his "peace" bed with Yoko Ono and dragooned him into coming to the campus to impart his wisdom to the students. In the spring of 1970, Allan chose not to run again, and I became student council president after a close two-way race.

During these two years, I had the chance to attend many Conservative meetings, both national and provincial. By the time I arrived at university I had already developed some sense of the gaps across the country that a national party had to bridge; I began to understand that becoming obsessed with single issues such as the Diefenbaker–Camp blood feud was the ultimate self-indulgence and conceit. The real issue was, could anyone build a national coalition around a series of essentially Conservative principles that reflected the will of a country to work together in a parliamentary system for specific policies?

It was an exciting time to be a Conservative. There was great ferment in the party, which Bob Stanfield encouraged. In 1969, he spoke at a conference in Niagara-on-the-Lake in favour of a guaranteed annual income, not as a left-wing or right-wing proposition but as a constructive way to replace the multiplicity of welfare, unemployment insurance, and other programs, which have never been terribly successful. His proposal would have dealt with dignity and self-respect for people, working or otherwise, who lived beneath the poverty line either by virtue of some handicap or a simple lack of jobs. The proposal was quite radical in its day and didn't go very far, but it could have been typified either as a Red Tory or as an ultimate neo-conservative response to the plethora of overlapping, uncoordinated, inefficient social welfare instruments that were, and are, wasteful and unproductive.

Around the same time, David MacDonald and I organized a small gathering at an Oblate Fathers' retreat on Little Whitefish Lake in the Gatineaus. Our purpose was to look at whether we could find a definition of "conservative" that broke out of traditional right-left rigidities. We came up with the notion of a kind of communitarian conservative option. We made the case that the Conservative Party should be active on social and economic issues on the streets between elections and that we should be a force for good, whether in government or not. Moving beyond the political party as just an electoral machine struck some people as strange, and we had some long debates. Stanfield didn't come to the meeting, but he was aware of it, and David kept him briefed.

What was a defining moment for me came when I found myself at the retreat doing dishes and washing pots and pans with a fascinating group of people. Nate Nurgitz, a lawyer from Winnipeg and the party's first vice-president from the west, Michael Meighen, a young lawyer from Montreal and grandson of a prime minister, Flora MacDonald from Cape Breton Island and the political studies department at Queen's, Roy McMurtry, then a lawyer in Toronto, Murray Coolican, who was on Stanfield's staff and the son of the chairman of the Ottawa-Carleton regional government, Jean Chevrier from Quebec, Rudy Dalenbeck, an agricultural economist from Macdonald College, Jeanne Carmichael, and Frank Tierney, a professor of English at Ottawa. I got a sense of the kind of family the party could be from east to west, and how the need to find some room for the party between elections was fundamental.

I also got a sense of how political cultures across Canada differed, the difference, naturally, being most emphatically pronounced in Quebec, where our organization was an amalgam of the old Union Nationale plus hangovers from the Diefenbaker period. There were always one or two people in Quebec who were of the view that the best of all worlds was a Conservative government without any seats in Quebec, so they could be the kingpins and not have elected people in the way. In the southern United States, such people used to be called Post Office Republicans, active Republicans who wouldn't work too hard. Democrats would sweep those states, but if a Republican captured the White House, then local Republicans got all the appointments with no elected people like congressmen or senators to muddy the waters. There were one or two Post Office Conservatives in Quebec.

But the major difference, which could be sensed both from party meetings and from life at Ottawa U., was that for the Québécois, the view of the state was quite different than it is in the Anglo-Saxon world. The view is that the state is the collectivity, and the collectivity is the storehouse of intellectual and material resources. Anyone has a right—in fact, a duty—to relate to that storehouse in some fashion that benefits his or her town, region, family, business, or industry. This is a very Gallic approach, found in France today as it is in Quebec, but not found in English Canada even during the height of the post-war government initiatives. This is not a character flaw nor evidence of any venality on the part of Quebeckers. It is simply a different historic structure with respect to the role of government, the governor, the *ancien régime*, and the state.

There is, however, a truly dark side to the power of the state, and it was revealed in October 1970 when Pierre Trudeau and his minister of justice, John Turner, brought in the War Measures Act. Armoured personnel carriers moved troops around our campus, making an intimidating show of force. Students and faculty who were members of René Lévesque's Parti Québécois were detained for no apparent reason. Offices were raided by well-meaning but essentially ill-informed police. Membership lists were taken.

In the Student Union Council headquarters, the PQ offices were on the same floor as the offices of the Young Progressive Conservatives, the Young Liberals, and various other political and interest groups. Two police officers came in and said, "We'd like to look through your building."

I said, "Sure."

"You can accompany us if you want, sir."

"That'd be great. I'll go along."

The building also housed the photography club, the campus newspapers, and the ombudsman's office. On the wall by the door of the photography club there was a poster, fairly common on campuses in those days, of an attractive young woman in a wet T-shirt. One officer called out to the other, "Hey, Harry. They've got better than a couple of 38s in here." The other officer ran over, thinking a gun had been found. They then shared a classic constabulary guffaw.

I said to myself, "These are the folks Pierre Trudeau has sent to determine which freedoms apply?"

These were cops used to sorting out domestic disputes, handing out tickets for double parking, and doing whatever else beat cops do, and here they were trying to figure out what constituted a political threat to the country. There was no roughing up and no breaking of doors; they could not have been more polite. But this was a sad state of events.

Members of the PQ on campus were detained for questioning, some for more than a day. I heard later that John Robarts was terribly offended when he found out that, while essentially enforced in Quebec, the act applied to the whole country and could have been been used just as easily to round up dissident students at York. No one to my knowledge was beaten or manhandled in any way and no one conveniently disappeared as might have happened in countries like Argentina, but it became clear that even in a society as fundamentally kind and decent as our own, you can find yourself in difficulty, mostly unwittingly, if you give the wrong kinds of power to police officers and soldiers not trained to deal with complex legal situations.

I called Bob Stanfield's office and spoke to his appointment secretary, Murray Coolican, about the detained students. Stanfield raised questions in the House, asking the solicitor-general why they were being held, only to get the standard response of "I want to thank the Leader of the Opposition for the question. I'll look into the matter."

Coming only two years after the world watched Russian tanks rolling through the streets of Prague, the army deployment in Ottawa engendered a strange feeling indeed. Naturally, not everyone shared the concern. The campus generally was engaged to the extent that any campus can be. The vast majority of students anywhere are not involved in student politics. They're involved in finishing their papers and getting through their exams. Maybe 10 percent of the student body became really involved. Students in the social sciences department organized a huge rally and invited Pierre Vallières and other such chaps to speak, although I begged the social sciences president not to provoke anyone.

There were no marches on the issue. People sensed that a march could bring out the troops and we could be into an entirely different situation. There was no will on anyone's part to promote that idea, although some on the more radical left would not have minded a confrontation for classic dialectic class purposes, perhaps creating a Kent State North. The Marxist-Trotskyite strain was very strong on campus. In some people's minds, the strain often rolled into the more extreme separatist position and the "struggle" against the establishment of the university and the Oblate Fathers who founded it. Both the English- and French-language newspapers on campus had to struggle with the issue of whether to print an FLQ manifesto.

The act said there were certain things citizens of Canada could not do, such as meet in groups of more than three or discuss pressing matters of the day. Our student council met anyway. A leading francophone radical, who was president of the Science Graduate Students Association, made a motion endorsing the FLQ manifesto and condemning the government for the imposition of the act and I knew this would produce swarms of police on the campus the next day, arresting students for no apparent reason and generally ruining people's lives. As council president, I argued that the motion was more than a touch foolhardy. We could express our concern, but to condemn the government and embrace the FLQ manifesto struck me as wholly irresponsible. But the resolution passed.

The next morning, I held a press conference. I said, "Unless that resolution is reversed at a special meeting I'm calling under section such-and-such of the constitution, I resign as council president." The threat didn't have much effect, but we called the meeting, got out our troops, and reversed the motion by a two-thirds majority. We then passed a resolution calling on both sides to work within the normal processes of the law, to respect civil liberties and human rights, and to set aside violence.

Students from civil and common law joined with me for an information session for all students about what the War Measures Act meant. We gathered in an auditorium for a meeting that was civil but very tense, chaired by a respected common law student and dear friend, Hugh G. Doyle. It gave me the sense that things that mattered greatly in life could easily be ripped apart by something like the War Measures Act. Normal distinctions like Conservative or Liberal and French or English don't add up to much when dissent is crushed by force.

I realized that it is a mistake to assume that Canadians intrinsically respect minority rights and civil liberties and are prepared to go to battle for them. If the waterhole gets smaller, the animals start to look at each other in a different way, which we saw with the Japanese and the other internees during the Second World War. We can become uncivil to each other *in extremis*.

For the vast majority of Canadians, the War Measures Act was not a personal threat and they were prepared to give *carte blanche* to the government in view of the alleged facts.

Maintaining order and stability is fundamental to maintaining any kind of genuine freedom, which makes me more of a Tory than a conservative, because Tories put order ahead of freedom. Looking at the October Crisis, the Winnipeg General Strike, or even the North-west Rebellions, a fundamental lack of order produces a context in which the most extreme and inhumane things tend to transpire.

Canadians have a noble commitment to order, but the flip side is that there is little evidence to suggest that they have as great a commitment to democracy as the British and Americans have. There has rarely been any significant outcry against abuse of authority, whether through the use of troops against striking unionists in Winnipeg, the use of a quasi-military force against strikers in southwestern Ontario, or the imposition of the War Measures Act by Pierre Trudeau.

Imagine an American president, faced with a secessionist movement in Texas, suspending clear across the country all the civil liberties and rights protected by the U.S. constitution. There would be uproar in the streets and a move for impeachment for violating democratic principles. Yet here in Canada in October 1970, four hundred people were arrested without charge in the middle of the night, held in jail for days with not one of them ever charged with so much as double parking, with police officers deciding who was a danger to the state, and with civil liberties—including the right to free assembly, the right to free speech, and other fundamental rights—suspended across the land.

This was bad government, pure and simple. It was panic on the part of Bourassa and, in my view, the worst kind of fascist totalitarianism on the part of Trudeau, Bryce Mackasey in Labour, and Marc Lalonde, the prime minister's principal secretary, a horrific jack-boot approach to their own people they felt comfortable taking because they had been elected in 1968 on the premise that they were going to "handle" French Canada. They were encouraged by the worst anti-French bigots outside Quebec because Trudeau stood with courage the day of the St.-Jean-Baptiste Day parade dodging flying bottles. Their mandate was to handle "those people," and if that meant calling out the army, so be it.

Certainly it was unacceptable that law enforcement agencies were unable to deal with FLQ cells that did, in fact, murder a minister of the Crown and did endorse the broad use of bombings, shootings, and other acts of violence to achieve political ends. It betrayed a lack of police intelligence on the ground and a lack of police capacity, maturity, and judgement in Quebec that we have yet to outgrow. The idea of British diplomats being kidnapped, cabinet ministers being abducted and murdered, and terrorists getting air time on radio is not the sense of order we believe in. But how order is achieved and what force is used when there is a breakdown of order are the measures of civility in society.

The War Measures Act was not the only vehicle available to the authorities. Marshal law could have been imposed. The army could have been invited in, as it was in Oka when the police were clearly overwhelmed. Any premier has the right under the constitution to request military aid to the civil power, but in that circumstance there still *is* a civil power, there still *is* a constitution, a Bill of Rights, *habeus corpus*, due process, and the law. All of that was wiped away, allowing police to arrest people without having any idea what they were to be charged with or without any reasonable suspicion of wrong-doing. They were arrested because they were on lists.

Bryce Mackasey implied in the House "that they would divulge the information that made them do it." To date, scholars have found nothing to substantiate even the hint of an insurrection. It is now commonly believed that the letters sent by Premier Bourassa and Montreal's mayor, Jean Drapeau, were written by, and carried to them, by Marc Lalonde.

The federal cabinet argued at the time that the police were too tired, overwhelmed, and needed the War Measures Act to help. But the RCMP didn't ask for it, the military didn't ask for it, the local police never asked for it. Politicians made the decision. Why? The only conclusion is that someone decided that it was appropriate to use the apparatus of the state to settle the score, which is the kind of serious miscarriage of democracy that citizens pay a price for.

This was the end of my political innocence. I began to understand that there are consequences to the rhetoric of arrogance and the consequences can be very unpleasant indeed. This is still a peaceable kingdom and a wonderful society. I remain a great supporter of the national defence department, but not for its use against our own people. When citizens see armoured vehicles patrolling on a campus in the centre of Ottawa, they know that something has gone terribly wrong.

My vitriolic dislike for Pierre Trudeau's policies emerged during this period. I developed an intense dislike for his arrogance, his condescension, and his readiness to impose his will even on people with whom he had argued across the kitchen table for twenty-five years. That act of rank repression shaped in me a profound and fundamental distrust of what federal Liberals had done constitutionally and a sense that our constitutional difficulties even today are very much the product of events that transpired more than twenty years ago. This was the point of departure and legitimacy for more extreme nationalism. Those who went on to advance the separatist cause in Quebec only reflected in a more extreme way the obvious conclusions the War Measures Act would have imposed on any thoughtful nationalist who wondered about his or her ability to defend Quebec's legitimate interests within Canada.

On campus, the result was that many French-Canadians who didn't take politics seriously started taking politics very seriously indeed. I saw an entire generation develop a sense of despair and a sense that those guilty of having a view outside the mainstream, especially in Quebec, might no longer expect the civility our society is said to embrace.

I also saw the inability of the Conservative Party to do anything about it. David MacDonald was the only member of the Conservative caucus who voted against the Public Order Act bill. Stanfield tried to ask questions of the government, but was badly treated by many in the press and by some in his own party because he refused to go lock-step with the Grits. Stanfield's instincts were clearly to oppose the act, but he knew he had to give the government the benefit of the doubt. If he didn't, the party would come apart, torn between those who believed in pre-trial sentencing for French-Canadians and others clearly opposed to the imposition. Rather than risk the collapse of the party, he had to take an essentially soft, pro-government position for the duration. That taught me much about how the reach of the Conservative Party can sometimes be a huge burden upon effective leadership positions.

As student council president and as a private citizen, I worked with David MacDonald to produce a pamphlet called *Not Strong and Free: In Response to the War Measures Act*. It contained a series of essays by distinguished Canadians about why the act was inappropriate, unnecessary, and in the long term extremely destructive to the national interest. Dian Cohen wrote on the economics of poverty in Quebec. Nate Nurgitz wrote about how there was no need for the legislation, given that there were sufficient powers under the Coroner's Act to detain anyone who might be in any way material to murder. Patrick Watson wrote about how the media censored themselves and caved in to the government line without so much as a peep. Jim Littleton from the CBC wrote about the lack of competent police intelligence-gathering during the process. Peter Desbarats wrote about the journalistic issues involved.

On the back of the pamphlet were the names of the people who sent money so the pamphlet might be printed, such as Alan Eagleson, Roy McMurtry, and an elderly gentleman from Vancouver, H. H. Stevens, who had begun the rescontructionist movement and had been part of the birth of the Progressive Party decades earlier. A number of New Democrats came on board, along with some people perceived as being from the far right, such as Sterling Lyon from Manitoba, who was very troubled about the implications for civil liberties.

Around the time of the crisis, there was a by-election in Lisgar, Manitoba, a seat the party had traditionally held and a seat Stanfield could not afford to lose. David MacDonald and I had gone west to meet with Wally Fox-Thecent, a professor at the University of Manitoba (and ultimately the chairman of Gary Filmon's advisory committee on the constitution), Sterling Lyon, and others in Nate Nurgitz's basement to work on the pamphlet. Nate was then de facto president of the party because Frank Moores had left the presidency to become premier of Newfoundland.

The day David and I flew home, Nate took us to the airport at the same time as Stanfield arrived to campaign in the Lisgar by-election, a constituency that had yet to accept the Red Ensign, let alone the Maple Leaf. Nate's biggest problem was to make sure the press at the airport didn't find David because he had stood alone against Trudeau's actions. Mixing the two issues could have cost us the by-election (we won comfortably), which was a further indication of how delicately those tendencies in the party have to be managed.

When Stanfield got off the plane, Nate said, "I thought your position on the War Measures Act was perfect."

Mr. Stanfield said, "Which one?"

Some days earlier, Stanfield was introduced at a meeting of southwestern Ontario Conservatives in London with, "Ladies and gentlemen, the leader of the Conservative Party, leader of the opposition, and the next prime minister of Canada, Robert Lorne Stanfield." No one clapped. Southwestern Ontario at that time was quite right-wing and very much in favour of Pierre Trudeau and what he was doing in Quebec.

John White, a wonderful man and John Robarts' minister from the region, stood up alone and began to applaud. It may have been only a few seconds until other people joined in, but it seemed like a few hours. White shamed them into showing respect for their leader, a decent man who was trying to bridge a serous gap without becoming a toady to the government. He gave the government the benefit of the doubt and they abused it, never giving him any information to justify or clarify why they did. Seeing that dynamic had a significant effect on young warriors in the party like me.

The event gave me the sense that the Conservative Party could be a force for balance and moderation in the English-French argument, a force that Trudeau clearly never could—and never wanted to—represent. His political view was black and white on such matters. There was no room for compromise, a stand that runs fundamentally against the nature of the country. Where the Conservative Party differs from the Trudeaus of this world is in the notion that more progress can be made through accommodation. A government doesn't have to sell the store or give up what it believes in, but progress can be made through an accommodation that provides an environment for a good country and some wonderful people.

On matters of the constitution, our party is about accommodation and is completely at odds with the Ramsay Cook–Pierre Trudeau–Michael Bliss school of thought that there is only one Trudeauesque cookie-cutter constitutional mould and mere mortals should never try to improve it or address its insufficiencies. Arguably, too much time can be spent on the issue, but the notion that a government can never discuss or hope to improve the matter is a strait-jacket that cannot withstand pressure from inside.

The party's agonies over the crisis deepened my emotional commitment to accommodation. The Tory party at its root doesn't fuss with the neo-conservative–Progressive Conservative distinction, which is largely illusory. It focuses more on the issue of how to maintain order and the social justice and opportunity that produce that order so that people have a sustainable and durable freedom.

Neo-cons and liberals are so sucked in by the notion of freedom first that they have an immature optimism about human nature. History couldn't be clearer. Remove structure and order, remove stability and institutional frameworks, and in the good times the result is predatory economic activity, greed, insensitivity, and intolerance. In the bad times, the result is rape, pillage, bigotry, racism, holocausts, and all the rest. In the kind of society we have now, so easily influenced by trends from outside and abroad, it is the ultimate naiveté to think that the worst excesses can't happen here.

There has not been similar violence since the imposition of the act, and thank goodness for that. But we've been fighting a more virulent strain of separatism every decade for the past quarter of a century. We have not yet paid the bills for that War Measures excess. It inflicted deep psychic wounds in Quebec, leading many Quebeckers to feel alienated from federal institutions, a feeling they passed on to their children. It seeded the clouds for the legitimacy of the Lévesque administration in 1976 and may have seeded the clouds for a far more serious threat to the country.

It also radicalized my Conservativism. I began working as an unpaid research assistant for David MacDonald, who represented the most humane and progressive wing of the party, writing questions for the House and committees to challenge the Liberals. After I finished my term as student council president, I was hired as his research assistant for $53 a week, plus all the meals I could afford in the subsidized cafeteria.

David was such an idealistic, hardworking, decent guy, he made Quentin Durgens look like a cynic and crass self-promoter. Working with him, I also began to realize that when Diefenbaker talked about the termites whittling away at his party power base, he was talking about MacDonald, Gordon Fairweather, Heath Macquarrie, and Mike Forrestall, people for whom I came to have great affection and respect. This made my position rather uncomfortable in the beginning.

I once quietly said to him, "You know, David, I was Youth for Dief."

He said, "I'm a Christian. We all carry around a bit of original sin."

I was never penalized for my enthusiasm for Diefenbaker. It was seen as an adolescent infatuation that could be grown out of. Being on that side of the fence, I also realized the intellectual importance of Dalton Camp's battle for a party that was civilized, urbane, and democratic, a party where the leader didn't have control over the membership in perpetuity, a party that said through conferences like the one in 1969 that we had to have a thinking process so that the party was not just about elections but about policy and people.

Working with David taught me about principle, humanity, and

idealism in Conservative politics and how those qualities had to mesh with political reality, constituency demands, and caucus dynamics.

Similar qualities became apparent on the provincial scene during the 1971 Conservative leadership convention in Ontario and the subsequent provincial campaign. Most people from eastern Ontario, including Maureen McTeer and others from the campus, supported Bert Lawrence at the convention, the member from Carleton East and a very well-liked and approachable politician. I chose instead to support William Davis.

As student council president, I believed Davis was a superb minister of university affairs who had, in a very Progressive Conservative way, introduced the notion of universal accessability to Ontario's universities and the colleges of applied arts and technology, which he had created. He said that no one who had the academic ability to continue beyond the secondary level would be prohibited from doing so for reasons of financial incapacity. That was a significant enrichment of what was available for people who came from poor or disadvantaged homes, and I was impressed with that. I had also met him during meetings of the Advisory Council on Student Loans set up to discuss the Ontario student awards program.

I spent the 1971 provincial election campaign as the youth canvass co-chairman with Maureen McTeer in Lawrence's constituency, which is where I first got to know Maureen well. We had known each other because we were both participants of the English Debating Society on campus, and after the election we became quite good friends.

In the provincial constituency of Ottawa South, Irwin Haskett, the long-time minister of highways in Robarts's government, stepped down and annointed Claude Bennett, a popular deputy mayor of Ottawa, as the Conservative candidate. A nominating meeting was scheduled at a local high school, and Bill Davis, touring across the province putting together his candidates, was to be the guest speaker. Because I was the PC Youth Federation national vice-president and from a local campus, I was invited to introduce Mr. Davis, which was quite an honour.

The meeting was the first time I saw him perform at close range in any meaningful way. He was impressive.

The nomination process couldn't begin because parents and students who wanted full funding for separate schools took over the meeting. The local alderman, the former minister, the soon-to-be-nominated candidate Claude Bennett, Davis, an aide, and sundry hangers-on stood behind the curtain on the stage. With the hall occupied by Catholic parents and kids, various cockamamee notions about how to deal with the situation arose. One person piped up with, "Let's call the firemen and just pull them out. Hose 'em down."

Davis looked aghast. He said, "That's not what we do in Ontario. I'll go talk to them. They have the right to talk to me."

He went out to hoots and jeers and sat on the end of the stage, microphone in hand. The crowd finally quieted down, if only to see what he was going to do. He said, "Look, you're unhappy about our policies. You have that right. That's what democracy's all about. Now, I am here for the Ottawa South Progressive Conservative nominating convention. But I happen to think the Progressive Conservative Party, when it holds a meeting, doesn't hold it so as to shut out people's concerns. So may I make a proposal? I will sit on this stage for one hour. You can ask me anything you want. I will answer to the best of my ability. At the end of that hour, you will allow the nominating meeting to continue as planned."

They cheered. For the next hour, they peppered him with questions. He said it many ways, but his message essentially was, "I'm troubled by the perception of unfairness, but I just feel way down deep that at this point in Ontario's history, dividing up our kids even more from each other is a mistake. The province is changing, the nature of our population base—multi-racial, multi-ethnic, multicultural—is changing very fast and it's important that our kids spend as much time together as they possibly can. I think spending grade eleven, twelve, and thirteen together is better, and that's why I'm not in favour of completing the funding."

At the end of the hour, he stood up and said, "Now, we're going to begin the Progressive Conservative nominating meeting. But I want to make it clear, none of you has to leave. You're welcome to stay."

When two-thirds of them stayed, participated in the meeting, and hung around afterwards for coffee, I realized that the premise of his kind of pluralism worked. That premise was a civility not often seen in politics. Compared to the arrogance of Trudeau, it marked a real difference in style. I decided there and then that this was about the best I was going to find in public life. There was an intrinsic moderation and decency that said that conservatism in Ontario is not exclusionary and doesn't have to be.

My contact with Davis and the people who helped elect him premier deepened at the 1971 general meeting of the federal Progressive Conservative Party. I had been appointed policy chairman for the PC Youth convention, held in the basement of the Ottawa Anglican cathedral. I then announced my candidacy for the national vice-presidency of the PCYF of Canada, which I hadn't planned to do before the weekend began. Alan Pope, the outgoing president, was really the person to put the student federation and the YPCs together into the PCYF nationally. But Darwin Keeley and a host of others came to the conclusion that this young fellow from Ottawa U.— bilingual, from Quebec, et cetera, et cetera—might be constructive as national vice-president. I announced my candidacy the day of the election, gave a fairly strong speech, and, quite to my surprise, won the post, defeating the thoughtful and capable Jack Houseman, who has had many political victories since.

I won with the help of the junior members of what was becoming a smooth political organization that would soon have a significant effect on politics in this country. Darwin Keeley, John Nicholls, Alan Pope, Bill Webb in eastern Ontario, John Hoyles in northern Ontario, Murray Coolican, Brian Armstrong, and Graham Scott, who had stood with Dalton Camp at the 1966 national convention as a YPC leader, were all around my age. I didn't know it at the time, but that was my first encounter with what became known, in the coinage of journalist Claire Hoy, as the Big Blue Machine.

The mythology about the fabled Big Blue is that it was the creation of Bill Davis or at least an Ontario creation born in Eglinton riding, home of Dalton Camp's advertising agency and where Camp campaigned for a federal seat in 1968. But the Big Blue Machine, to the extent it ever existed as a cohesive entity, as opposed to being an elaborate figment of many people's imaginations, was actually created by Robert Stanfield. After the debacle of the 1968 general election, he was determined to build a modern political organization.

In the 1968 election, every province and every riding made its own decisions about local federal activities. There was very little central advertising, except for a few newspaper ads. The tour was built around which riding was prepared to put on a meeting Stanfield could speak at. Speeches were written in a way that responded to the rhythm in the press, but were tied only to the way policies played in the press, not to any research data. There was no link at all between public-opinion research, policy analysis, campaign structure, when and where the leader went, or who was used where. All that just happened. Maybe it worked, maybe it didn't.

The lesson was learned in 1968. The party said, "Never again."

Malcolm Wickson from British Columbia, a former national director of the party, was invited to become campaign chair in the early seventies. He went to Ontario to see whom he could assemble from amongst those who had worked for provincial cabinet minister Allan Lawrence in the leadership campaign, almost defeating Bill Davis in the process. He assembled the moderate Michigan Republican Bob Teetor, Norman Atkins, who ran the Camp agency, and others.

The notion the team developed was that in campaign strategy and tactics, there might actually be some relationship between the party's policy, the best way that research said to advance that policy, what the team did on television, where the leader went, what the leader said, and what the advertisements said about the campaign. Today, this strikes everyone as quite normal, but it was revolutionary for any Canadian party in the late sixties and early seventies. Stanfield lent the Big Blue Machine to Bill Davis for his 1971 campaign to see if the integrated system could work.

I had run into the best of the Big Blue Machine when they helped me get elected as PCYF national vice-president. I soon ran into one of the most troubling aspects of it. After my victory, I went across to the Château Laurier Hotel for the senior party meeting. The battle for national president was between Don Matthews and a lawyer from Alberta, Roy Deyell. It was important to the Big Blue Machine that Deyell win the post. The party constitution specified that the first vice-president had to come from a region not represented in the president's office, so the only way Roy McMurtry, a Tory activist in Toronto and part of the Machine, could become national vice-president was if Roy Deyell became president. McMurtry, as vice-president, could then cement the relationship between the Davis and Stanfield people.

Don Matthews was really the Ontario candidate for president. He had the support of John Robarts and Tories from southwestern Ontario and he ran one hell of a campaign, directed largely by his daughter, Debbie, who was by far the smartest politician in the family.

While I was on the convention floor, a senior Blue Machine organizer, Paul Weed, who would later become a great friend and supporter when I ran for Parliament, came over, stood about an inch from my face, and said, "Young man, if you want a future in this party, you will vote for Roy Deyell for national president."

I had no strong view on the matter. But on the first ballot I voted for Deyell. On the second ballot, I was canvassed by Debbie Matthews. Her argument and presentation were compelling and I immediately switched my vote to Matthews.

Despite some reservations about the strong-arm tactics used on the floor, I began to develop a relationship and a sense of family with the Big Blue Machine and with Bill Davis. This was the kind of relationship that people in the Reform Party and the neo-conservative extreme hate the most about Tories in Canada and traditional Republicans in the U.S., a relationship built on a structure of loyalty, partisanship, and a sense of duty not driven by ideology. The bonds of kinship, fuelled by passion, are nourished by having fought in common cause, and being counted together in winning and losing campaigns. My college years had deepened my understanding of the party—as a national instrument with weaknesses and strengths—and as an extended family with friends, "in" crowds and "out" crowds, and many different subcultures. It was, more than ever, home.

3

BLOODIED IN THE MARCH
OF THE UNDISCIPLINED

BETWEEN 1968 AND 1972, Liberal policy conceits around unemployment, the deficit, and federal–provincial relations, as well as many examples of corruption now forgotten, reduced Trudeau's popularity substantively in many parts of the country. Given Bob Stanfield's careful, step-by-step approach to policy development, candidate attraction, and campaign construction, 1972 looked to be the key opportunity to see a significant Conservative redress of the electoral excesses perpetrated by Trudeaumania in 1968.

Trudeau's view of process had come to a grinding halt. His foreign-takeovers bill was excessive and Edgar Benson's white paper on tax reform was an unmitigated disaster. The prime minister had told strikers on Parliament Hill to "mangez de la merde," and his arrogance, impatience, and condescension were starting to play in the minds of voters. The complacency—in the face of high unemployment and economic disparity— of "The Land is Strong" campaign he launched in 1972 spoke to a Liberal contempt for those in the fisheries, on farms, or on the unemployment lines who were not doing so well.

The Stanfield campaign was based around the concept of "There is a better way." The campaign was about Trudeau's insensitivity, reconstructing a more cooperative federalism, fighting unemployment, helping the poor, and building a greater social safety net for senior citizens. It wasn't a campaign from the right, although it dealt with issues of waste. It was a populist campaign about giving people a fair chance, broadening the economic mainstream, and dealing with unemployment at its roots as opposed to through government giveaway programs such as Opportunities for Youth and the Local Initiatives Program.

Only two things stood in the way of Bob Stanfield becoming prime minister. One was John Diefenbaker, the other was Quebec.

The Diefenbaker factor—a former leader in the caucus and in an office that was, because he was a former prime minister, well staffed—produced an overhang that constrained what the current leader could successfully execute once he decided what it was he should do. The problem was made worse by the degree to which Diefenbaker's presence in the caucus legitimized dissidence, disloyalty, and disunity. It was no accident that Trudeau, John Turner, and other Liberal luminaries fawned over Dief while he sat on the opposition benches. They knew that magnifying his importance only served to divide the Tory caucus and burden Stanfield in the party management responsibilities every leader has as a fundamental priority, particularly if the leader happens to be a Conservative.

The Diefenbaker factor interplayed with the Quebec factor in a fascinating way. Stanfield's efforts to make headway in the province had been consistent and well financed, and were much benefited by such tireless volunteers as Jean Bazin, Brian Mulroney, Michel Cogger, staffers Richard Lelay and Tom Sloan, Bernard Flynn, and speech-writer François Morrissette. He recruited outstanding candidates like the popular judge and former provincial justice minister Claude Wagner, popular lawyer and party secretary Michael Meighen, and others who brought forward the concerns their communities wanted to see expressed in Ottawa. Stanfield visited the province frequently and, in his fifties, went from zero fluency to a fairly elegant French more grammatically correct than that spoken by many native-born Quebeckers. It may have been slightly halting, but then so was his English.

But his fundamental problem in Quebec was that, since the advent of the Union Nationale, his party had no roots in provincial politics. Many Quebeckers, including many in the press, had an enduring respect for Stanfield, but that could not bridge the gulf cre-ated by the lack of any identification between the party and the modern reality of Quebec.

That problem was made more difficult to manage by the Diefenbaker–Jack Horner cadre, which Trudeau used effectively to undercut and, in the end, destroy any progress Stanfield's hard work might have achieved. When the Liberals introduced resolutions to reaffirm the Official Languages Act, they did so not only to reconstruct their base in Quebec but also to see how far and deeply they could divide the Conservative Party. They knew the division would be harmful not just in Quebec but in northern New Brunswick, parts of P.E.I., and in many progressive parts of Toronto and Vancouver, where a party had to be seen as national in scope to garner local support.

Diefenbaker not only went for the bait but led a rump of Conservatives who voted against the act not once but twice. He repaid all the unnecessary kindness heaped upon him by Trudeau, producing a deep rift in the Conservative caucus and putting severe pressures on Stanfield that diminished his capacity to run the party.

What were people in Quebec to make of a leader like Stanfield—modern, progressive, and becoming more articulate in French week by week—and his excellent team of candidates when, on his own front bench, sat people opposed to the principle of fairness and the use of French in appropriate federal institutions? What were they to make of that in comparison to Trudeau's front bench, with so many prominent Quebeckers from the salons of Outrement and Westmount, the University of Montreal, established law firms, and the business empires of Paul Desmarais and others? It was hardly a fair choice.

When Stanfield removed the official-candidate status from Len Jones, a candidate in Moncton opposed to the languages act, he stayed consistent with the party's history and its mission, which has accommodation of French and English political aspirations within its very soul. But he went into the campaign with the Diefenbaker albatross firmly around his neck.

I decided to join him. My first exposure to the idea of getting involved federally emerged out of working as a canvasser for the provincial party in 1971 for Bert Lawrence in Carleton East and later helping out Gary Guzzo in Ottawa Centre. Working in those constituencies, I came across the Mann sisters, Laura and Agnes, who lived in Ottawa South. They were supporters of the provincial member, Claude Bennett, and also great Diefenbaker supporters from the old days. They encouraged me to give some thought to a federal nomination.

I was not scheduled to graduate until the spring of 1972, but while working part-time with David MacDonald, I had again been toying with the notion of running in my home riding of Mount Royal, against Trudeau. But riding president Barney London again demurred, encouraging me to cut my political teeth in Ontario.

I felt that to get young people active in the party, we had to stop being youth organizers, youth canvassers, and youth chairmen and start to participate in the substance of politics, seeking a seat for the House of Commons. I also felt that unless I took on a tough seat and went through the experience of running for Parliament, I would never understand the essence of politics.

It became apparent that if I wanted to enter the lists, I would have to look for a long-held Liberal seat that did not appear to hold much hope of switching. The English-speaking seat that had the most substantive qualities in that regard was Ottawa Centre, a constituency that had voted Liberal for at least fifty years by huge margins. It had been held by George McIlraith, the Liberal solicitor-general and minister of public works, for the better part of a quarter of a century. It was so Liberal that Charlotte Whitton, the popular mayor of Ottawa, could not break the hold as the Conservative candidate even during the Diefenbaker sweep of 1958.

A good friend I had met in the provincial campaign, Jerry Lampert, was the president of the student government at Carleton University at the same time I was president at Ottawa U. We decided we would get a committee together to win the nomination. His vice-president, Brian Hamilton, joined our young crew of insurgents.

Party headquarters had a very different view. They wanted a substantial, well-known, locally rooted professional or business person to carry the colours, not because the seat was so winnable but because it was the seat in which Parliament Hill sat and where people who were opinion-makers nationally, including members of the parliamentary press gallery, lived. A strong, substantial candidate would convey the notion that the Stanfield team was a well-organized, high-profile, quality organization that could win the election. A yet-to-graduate student wouldn't do.

The party did not actively discourage a student from running. Yet there was no encouragement to speak of, either, save for a letter Lowell Murray, then working at CN in Montreal, wrote to Graham Scott, Stanfield's executive assistant. Murray reported that there was a young man who had worked in the provincial campaign in Ottawa who seemed to be liked by both the left and the old Diefenbaker crowd, which was unique. He said it would be "a good thing" if the party could get that young guy to run for them. David MacDonald was also encouraging, but was troubled by anyone getting into politics too young and getting burnt out too soon. Understandably, he was also focusing on his own constituency.

All things being equal, I concluded that if I waited for an easy seat to be delivered, chances were it would not happen, certainly not at age twenty-one.

Jerry and I gathered a committee and began working towards the nomination meeting in April, a month before my graduation. The establishment had lined up behind Ed Foster, a well-known and well-respected local lawyer. He had the support of provincial cabinet ministers and the federal powers in the area and he ran an aggressive campaign selling memberships. Jerry Lampert, Brian Hamilton, myself, and others on my committee determined early on that the way to make the campaign work was to shape an intergenerational battle but to cut it a little differently. We already had great support from Young Conservatives at the two universities, who were the hardworking organizational core. So we focused on senior citizens.

I spent much time in senior citizens' homes and apartments and at the Rex Lelacheur Choir Studio on 5th Avenue with an organization called the Capital Ward Women, made up of older women who had supported Charlotte Whitton in her many municipal campaigns. As a young bachelor living in town on my own, I kind of got adopted by the Capital Ward women, and they took a special interest in my campaign. The Mann sisters, Laura and Agnes, worked day and night.

Some unexpected people came out of the woodwork to show support. Ivan Sparks, who had been president of the riding association for many years, was an elder of the United Church and proprietor of one of the largest moving firms in the city. He was a long-time Conservative activist who decided to get in lock, stock, and barrel. Rick Clippingdale and Bob Keiserlink, professors in the history department at Carleton University, joined in very intensely and made huge efforts to help the campaign come together, along with Helen and Tony Lemay, and Osie Howe, an ancient but loyal Tory lawyer from Centretown. But it was the senior citizens who put their shoulder to the wheel and hit the phones something fierce. Laura Mann was on her phone all the time.

On the night of the nomination I stood with my campaign team in the auditorium and looked across the crowd. All the Foster signs clearly indicated an early win for my opponent. Then a fleet of vans showed up at the door, each one letting out up to twenty seniors. With a relatively strong speech in English and French, with a bit of Italian thrown in, I was able to win on the second ballot.

Now we needed a committee room, but were completely without funds. Tom Assaly, who had been active in local politics and the construction business, spoke to the vicar at a small High Anglican church, and the attic of St. Barnabas Church became, until further notice, our primary committee room.

I made courtesy calls on all the ministers and priests in the constituency, including Monsignor Lesage. I was curious about the chance of area Catholics lending their support. He was polite. It was zero.

I called on Canon Borden Purcell of St. John's Anglican Church on Elgin, which was quite an activist congregation, with sit-ins against Vietnam and the like. After chatting for a bit, he said, "Do you have a committee room in this end of town?"

"No, I don't."

"Well, you do now. Our basement."

Thus began an Anglican Church-based campaign for a humane Conservative tomorrow, led by the Progressive Conservative candidate for the riding of Ottawa Centre, relatively fresh from fourteen years of education in a pre-rabbinical Hebrew school.

We had no money. Jean Pigott, a local activist, business leader, and Tory, undertook to be our finance chairman, but, as I was informed, reported back after a couple of weeks that she was not having great success raising funds for an unknown, especially one from a minority religious background. Someone suggested we talk to Irwin Haskett, former MPP for Ottawa South and the highways minister for John Robarts. A patent agent by trade, Haskett had retired gracefully from politics and was one of the grand old men of the Conservative Party. Jerry Lampert, Brian Hamilton, and I paid him a visit to get financial advice.

He looked at me intently and said, "Young man, anybody who carries the Conservative colours must either have the personal money to pay for it or have the capacity to raise it."

I said to myself, "This is not going well."

He walked over to the window, looked out over the scenery, turned around, and said, "I'll be your financial campaign chairman. You're a young guy and you're in this for the right reasons. I'll do it."

He produced about $16,000 out of nowhere, so we ended up with a real committee room and storefront just like everyone else. This being the days before disclosure, I never quite figured out how he raised the money. My sense was that he went through some old lists and approached highway pavers and construction people, not all of whom shared an Anglo-Saxon background, and said, "This guy Segal ... get in on the ground floor." That Ottawa didn't build highways and had no jurisdiction to do so may have been lost on them.

Shortly after we opened our committee room above Scrim's florist shop on Slater Street, Jerry Lampert got a call from a lady who asked, "Segal, Segal, Segal. What kind of name is that?"

"It's kind of a Canadian name," he said.

"No, no, no. Just tell me, is he or is he not a Catholic?"

"I can assure you, ma'am, he is not a Catholic."

"That's great. I'll be sending you $2,500."

Once alerted that I wasn't Catholic, the Orange Lodge, which was still alive, invited me to speak on a Saturday afternoon while games of whist were in progress. They gave, I believe, the second-largest campaign donation of anyone in the riding, simply on the grounds of my non-allegiance to Rome.

The campaign began to roll. Our sign man, Tom Formanczyk, who was a wonderful person, a butcher by day and painter by night, volunteered to screen-paint all our signs. Unfortunately, he chose to paint them pink and blue in a wonderfully psychedelic style that conveyed no message and rendered the signs unreadable. It's tough to deal with an artist who thinks he's created something complex and compelling when the purpose of the exercise is to be simple. He agreed to make a modest correction.

Jerry and the team had me canvassing every day, if only to keep me out of the committee room. To keep myself happy, I whistled the campaign tune as I walked up and down the streets.

I knocked on one door and a guy said, "You're that bilingual Conservative candidate, aren't you?"

"Yes, sir, I am."

He slammed the door in my face, the first of many to do so over the coming weeks.

On my second day of canvassing, Jerry sent me down to Renfrew Street. I knocked on one door and a woman in her fifties answered. She said, "Oh, you're that nice Conservative candidate. I've heard so much about you. Won't you come in?" In I went and out came the tea, biscuits, and scones as two older, very pleasant women said, "Tell us about your policies. Tell us about yourself." We chatted for forty-five minutes.

Unbeknownst to me, my campaign manager was going nuts trying to find me. When I got back out on the street, the canvass chairman tracked me down and said, "Which house were you in?" I gave him the address. He said, "Those are George McIlraith's two spinster sisters and they just played the goddamn game of 'get the Tory off the street so he can't knock on any doors.'"

I canvassed in an apartment building with Maureen McTeer, each of us taking different floors. A very attractive young woman sheathed in Spandex responded at one door and said, "Are you that Hugh Segal, the Conservative candidate on TV?"

"Yes, ma'am, I am Hugh Segal."

She was stunning. "You know, I've always believed in the Conservative Party. Bob Stanfield." She went out of her way to let me know I would feel extremely welcome should I wish to spend time in her apartment discussing the issues of the day.

It's unclear where my young bachelor's head was, but I believe it was heading in the general direction of her foyer when the elevator door opened and out stepped Maureen. "We have more floors to canvass."

"Absolutely," I said. "Let's get on with it."

In the Italian area, I had a little spiel prepared. I would knock on the door and say, "Bon giorno! Sono il candidato progressivo conservatore por questa zona." If they spoke back to me in Italian, I was dead. One couple was so excited that I could speak Italian at all that they invited me in, sat me down, and poured me a glass of homemade grappa. I thought, "How harmful can this be?" Without the benefit of the approbation of the Liquor Control Board of Ontario, the stuff must have been 190 proof. I took one sip and had to be helped back to the street in a state of substantial disrepair.

My Liberal opponent was McIlraith's successor, Hugh Poulin, a local lawyer who had been McIlraith's campaign manager for decades. He was a gentle soul, then married with a large family. The NDP candidate was Irving Greenberg, a wealthy local developer and philanthropist, one of the major shareholders of Minto Construction, the largest housing construction firm in the city.

During the campaign, I learned many things. I learned that a candidate can win almost every debate in an election and do himself great harm. We had many debates in school basements where I would often win, but it would be clear at the end of the evening that it would have been better not to have won. There was a bias towards candidates whom voters could trust, understand, and identify with, rather than those who appeared to be too clever by half.

I also began to get the sense of "innocent hostages" in politics. I found it hard to be intensely critical of Hugh and the Liberals when his wife and children were in the audience, which they often were.

In a meeting during the third week of the campaign, someone stood up and said, "I wonder if I could ask all three candidates how it is that the ass-out-of-the-pants student is running for the Conservatives, yet one of the wealthiest men in the riding is a New Democrat?"

I went to the mike and said, "If I had Irving's money, I could afford to be a New Democrat too. But all of my people have had to work for a living all their lives and, I suspect, so will I. Therefore, I'd better be a Conservative because we actually believe in working for a living. We believe everybody should. We believe it's quite a good thing."

At another meeting, a group of pro-choice activists was pressing the matter of abortion. I had not ever thought about the issue seriously. I was young and single, and family formation was the furthest thing from my mind. I took what was essentially Stanfield's view, which was that this was a private matter between a woman and her physician and, while there may be some role for the Criminal Code, we shouldn't be overregulating or micromanaging these sorts of things.

Hugh Poulin took a different view, a position of principle dictated by his strong Catholicism. When he articulated a pro-life stance, some women booed and heckled him. Something snapped. I said, "Those of you who are booing and heckling probably agree more with my position than Mr. Poulin's, but he does have a right to his position. He does have the right to articulate it here tonight without being harassed. If you don't like it, make your electoral decision accordingly, but you have no right to be demeaning with respect to his position." That produced a call the next morning from Monsignor Lesage, who said, "I don't agree with your position, but that was something quite special for you to do."

As the campaign went on, we could see a shift in the northern part of the constituency between the Queensway and Parliament Hill, where highrises housed younger civil servants who were beginning to identify with our campaign, with Stanfield, and to an extent with me personally. In the southern part of the riding, which was less populist but more of a street community, with more home ownership, there was continuing anxiety over the bilingual question and some discomfort with a candidate who supported Stanfield's commitment to the Official Languages Act.

Except for our champion in Ottawa East, I was the only candidate in the region to support the policy unequivocally. In Ottawa at the time, any English-speaking public servant whose career did not take the trajectory he or she had in mind blamed it on the official languages policy. Certainly, in the early days of its application there was some hamhandedness and unfairness, but there was little evidence that the legislation was the reason for career changes or setbacks. Nor was this a reason to be against the principle that Canadians have the right to be served by their national government in their choice of English or French.

Other Conservative candidates in the region, such as Walter Baker, Peter Reilly, and Paul Dick, offered a healthy strain of criticism and a commitment that the legislation would be changed. By doing so, they seemed to have some hope of being elected. (They all were.)

Wally Baker in Grenville-Carleton was for changing the policy substantially, which produced ground-swells of support amongst traditional Conservatives. I wasn't prepared to support that. I thought it was unfair.

Peter Reilly, our candidate in the next constituency to mine, did not equivocate on the policy, but made a lot of noise about changing the implementation. Reilly had had a pretty checkered career. He had taken on Trudeau over the War Measures Act, which was difficult for a CBC journalist to do in those days. He had a significant following as a local broadcaster, but there was some personal animosity in his constituency. At one nomination meeting, George Hees was giving a marvellous speech in support of Peter when some guy at the back hollered, "Peter Reilly is a no-good, stinking, divorced, drinking bum."

George said, "Nevertheless, he's our man, and he's wonderful."

During the question period, someone said, "Mr. Reilly, I'd like to know. Is it true you've been married three times and have a drinking problem? Yes or no?"

Peter walked to the microphone and, without missing a breath, said, "Don't you think if you'd been married three times you'd have a drinking problem too?"

He got a standing ovation.

Going through two parts of the constituency—Mechanicsville, which was largely francophone, and what was referred to as Little Italy, a depressed industrial area with a high concentration of Italian-speaking people—I found some fascinating things. Hugh Poulin could not and did not speak a word of French, but his name was French and mine wasn't. Liberal support in Mechanicsville was very strong. In the Italian area, there was great loyalty to the Liberal organization because of McIlraith's patronage and involvement in public works and also because of Liberal prominence on immigration issues. Those two clusters, composing about 30 percent of the riding, were solidly Liberal and wouldn't move much. While the densely populated area north of the Queensway was traditionally Liberal, the area south of the Queensway was historically very mildly Tory, which was how we would lose elections.

We made real progress during the campaign. Nationally, the momentum slowly moved towards Stanfield while the Liberal "The Land is Strong" campaign began to fall apart.

As the campaign progressed, we held a huge rally at the McNabb Arena. Even though I was a twenty-one-year-old candidate who had not lived in Ottawa except to go to university and, classically, had neither a pot nor a window, Bill Davis came to the rally. Fresh into his first term, he was at the zenith of his popularity. The party tried to get him to come to as many rallies as possible, with people brought in from across the region to generate enthusiasm and hard work. Davis would always introduce Stanfield, implying that Bob Stanfield was right for Bill Davis's Ontario. Then Stanfield would speak.

Davis came to the arena because he had genuine respect and affection for Bob Stanfield and he because he wanted to help a young candidate who didn't have much of a chance. His presence helped take me—an obscure student running in a seat Tories traditionally lost by 7,000 to 15,000 votes—to contender status, which significantly boosted my capacity to have influence in the party.

There were moments of great personal sadness about two weeks before election day. My mother, a smoker since 1950, went into hospital to deal with what appeared to be a bad case of bronchitis, but the physicians found lung cancer rampant. I went home to Montreal for the surgery and to spend time with her and my brother Brian before returning to the fray (my brother Seymour was in Australia). I campaigned with quite a heavy heart the last two weeks, which put the political side of things in some perspective.

The anxiety also added to the fatigue that inevitably sets in after a long campaign, and which can play havoc with any candidate. With about two days left to go, I found myself at another senior citizens' home. I had integrated my speech on unemployment with my speech on pensions. Having made maybe three speeches a day for twenty-five days and having knocked on thousands of doors, I stood at the front of this hall at four o'clock on a Friday afternoon and looked around the room. There were about 150 senior citizens attending, some of whom were semi-awake, some a little hydrocephalic, some a touch incontinent, some having suffered from strokes and other illnesses.

As I spoke, the thought that I was appearing in a Monty Python sketch kept intruding into my mind. The thought occurred to me, "This has got to be the most ludicrous context I could ever be in. Why would any of these people care about anything I have to say? Why am I here?"

The insanity of it all began to destroy my composure. Fighting valiantly to not laugh uncontrollably was not a very high-minded way of making perhaps my last speech before election day. When I began talking about pensions, I lost it. I said, "The Conservative position ... our position on pensions ... our position ..." I started to laugh and couldn't stop. I recovered long enough to say, "You know why that's so funny? That's so funny because when I think of the Liberal position on pensions, I tell you, that's even funnier!"

Everyone started to laugh, except my campaign team, who were standing at the back hoping their candidate could be reconstructed before election day. I took the incident to be a way of understanding that you must never take yourself too seriously in politics. If you do, you have a fool for a candidate.

On election night, along with some friends and family, the campaign team gathered in a suite at a small motel, the Lord Elgin, to watch the coverage. As the results poured in, Ottawa Centre became the see-saw battle of the night. It took until almost midnight for the result to be clear. The Liberals squeezed out a victory by about 550 votes, an 1,100-vote margin, down from an 8,000 margin in the previous election.

I took polls in the north part of the constituency that had been Liberal for forty years. I didn't take them by much and didn't take a majority of them, but I took a higher percentage than a Conservative ever had before. The Liberal hedge in the Italian and French areas stayed solid. But the Tory area, which should have come through with flying colours, was more mildly Tory than ever, largely on the linguistic issue and because some who had supported Eddie Foster never forgave me for winning the nomination.

Nationally, Conservatives saw the election as a victory. We came first in the popular vote and first in every province except Quebec, where we could hold only a few seats. In view of the two-seat difference on election night and the loss of one seat in Ontario by fewer than five votes, this was really a five-vote election decision. A gap that narrow represented a stupendous leap forward for a party that had been down in the low teens of popularity after Trudeau had racked up huge numbers after the War Measures Act as English Canada's best bet for taking the boot to his own province.

The loan of Bill Davis's organizational people, along with Davis's own popularity and support, produced an impressive increase in PC seats in Ontario. Similar support from Peter Lougheed in Alberta, Richard Hatfield in New Brunswick, and Tories elsewhere aided what was a fine-tuned and tactically superb campaign run by Norman Atkins, Malcolm Wickson, Finlay MacDonald, Paul Weed, Rich Willis, Tom Scott, Ross Monk, Nancy McLean, and, chairing the youth campaign, my old Ottawa U. roommate, Ian Green.

David Lewis's corporate-welfare-bums campaign shaved support from the Liberals' left while the Stanfield campaign turned support away from the centre and centre-right of the Liberal base. The Trudeau drift was rebuffed, and Liberals were left with little more than a rump of ethnic seats plus Quebec.

Tories would be coming to Ottawa with a 40 percent increase in strength and with an impressive new caucus, with such stars as Flora MacDonald from Kingston, Ron Atkey from Toronto, Bill Jarvis from southwestern Ontario, and Joe Clark from Alberta. Conservatives even managed to elect Claude Wagner, despite the bad fortunes for the party in Quebec overall.

Down at my campaign headquarters, the workers staged a victory party. I'm not sure why it was a victory party, but it was. Everyone was so excited about how well the campaign had gone and how close Stanfield had come; there was a sense of having been part of something very important. I got carried in, which is no mean weight-lifting feat, to make a speech to the troops. The team presented me with a picture of John A. Macdonald, signed on the back by every person who had worked on the campaign. We all went to bed not sure whether Stanfield had more seats than Trudeau or vice versa.

As far as the papers were concerned, I won. They understood that Hugh Poulin had managed a victory, but his small victory was displayed by the press as a huge setback. My near win was displayed as a great step ahead. A post-campaign analysis to find where that 550-odd votes might have gone showed that Poulin's leads in traditionally Liberal polls with highrises, public servants, and young people had been either eradicated or cut massively, aided by the strong NDP campaign. The Tory polls in Ottawa South produced victories, but victories smaller in percentage than in other Tory polls in the region.

I was rejected *en bloc* by francophones simply for being a Conservative, and I saw the price the party paid for the divisiveness of the Diefenbaker caucus. The larger message was what the Diefenbaker situation did to the party's capacity to build any kind of momentum amongst French-speaking voters. Despite the party's massive victory in English Canada, Diefenbaker and his caucus cohorts robbed Stanfield of victory by a handful of votes.

My campaign produced a call from Graham Scott in Stanfield's office to join his staff as junior appointments secretary and legislative assistant. On my first day, I was informed that Mr. Stanfield was due for a haircut before the House met. We were trying to work that into the schedule to make sure there was time for briefings on questions before the meetings of the House and caucus. I said, "Well, how long can a haircut take? This is Bob Stanfield. He's just about bald."

I felt a tap on my shoulder. I turned around and turned sheet white as Mr. Stanfield said, "Been here long?"

Everyone who worked for Bob Stanfield went through three phases. In the first, you were so much in awe of him and his decency, commitment, and integrity that you wondered what the hell you were doing on his staff. In the second phase, after deciding you had all the answers, you wondered what the hell he was doing in the leader's office. In the third phase, which was where most of us ended up, you wondered how you could ever leave.

He had such a strangely compelling personality. He had the same lunch every day—a club sandwich and a glass of milk—then had a little nap. At one-thirty, we'd tap on his door and brief him on questions. Senior policy officer Bill Grogan, John Rolph, and others would come in with serious, intense questions. Stanfield would play with the words so by the time he asked the question in the House it would be softer, less accusatory, and less unfair than partisans might otherwise hope.

The mood of the House was very much of a Tory momentum. When I first joined the staff, I went to the prime minister's office to meet my counterpart, Trudeau's legislative assistant, Joyce Fairbairne. On her door was a poster of a kitten hanging on to a window sill by its claws, with the slogan "Hang in there, baby." That pretty well summed up the Liberal mindset.

The core question was, could Liberals reconstitute to fight back or was a Tory landslide in the next election inevitable? Clearly the Liberal-NDP strategy in their de facto coalition was to stall, hoping for a shift in public opinion and the healing powers of time. The NDP's price for support was not inexpensive. The Foreign Investment Review Act, Petro-Canada, wage escalations in government bargaining units, expensive UIC enhancements, and huge social-spending programs produced a deficit so massive it worked itself into the very sinew of the country's fiscal structure.

In Stanfield's office, the mood was upbeat and cheery, but not without traditional Conservative tensions. John Diefenbaker, truly Trudeau's secret weapon, continued to cause the leader great grief, despite unending civility on Stanfield's part. The glare associated with a government-in-waiting was put on every question in the House and every policy position in committee.

Working with Bob Stanfield was a singular privilege. I got the chance to see something powerful at work in the party's interests: modesty and humility. If understatement stunted growth, Bob Stanfield would have been three feet high. In fact, he stood taller than most peope in public life. Most politicians make promises easily, then worry about how they might be kept. Stanfield was the opposite. He agonized over ensuring that hopes were not unfairly raised, ill-considered propositions not too rapidly advanced, nor simplistic solutions easily embraced.

He was very much for the underdog in almost every situation. In the Middle East in those days, the Israelis were no longer seen as the underdog, and Stanfield was quite interested in making sure the Palestinian case got fair coverage and that the party treated them fairly. After the 1973 Yom Kippur War, all the Arab ambassadors came to see him to rant against Israeli conspiracies and U.S. imperialism. He listened to it all, not terribly impressed.

In the end, he said, "Now, I want you gentlemen to understand that we have an open-door policy here. Any time you have a concern, I want you to call this office. My man Segal, here, is your contact."

For the next six months, I had four Arab ambassadors on the phone almost daily. Stanfield would poke his nose into my office every day and say, "How are our friends doing in the Middle East?" He took great joy in putting that burden on my shoulders. It was his way of educating me a bit to other side of the question.

The simplicity of his values—which I took to be thrift, integrity, and compassion—was balanced by a complex view of issues. He saw them not only as a federal politician eager to win election but as a former premier of a have-not province who had dealt day-to-day with real problems.

He showed very little rage when Trudeau once again used an artificial resolution on the Official Languages Act just to see who he could pick off in the House. Of course, with Diefenbaker's support, he picked off a small row of Conservatives. Stanfield seemed to disregard the implications and responded more with sadness and disappointment that a prime minister would act in such an adolescent way.

His approach to party unity was similarly stoic. The general meeting of the party in 1971 had seen Don Matthews elected party president. His relations with Stanfield, largely because of Matthews' suspicion of the Big Blue Machine and vice versa, were correct but rarely warm. When I became Stanfield's legislative assistant, Lee Richardson was on Diefenbaker's staff and Bill Liaskas worked for Matthews. This being the party pre-Mulroney, there were many times when the national president and the leader weren't talking to each other, and most of the time Diefenbaker was not talking to Stanfield. This made communication between the offices difficult.

Lee, Bill, and I worked tirelessly to ensure as few misunderstandings as possible. The secretaries, who were loyal to their bosses and in tune with their petty points of anguish, would not hand messages between the three offices because of old battles, so when we left messages for each other, we would always say, "Please have him call Howard." When any of us saw a pink message slip with "Howard" on it, we would simply call the other two and connect.

The caucus had broad cleavages—right–left, urban–rural, and pre- and post-1972 membership. The pre-1972 caucus had a search-and-destroy view of an opposition's role. The new caucus was interested in constructive alternatives and fresh beginnings. There was a perpetual tussle going on for control of the Quebec organization, which, in view of its fractiousness and lack of electoral success, was not that great a prize in any event. Through it all, Stanfield had to maintain campaign preparedness, perpetual fundraising, and steady policy development, all of which he did with good humour, grace, and a self-effacement that just deepened this young staffer's loyalty.

What struck me forcibly was that every time we went to Quebec, there would be Brian Mulroney. Nothing then could have brought a person greater disrepute or even humiliation in Quebec than being an active Conservative. There was nothing in it. There were no appointments, no legal work, nothing. Yet there was Mulroney, all the time. His father had passed away, he was trying to get his mother and the family moved into a home in Montreal, trying to make a living for everybody, yet he was hanging in with us despite the setbacks. I had a sense of a guy who was there for the right reasons. He could have gone over to the Liberals, who would happily have had him as a candidate or as a judge. He could have sold his soul eighteen different ways, but the thought never occurred to him. He was a Conservative and he was always there for Conservative MPs and for Bob Stanfield when there was no one else to meet him and no one else to offer advice.

What also struck me during trips to Quebec was how different the practice of politics was there. In Quebec, issues of status were of immense importance. Who sat where, who was on the dias, and who got to speak were critical. Such matters are not without meaning in English Canada, but in Quebec, they matter a lot. It was important that there be a limousine for the leader, even though the party had no money, because the leader couldn't be seen travelling around the city in something less than an appropriate vehicle. To do so would speak ill of the substance and importance of the party. In other parts of Canada, the more humble the vehicle, the happier people would be. A pick-up truck would be great if organizers could find one that was beat up enough.

For anyone brought up in the politics of Montreal, the compass about what constitutes importance and conveying the notion of importance as a leader and as a person is very different than it is to someone growing up in, say, Brampton or Regina, where a minimalist approach to the accoutrements of government is culturally appropriate. Even in Quebec today, businesspeople can get together and buy an official residence for the premier. If anyone tried that in Ontario, Crown attorneys would press charges. In Quebec, it's appropriate. No one means anything negative by it. The style reflects similar differences in theatre between an English "audience" that expects to hear something and French "*spectateurs*" who want to see the spectacle of it all. Many journalists, unfortunately, have taken that style to mean an implicit acceptance of corruption, which is a bigoted view of what is simply a stylistic difference.

That difference always made Stanfield uncomfortable. He hated the stretch limousines that always showed up in Quebec. In Ottawa, he walked halfway to work and preferred to drive his own blue assembled-in-Nova-Scotia Volvo rather than have a driver. His sense of propriety and frugality was immense. He always flew economy class, refusing to be whisked into lounges or to the front of the check-in line. On my first trip with him on Air Canada from Ottawa to Montreal, he literally fought me for his bag. Not only did he carry his own bag, I was lucky to hold on to my own.

He insisted that the party write him a monthly cheque to cover the cost of upkeep and staff at Stornoway, then (this being pre-disclosure days) quietly wrote a cheque to the party for the same amount, establishing the principle that a leader would get some support for duties related to his job so that people of all economic backgrounds could consider running for high office. He personally subsidized key by-elections when the party couldn't raise the cash it needed. In a by-election in Central Nova, the Grits were desperate to win and were throwing the kitchen sink into it. We had a good young candidate, Elmer MacKay, but not much money, so Stanfield wrote a personal cheque so there would be a strong campaign.

Of course, in the period of national adolescence engendered by Trudeau and his diving board, the values of integrity, quiet frugality, and unheralded compassion were about as relevant as a bespoke tailor in a nudist colony. The media and the Liberal ethos had much more interest in the vacuous, self-centred, the-state-has-no-place-in-the-bedrooms-of-the-nation approach than in such anachronistic qualities. Appealing to a self-indulgent, youth-focused society's desire to have their "bedroom freedoms" elevated to the national agenda by a trendy politico was far more politically astute than trying to deal with the grinding but dull problems of poverty or income disparity.

The state was far too busy burrowing into our pockets to have much time for our bedrooms anyway. The rate of inflation engendered by massive government spending began to raise the cost of living, hurting the most defenceless among us, those on fixed incomes. Ironically, inflation increased the government's revenues, thereby removing any incentive to get inflation or inflation-causing spending under control.

Inflation became a compelling issue as the minority government looked to be readying itself to go to the polls in 1974. For the major thrust in the coming campaign, Conservatives settled on a proposal by Conservative MP Jim Gillies, the MP for Don Valley, for a ninety-day freeze on prices and wages. This proposal would have no effect on people who were either self-employed or employed by others (namely, all the working population), nor on anyone who had a salary set for the coming year. But a freeze on prices would have the direct effect of ensuring that the price of bread and milk and rent and a host of other things did not rise for a while, allowing people to take a bit of a breath in what had become quite a horrible inflationary spiral.

As the election approached, I re-enlisted in the crusade. Stanfield decided I couldn't stay on his staff as well as be on the public payroll. Of course, the Liberals had for years had executive assistants, special assistants, and nominated candidates feeding from the public trough right up to an election and sometimes through it, but Stanfield wouldn't stand for that. I moved down to headquarters as director of communications, and moved off the publicly funded Opposition Leader's staff.

The nomination for Ottawa Centre was contested by a decent and heavily accented professor of mechanical engineering from the University of Ottawa with the unfortunate first name of Adolf. I won the nomination handily.

One of the happiest moments in my life came when, after winning the nomination, I introduced my mother in the audience from the stage at Ottawa Technical High School. She had recovered from surgery and had had another two years of an almost normal active life, travelling, staying in the workforce, and doing things that mattered to her. It was a huge physical effort for her to be at the nomination, but she was immensely proud that one of her children would be a candidate for a major party. She connected with the crowd immediately, as they did with her, and became the centre of attention. It was one of the great nights of my life watching her enjoy herself so much. Sadly, she did not live through to the campaign.

In this election, I didn't face many of the same problems I had two years earlier. Because I was seen as the likely winner, the money rolled in. Irwin Haskett raised many times our 1972 budget. With that kind of financial clout, we had TV and radio ads, billboards, three storefront committee rooms, and mobile committee rooms. We managed five literature drops and a series of canvasses. Claude Wagner campaigned for me in the francophone sections of the riding. In the end, it didn't matter.

There was a helpful moment when Michael Meighen spoke to a service club in Montreal and called for freezing both the salaries and the size of the civil service, which, when you are a candidate in downtown Ottawa, produces an interesting effect. Pierre Trudeau's "Zap, you're frozen" response to our main policy was also having a great effect, especially in Ottawa. Civil servants were quite anxious about the policy for reasons I can't fathom. If anyone did not have to worry about salaries being frozen on a ninety-day basis, it was civil servants.

At Party headquarters, there was some concern that the Tory message wasn't getting across. Going door to door, I knew otherwise. I called Bill Grogan, who, along with Dalton Camp, was writing the major campaign speeches, and said, "Bill, I've got bad news and good news for you and I'll give you the good news first. They know our position on wage and price controls. Don't you worry, the message is getting through. The bad news is, they hate it."

We determined by about the third week of the campaign that we could save a lot of money by closing our committee rooms and shutting down the phones. But that's not what a Happy Warrior does, so we kept on slogging.

The truth was, however, that the position finally advanced by the party did not come apart in substance, although it faced ruthless and shameless attack. It came apart because the caucus came apart. Diefenbaker spoke in favour of controls on prices but not on wages. When the pressure from other parties intensified, Jim Gillies moved off and advocated a slightly different policy. Jack Horner advanced yet another one.

At meetings, I tried to defend Stanfield's position. After I'd made an eloquent case for the policy in one school basement, Hugh Poulin wandered forth and said, "I'm not troubled by Mr. Segal's explanation of price and wage controls. But I don't know whether the policy up for debate is his version, which is Mr. Stanfield's version, or Mr. Horner's version or Mr. Diefenbaker's version or Mr. Gillies' version, because they all purport to be Conservative positions."

At that moment, I knew I was cooked.

Adding to the problem was a media bias against Stanfield, which had quite an influence, given the radical increase in TV coverage of politics. A thoughtful, considered leader given more to thoughtful understatement than to glib one-liners was simply beyond the media's capacity to understand. Reflective consideration was portrayed as halting, uncertain leadership. Inclusive, reflective policy-building was dismissed as uninspiring rube-style obfuscation. This was not a time for patience. Instant gratification had arrived in politics, with Trudeau as the schlockmeister and the media as carny barkers. Stanfield could not compete in that field.

We went into the campaign against odds that were not to be overcome. Nationally, Trudeau returned with a majority. I got more votes in 1974 than I had in 1972, but the NDP vote, which had come largely from the Liberals in 1972, collapsed back into the Liberal totals, so I was swept out to sea.

In the election aftermath, Keith Davey said Liberal polls had shown there wasn't massive opposition to price and wage controls. The perception of confusion about our policy and our inability to advance it had a far more deleterious effect on the vote than the policy itself. That was an important lesson about how even the best of policies can be screwed up when the party unity isn't there to sustain it. The long arm of divisiveness and the Diefenbaker caucus conspired to do to Stanfield's chances on this issue what it had done with Quebec in 1972.

For me, and for people who had worked tirelessly between 1972 and 1974—like Brian Mulroney, who as a volunteer organizer in Quebec had put together a good slate of candidates—seeing all this potential go down the drain because of the party's inability to maintain unity had a huge effect. It taught a lesson to every child of the party.

Having defeat snatched from the jaws of victory time and again became the metaphor for the Stanfield period. Here was a man who made Adlai Stevenson look like a savage—decent, caring, Harvard educated, down to earth, understated, and with healthy roots in provincial government—but folks would not follow him across the street because they decided he could not maintain a position.

That meant the end of Bob Stanfield as leader. He then moved into a kind of sainthood status in official Ottawa, a good measure of which was earned by his humanity and genuine concern for the disadvantaged. He believed Conservatives had a primary responsibility to address that concern if the right to excel, earn profits, and benefit from them was not to be perceived as being won at the expense of those less able to participate in the economy. His interest in the guaranteed annual income and his support for progressive social measures were tied to that fundamental concern.

But if you are a Conservative, the other critical gateway to sainthood in official Ottawa is passed through simply by losing. The role for which the post-war Conservative Party has been most appreciated is legitimizing the permanent, natural government, the Liberal Party, with its acolytes in the public service, the RCMP and the CBC, the cultural and business centres, and the university community. Canadians become instantly suspicious of Conservatives in government because, frankly, it is not where they are supposed to be.

Nothing could be better for the Liberal view of government— supine intellectually to the use of government as a tool for social engineering and intervention in provincial jurisdiction—than Stanfield's defeat on nothing less elegant than the collapse of party unity on policy during a campaign. This fall was particularly attractive to the permanent brunch crowd in Rockcliffe Park, which prefers no interruption to the natural course of events and whose hardcover and paperback focus on foibles, excesses, and alleged corruptions never seems as urgent when Liberals are in office.

The loss was not just the loss of what many Canadians believed literally was "the best prime minister we never had." It was the loss of an opportunity for the country to consolidate after a period of excessive Trudeau spending and dominant federalism. It could have been a period of a rational and pragmatic balance that would have seen taxpayers' rights protected and fiscal capacity conserved.

Bob Stanfield led the Conservative Party with dignity, elegance, grace, and competence. But he lost thanks to Diefenbaker and the divisions within the Tory family that the former prime minister helped sustain. The loss to the country was probably far more serious than the loss to the Conservative Party of an opportunity for victory.

4

BRAMPTON LEGIONS

SOON AFTER WE LOST THE 1974 ELECTION, Ross DeGeer, executive director of the party, and Hugh Macaulay, kind of an unofficial chairman and volunteer adviser to Bill Davis, came to see me in a little office at party headquarters in Ottawa, a building so old we had to shout to be heard over the radiator. I was director of policy, planning, and communications at national headquarters, working towards the party's 1974 general meeting.

They asked if I would be interested in joining the team they were putting together in Ontario to fight the provincial election expected in 1975. They said, "We'd like you to come on board as campaign secretary. It's important. It's a tough job and you'll be the most junior person on the committee, but we need fresh blood. We're in trouble."

Thinking about the situation, I came to two conclusions. One was that William Davis had been there for me when I was a student and a candidate. Two was that it was an honour being asked to help him at a time when the Conservatives in Ontario represented the core of what was urbane about the party, the core that reached out to people of diverse ethnic groups and of varying religious and other persuasions. Not that the federal party didn't also do that, but in many parts of Canada where the federal party was strong, there weren't many ethnic voters to reach out to.

I said, "I really can't leave here until Mr. Stanfield decides whether he's staying or going. If he decides he won't stay, fine."

To his credit, Stanfield announced at the general meeting that he didn't want to lead the party through another election, so I felt free to go.

I joined the Ontario team as campaign secretary in May 1975, a posting that exposed me to the structural side of party organization. The election call seemed likely to come in the fall, and the Davis government was trailing the Liberals badly.

The Davis era in Ontario had started well. After winning the leadership convention in 1971, one of the first acts of this MPP from Brampton—a suburb of Toronto in Peel Region—was to cancel the Spadina Expressway, an autoroute poised to cut from the suburbs through to the downtown core of Toronto. Every newly minted leader of every political party has to find a way to establish that generational change has transpired, that a fresh perspective exists, that the party has voted for change, and that change has actually occurred. How the leader does that is as important as the way the leader broadens the tent at the moment of victory to let everyone in and become inclusive. The Spadina decision was a way to say, "This is not a mechanistic party of gas-guzzlers insensitive to the issues of environment, quality of life, family, and neighbourhood. Quite the contrary. There can be a balance between economic growth on the one hand and those other virtues on the other."

Spadina was the way to make that happen. It was not only the right decision but was an instrumental decision that had to be made before the election so that people could understand precisely how Bill Davis was different.

What is fundamental is that no Conservative wins an election in Ontario by getting only Conservative votes. The Conservative core on a good day is 24 percent. A Conservative can win an election in the province only if a lot of people who normally vote otherwise decide the leader can be trusted for the next four years. Bill Davis understood that. He had seen Tom Kennedy, Leslie Frost, and John Robarts do it. It became fundamental to find a way to establish that trust, because otherwise the province could lapse into the middle ground of Liberalism, which is the enemy. It is the enemy for good, solid, historical reasons. Liberalism is a threat. This is not a battle between warring elites. This is serious. As citizens, we always pay a huge price for a Liberal period in office, so not letting them be in office is fundamental to everyone's best interest.

Premier Davis's office was run between 1971 and 1974 by Jim Fleck, an affable MBA-daytimer-at-the-ready type who had been secretary to John Robarts' committee on government productivity. The committee had proposed a radical reorganization of government to keep it "tight" with modern times. Davis's long-time aide Clare Westcott used to say that the machinations of the Harvard Business School had done more to destroy democracy than any initiative since *Das Kapital*. True or not, it was not hard to accept that during Fleck's time the Davis government had become remote, disengaged, and a touch mechanistic for real-life Ontario. Greenbelts, regional governments, superministries, planning envelopes, Toronto Centre Region Plans, land transfer taxes, land speculation taxes, and a host of other matrix-like solutions emanated from Queen's Park in a way that erected a sound barrier between the government and its employers, the people.

All these initiatives boasted a rational, thoughtful, strategic public-policy purpose, but none could be explained in under eight paragraphs, single spaced. Voters heard none of the explanations; the explainers rarely heard the people.

In the fall of 1974, I worked in two provincial by-elections on the policy side—Stormont-Cornwall and Carleton East—where Tory seats were lost despite high-profile candidates. We came second in Stormont and third in Carleton East. These losses, and a previous loss in the Goderich, Ontario, riding held for years by former treasurer Charles MacNaughton, sent a serious message to the Davis organization. The roots had become shallow, the links frayed, and trouble was on the horizon.

That governments get into trouble is normal. What distinguishes durable governments from the David Peterson flash-in-the-pan variety is that they get the message and change their ways. When Ed Stewart replaced Fleck as deputy in the premier's office and, subsequently, as secretary to the cabinet, the stage for real repositioning and pragmatic, hands-on political decision-making was set.

With the election looming in September 1975, I went to Toronto from my home in Ottawa two or three days a week. I shared a hotel room with Norman Atkins and worked on campaign planning and organization.

Davis started the election fourteen points behind Robert Nixon's Liberals. Nixon was recruiting fancy candidates, among them former Toronto mayor Phil Givens, and the general impression was that Bill Davis was almost certainly going to lose.

Classically, the campaign secretary is the one who, after a committee meeting where thirty people all decide they are going to do something, calls each of them the next morning to say, "You said you'd put together a list of new advance people we could use as volunteers. I know and you know that I'll call you until the list is in. Every day. If you want me to stop calling, give me the list." If the campaign secretary doesn't do that, commitments, whatever they may be, fade away, particularly when the committee is made up mostly of volunteers who have real jobs elsewhere.

A campaign secretary also tends to do everything at headquarters, including answer the phone well into the early hours of the evening. One night during the campaign, I answered a call and a voice said, "Would the campaign chairman be there?"

I said, "I'm sorry, Mr. Atkins is in a meeting."

"Oh. Do you think he'll be free soon?"

"Well, I don't know. He's pretty busy. Do you want to leave your name? I'll be glad to have him call you."

"Would you tell him it's the candidate."

"We've got 125 candidates, sir. Which candidate is it?"

"The one in Brampton."

We had something in the campaign organization called the Grand Klong, which was awarded every week to the person who made the biggest mistake. The award was a brown heart, reflecting what happens when all the excrement in one's body goes directly to that organ. I received the award that week.

In the campaign, the core issue was rent control. *The Toronto Star* ran with it something fierce, publicizing NDP leader Stephen Lewis's litany of horror stories about senior citizens, single mothers, and the poor being gouged by rapacious landlords. The paper's journalists had researched the issue well and had come out with anecdotal stories that dominated the front page day after day after day. If we lost the apartment dwellers in the highrises of Scarborough, Mississauga, and downtown Toronto, we would lose the election.

At first, we tried to fight back by saying, "Oh, don't worry, the Unconscionable Transactions Act can be used against usurious rent increases." This was true, but both tenant and landlord would have passed away before the matter was ajudicated.

We quickly had to make a critical decision. Did we want to give the keys to the store to the other side? The developers and other people in the apartment business didn't want us to impose rent controls, but they didn't stop us. The numbers clearly showed that if Nixon adopted rent control as Liberal policy, he would sweep Metro and win. He didn't. I concluded the developers had gotten to him when they couldn't get to us. That decision, along with his performance in particularly nasty and bitter TV debates, cost him the election. Notwithstanding the popular vote, Nixon came third in the seat total and Stephen Lewis became leader of the opposition, fundamentally changing the political dynamics in Ontario.

On election night, I went to Brampton. Everyone seemed awfully upset because, although we were still the government, we had won only a minority. There hadn't been a minority Tory government in Ontario since George Drew's in 1943. I walked in higher than a kite. I thought this was a perfect rebalancing of the political process. People looked at me as if I were nuts. Mrs. Davis was particularly down.

I said, "Kathleen, with the greatest respect, I come from Ottawa. This looks wonderful. This is a new start. This is super. We've got a fresh beginning, and the other guys now have to put up or shut up. All these wondeful ideas they have, they have the votes to put them into effect. Let's see if they will."

After the campaign, still happy with the result, I headed off to P.E.I. to take a couple of weeks' rest at David MacDonald's place in Alberton. At the end of the first week, Ed Stewart, clerk of the Davis cabinet, who was not very partisan—quite the contrary—called and said, "I'm led to believe that you were involved with Mr. Stanfield during the minority government in Ottawa."

"Yes, sir, I was."

"Well, apparently, there's nobody around here who's ever been involved in minority government and there's some thought that you might not be a bad legislative assistant. Now, I'm not personally totally sold on this idea, but if you'd like to come up and have a chat, I'd be more than delighted to do so."

I said, "I would be honoured to come and have a chat."

I put down the phone and said to David, "Not the most enthusiastic recruitment call I've ever had."

I began work as legislative assistant to Premier Davis in November 1975. The next two years were the happiest of my life. I broadened my sense of the Tory family while establishing a family of my own. I was best man at the marriage of my roommate from Ottawa U.,

Ian Green, at which the maid of honour was Donna Armstrong, a wonderful woman of great intelligence and beauty from Kingston. In 1976, after a determined courtship on my part, for which Donna argues she helped pay through substantial Visa account balances, we married, surrounded by a fascinating mix of people. Joining with my family from Jewish Montreal and Donna's half French-Canadian, half Maritime-Scottish family were some whose roots were extremely humble like my own and who had grown up in this country from immigrant stock. Others, like Claude Wagner, Bob Stanfield, Bill Davis, Ed Stewart, Eddie Goodman, and Ian Green could be seen as representatives of older traditions and governing elites. The entire group, along with David MacDonald and various other members of the Progressive Consevative family, formed a picture I will never, ever forget.

Everyone approved of Donna, seeing clearly, as I could, that she was one of those people who had her head screwed on firmly and who would never let the successes or failures of politics get in the way of keeping our heads straight over what really mattered. If I ever came home with an impression of myself slightly larger than reality might suggest was appropriate, that impression would certainly have a short shelf-life.

The wedding canopy was held by my two brothers, Seymour and Brian, and Donna's two brothers, Fraser and Roy. The service was in French, Hebrew, and English. Donna's parents were supportive, as were Brian and Seymour. The event was warm and intense—which is what you might expect from an event mixing French-Canadian, Scottish, Jewish, and political sensibilities.

Beyond the personal and into the professional, in those years I became awestruck by how the Davis organization operated, because it operated for a policy purpose. It was not, as its detractors suggested, a mechanistic organization that was about patronage, influence, power, and all the rest. It was about gathering up and regenerating new groups of volunteers across the province with abilities in policy, orga- nization, fundraising, volunteer development, and the creative arts, all in support of a particular approach to public policy, which was the Ontario Progressive Conservative bias, best described as progressive social policy and very conservative fiscal policy.

I also developed a sense of awe about how the government of Ontario worked. What was most awe-inspiring was not the mechanisms or structures of government but the degree to which government was so much more down to earth than anything I had seen in my opposition days watching the federal government. Ontarians knew what the government of Ontario did. The government there financed the schools, ploughed the roads, and kept the hospitals open. If there wasn't a war on, citizens couldn't say what Ottawa did except tax and pontificate.

The most important single attribute of Bill Davis's conservatism was its rootedness in everyday life. The Toronto Club may have been the prism through which key business leaders saw the world (and there is nothing wrong with that view, if you do not mind limited views), but Davis's conservatism was more resonant at the Rotary Club or the local bowling league. His government sported these roots with real and compelling pride. This was not so much because of philosophical biases as it was because of individuals who peopled his administration at its best, beginning with himself.

Whatever the policy coming from the civil service or the party, Davis had a wonderful capacity to deal with it. He had an ad hoc group of kitchen-table types he gathered regularly to make sure he wasn't missing something in caucus relations, and he had an ability to pick up the phone and talk to a regional office manager for the ministry of education in North Bay, if need be, to find out what was really going on. He may not have always done it himself, but he knew it needed to be done. His was a government that went through periods of disconnect, for which it paid heavily, but was never actually disconnected. It would go through periods of intense connection with the reality on the streets and concession roads, on the farms, and in the stores of the province. These were the times when his government was at its most effective, most able, and most agile.

These were days when there were family-law reforms and when Davis quietly went about building more French schools because it was the right thing to do and because the population demanded and required it. The Ontario French-language school system was the largest non-denominational school system operating in the French language anywhere in the world outside France, yet it was constructed without much of a backlash, especially in light of the backlash Trudeau engendered by the way his Official Languages Act was put into place over the same years in Ottawa.

The focus of social policy was seniors. A series of studies made it apparent that too many senior citizens, particularly women, were living at or beneath the poverty level. There was a thrust in social policy through the Guaranteed Annual Income payment, or GAINS, the senior citizens' tax rebate, and the establishment of a seniors secretariat to recognize that the people who built the country and had invested so much in its development were now trying to live out the remaining years of their lives during the Trudeau-generated period of high inflation, when rates of 8 to 9 percent inflation a year or worse were, over four years, collapsing by 50 percent the value and buying power of their pensions.

The Ontario government stepped in. Darcy McKeough, the minister of finance, treasury, and economics, allowed me to come along as a junior member of the delegation when he attended a federal-provincial fiscal-relations meeting chaired by Trudeau's minister of finance, Donald Macdonald. The Liberals were trying to ram through a revenue-guarantee rule in response to the Benson white paper on taxation, which would have radically changed the fiscal floor upon which all provinces operated. It took a tremendous effort by McKeough and others to keep the federal government from doing something that would have dislocated the tax structure across the country.

In those meetings, I had my first real glimpse of how arrogant the federal government could be and how unrelated it could be to what was going on in the streets and on the farms of the country. It made an indelible impression upon me and my view of how out of touch the federal bureaucracy was then and is now.

Ontario under McKeough brought in a rule between 1974 and 1976 that basically said, "Whatever the rate of inflation, we will spend at least 2 percent less." The rate of inflation would increase our revenues by that amount, so we would spend 2 percent less and the difference would be used to retire the debt or pay down the deficit, which was done to bring some fiscal restraint to the system. Inflation was ratcheting up revenues and costs, becoming a machine that fed itself. Heading towards usurious and problematic levels of inflation and towards the 1974 election campaign over price and wage controls, Ontario used the situation as an opportunity not to increase its revenues but to stabilize its debt and the rate of growth of its deficit.

In the years I was at Queen's Park, we never had a deficit much in excess of a billion dollars. There were several years when the books would have almost balanced, except that to keep the interest costs down for hospitals, universities, colleges, and municipalities, we would advance them the money so they wouldn't have to borrow. That would also keep our books from going into an artificial balance we knew we couldn't sustain during a recession. There was no need to create an expectation that couldn't be met.

All this was done at a time when the population was growing by leaps and bounds, and the demands on the system—on universities, colleges, and hospitals—were increasing at an incredible rate. Davis managed to navigate through all that with his very moderate sense of down-home values.

He mentioned Brampton everywhere he went, not only to promote Brampton but to remind people that he knew where he was from. Whether he was at a bankers' meeting in Zurich or a rating agencies' event in New York City, whether he was in another part of the province or at a fancy first ministers' conference in Quebec City, he knew who he was. Brampton became synonymous with values of parsimony, generosity among people, community life that meant something, volunteerism, and a family structure that was the centre of life.

I would go to Brampton with Ed Stewart on Wednesday mornings to pick Davis up before cabinet so Ed could brief him about the agenda. In his little office at the house would be three or four Bramptonians with problems. The family dog, a touch arthritic, would be coming in from a night on prowl and Kathleen would be blasting a hair dryer on old Thor's hips so he might possibly walk again. Ed and I would try to get a cup of coffee while the kids ran around getting ready for school.

This was the real world. This was not a house with paid staff. This was a house, inherited from his father, where a busy family was going about its business. Here was a man trying to be a father and a husband and a premier at the same time. It was so different from the cerebral, heavenly detachment the Pitfields and Trudeaus displayed as they perambulated around Ottawa dealing with the "larger" issues.

I suspect Bill Davis slept in fewer hotel rooms than any other first minister in any jurisdiction in the world. Every night, if there were a plane that could get him home, he went home. It didn't matter if he were in Moosonee until the wee hours, he went home. The odd time we were too far away, we would stay in a hotel, but those times were rare indeed. It would strike the press as strange to be sitting in Windsor contemplating a four-hour trip back to Toronto. Aides, reporters, and everyone else in the entourage would get to their hotel rooms and flats at 2 A.M., but at the same time Bill Davis would be in his bed in Brampton. He simply believed people should go home. He believed that when politicians, businesspeople, or sports stars stay out on the road, they forget what is important and lose contact with their kids and their community. Bill Davis went home every night, which made a big difference in the staff's perception of him and his perception of us.

He structured his staff in a fascinating way. Ed Stewart was utterly non-partisan. He had come up through the ministry of education and had been a teacher, a local superintendant of education, assistant deputy minister of education and university affairs, and a deputy minister under Davis. Ed was the most down-to-earth guy anyone could ever want to meet. He was completely unimpressed by the trappings of government; he found them a touch tiresome and bothersome. Whatever the politicians had in mind, civil servants knew that Ed would always speak the truth in the Premier's Office.

The son of a Scottish autoworker from Montreal who had lived in Windsor, this remarkable public servant advocated two simple principles. To the partisans, he would say, "Good, honest, and simple government is the very best politics, whatever the affiliation of the government of the day." To his colleagues in the civil service, he would say, "Our job is not to act as if we manage warring departmental turfs with different priorities but to remember that this is one government, accountable to the people, who have every right to expect frugality, common sense, compassion, and honesty."

Ed could be found in his office from 6:15 A.M. on, reading the papers, drinking the world's worst instant coffee, and listening to big-band music as he planned the day's events. His door was always open, and deputies learned quickly that failing to avail themselves of that open door and letting a problem simmer beyond the point of retrieval was not likely to be a career-enhancing move. He ran the senior civil-service appointments process in concert with other senior civil servants and guardedly insisted that partisanship play no role. If someone was brought in to perform clearly partisan policy work, he believed they had no right to aspire to or hope for a civil-service commission, and they simply did not get one. If there was any hint of scandal or lack of probity, he either called the OPP himself or made it clear that all who reported to him or through him had a primary duty to do so.

What saved the government from its own potential excesses was the integrity and frankness Ed brought to the job, his belief in the imperative of a non-partisan public service, and his belief that politicians who were duly elected required a full range of the broadest possible inputs to make well-informed decisions. No deputy or minister who tried to hijack the premier's prerogatives or government priorities could get around Ed.

Clare Westcott dealt with the vast array of issues a premier has to address in a methodical and uncontroversial way. The provincial diplomatic corps, refugee families in trouble, messages to families of slain or wounded police officers, people who fell through the cracks of the welfare system—all these fell to Clare to attend to, and he did so with grace, self-deprecating good humour, and the odd burst of advice that kept everyone in the office on their toes.

Clare had been Davis's executive assistant in the ministry of education and an executive assistant for Bob Macaulay when he was minister of trade. He was pure politics from Seaforth, Ontario, where he had been a hydro lineman, and became kind of a fifties version of Mother Teresa. If a journalist's wife were sick but couldn't get into a nursing home, Clare got her into a nursing home. We had a rule in Ontario that all ambulances had to be disassembled after so many miles so they couldn't run again, but if there were Caribbean countries that had no ambulances, Clare would get them reassembled and shipped on Armed Forces flights to the Caribbean. If there were kids at an orphanage or a church school in the north who had never been to a Maple Leafs hockey game, he'd get them tickets and a bus company that would drive them to the game. Using the authority of the Premier's Office, he would say, "The premier would really think it was nice if these kids could get to a game."

He did these kinds of things incessantly. Clare could reach down into the system because he had been in it for thirty years and knew everybody. There was no such thing as a textbook thrown out in an

Ontario school as long as Clare was in the ministry of education. Textbooks were bundled up and sent to English-speaking schools in Uganda, South Africa, or the Caribbean. Anybody who could use some got some. In his office could be found people from the Holy See, consulates, or old folks' homes needing help. It was like a World Vision operation going on down the hall from the Premier's Office.

Laird Saunderson, the appointments secretary, found a way to make everyone from the captains of industry to the most local and humble of organizations feel that they counted and that the premier considered their needs, whatever the time pressures involved. Lyn Hillborne did the same for the premier when he travelled from Queen's Park across the province, the country, and the world. Helen Anderson, whose service to Ontario began as a file clerk under Mitch Hepburn, was a confidential secretary who had been with the premier since his days in Education. "Miss A." redefined for all time the confluence of grace, loyalty, and hard work under pressure.

Ray MacNeil aided Ed Stewart as a troubleshooter from within the system, and he became an early-warning system about the inside of government and the appointments process that would put the DEW line to shame. Sally Barnes and Vince Devitt in the press office, two old hands with experience in newsrooms across Ontario, never tried to manage the press. They both simply argued for telling the truth, on the assumption that it is only when you fudge the truth that the press has any real leverage. They usually prevailed.

Eddie Goodman was outside the circle until 1974 for reasons likely more related to petty jealousies than to any substantial issue. Eddie was the guy from the real world of law, business, and politics who brought common sense, humour, and the odd flash of wisdom to the process. He was not burdened by shyness. He was a sparkplug for everyone and a constant mentor to me.

What I learned from this team, as campaign secretary and, after 1975, legislative secretary, overwhelmed any contribution I was able to make. These were Davis people on the inside, bolstered by a modern, frank, down-to-earth campaign organization run by Norm Atkins and shepherded out of party headquarters by Ross DeGeer.

I was the political guy. My rule was always to ask, "Are we doing this because as Progressive Conservatives we believe in this? Are we doing this because it corresponds to the Progressive Conservative notion of what is in the public interest?"

Ed Stewart would ask, "Is it in the public interest, notwithstanding what the hell the PCs may or may not think? What is the public interest?"

The Progressive Conservative Policy Committee, of which I was secretary, grouped party officials, MPPs, rank and file, and spokespeople from small business, agriculture, and the wider Ontario community beyond Metro Toronto's self-centred gaze, meeting monthly under the able chairmanship of Darcy McKeough, perhaps the most competent Treasurer of Ontario ever to that point.

A subset of this group met every Tuesday morning for breakfast to look at issues, offer advice, and add to other forms of political intelligence from the caucus and rank and file. It included the ex officio party president; the campaign manager (the affable and always politically acute Norm Atkins); the party director, Ross DeGeer, one of the most efficient and pragmatic organizers in modern Canadian politics; policy advisers such as Tom Kierans, Eddie Goodman, and Hugh Macaulay; and key ministers such as Roy McMurtry, Tom Wells, Bob Welch, and, over the 1975, '77 and '81 elections, Frank Miller, Bette Stephenson, Larry Grossman, Bob Elgie, and others. All of these ministers has their own strong advisors. Roy McMurtry had Bill Saunderson and David Allen. Larry Grossman had the brilliant and sage Alan Schwartz. Frank Miller had Tony Breloner and Hugh Mackenzie—all of whom reflected different professional, ethnic, and geographic constituencies.

Some on the far right of the party were troubled because they thought there were too many people around Davis and that those people were far too moderate, but everyone had a way into the system. Everyone had someone they could talk to. Whether the group in charge was called the Big Blue Machine or the Park Plaza Breakfast Club, it was a group of people, largely volunteers, who were part of the process. Tom Kierans on the right, Eddie Goodman on the left, Norm Atkins wearing the advertising man's hat thinking about how it all would sell, and ministers as far left as Larry Grossman, Roy McMurtry, and Tom Wells, and as far right as Darcy McKeough and Frank Miller, all sat around the table.

The purpose was to offer frank and undiluted advice and deal with bad news dispassionately. It became not an elite division between those in the room and those outside, as some observers often implied. Rather, it became a key point of contact wherein the networks of all those in the room supplemented the bureaucratic and formal networks that often worked too slowly or less frankly. All the decisions were made either in cabinet or in caucus.

About twice a year, Davis would take people away on retreats, including people from the left and the right, in the party and out of the party, from a wide reach of Ontario life—labour, health care, industry, and the community and volunteer sector—all invited to "come and reason together" in Ontario's interests. There was also the Ontario Business Advisory Committee, co-chaired with the Chamber of Commerce, supplemented by the annual meetings of cabinet with the agricultural federation, the teachers' federation, the Ontario Federation of Labour, the medical association, and others, rounding out a planning and listening process that kept the government on a straight and well-balanced course.

The Davis style of government was not top-down, with the premier *über alles*. It was "Let's have a debate here. Let's see how people feel. Let's get it on the table." He would listen to the discussion for two or three hours and say, "I think I hear where you're coming from. I think I sense where the right path is, and this is where we're heading." No premier can do that that to a cabinet or a caucus unless in the end the members agree with the leader's judgement.

Cooperating with labour in the interest of greater productivity, the LaMarsh Commission on Violence in Television, the rejection of a UN Law Enforcement Conference in Toronto because the terrorist PLO planned to attend under UN auspices, all emerged from this process, along with many other tonal and substantive changes.

In many of these initiatives, many thought they detected the shadowy presence of Dalton Camp, although he was not very visible around Queen's Park beyond the early seventies. I had come into more contact with both Dalton and his brother-in-law, Norm Atkins, while on Stanfield's staff. Dalton was a frequent adviser on policy, while Norman was a frequent adviser on policy, communications, and organizational matters. I couldn't do my job in Ottawa without working with them, getting to know them, and unavoidably coming to like them. When I came to Queen's Park, I got to see them not as the mythology portrayed them but for what they were.

Dalton, one of the most erudite and literate people in the party, successfully led the process for democratization in the sixties. He made us into a modern political party, then was turned into a pariah by some who feared the clarity of his approach. While most everyone in the party in 1966 was of the view that the time had come to address the Ceasar problem, and a majority had voted to do just that, there wasn't much affection for the man who led the charge, which almost put him in a position of exile, unduly and unfairly. Fortunately, because he was relied upon by people like Bill Davis in Ontario, Hugh Flemming and Richard Hatfield in New Brunswick, and Frank Moores in Newfoundland, the benefit of his intellect and background wasn't lost to the party.

Both Dalton and Norman were stereotyped from the outside as a kind of cabal that manipulated events in their own interest, especially in gaining government advertising contracts for Camp Associates Advertising Ltd., an agency taken over by Norman in the late sixties and which Dalton had almost nothing to do with after 1972. In truth, other agencies received far more work and the process was far more open than it ever was under a Grit regime, but the perception remained. There was never any question of competence. The agency did some of the most creative, impressive work ever done in this country in tourism and other areas.

Some inside the party, particularly on the right, were almost as distrustful as those on the outside. But both Dalton and Norman were driven by the clear perception that the Liberals were the enemy, just as Dalton was driven by the need to have a premier in New Brunswick who would be fair to the 40 percent of the population who were francophone, and just as he supported Stanfield for leader because he perceived the need for someone with policy breadth and a fundamental moderation and decency to open up the party in Quebec and urban Canada.

I did not agree with all their views. We differed on many things. But their purpose was essentially to argue for a common-sense pluralism without which the Conservative Party is irrelevant. The people who related to them in many ways in the process—Roy McMurtry and Tom Wells in Ontario and people at the federal level such as David Crombie—all reflected that strain in the party. That strain isn't always right. Sometimes, there is a need to move to a more conservative position because a Liberal or NDP government has pulled things so far to the left that unless a new leader and cabinet get back to a traditional conservative position, it's impossible to move a government towards the centre. But, in general terms, when in government, humanity and moderation are what matters.

What I learned from Bill Davis, Dalton, Norman, and, to an extent, Ed Stewart was that a government's distinction emerged more compellingly from things it had the courage not to do than from things it decided to do.

Among the staff, we used to say that Davis's exhortation to cabinet was, "Never put off to tomorrow that which you can avoid altogether." It was only partly a joke. He learned his lesson from 1971 to 1974, with the land transfer tax, regional government, and other reforms dealing with every inadequacy and inequity in the system. Many people said, "What is he fixing? A bunch of things that aren't broke, that's what. And he's tearing up the place in a way that's quite counterproductive." That view just about did him in. He didn't almost lose the 1975 election because he had been too conservative. He almost lost because his government had been too activist. The agenda was jammed full and ministers were getting in people's faces all the time, violating the rule that the Ontario government should be like a cleaning lady: dependable, efficient, as low-cost as possible, and, above all, someone who doesn't break anything. He would not make the same mistake again.

The minority situation was not sustainable for long. After a year and a half, many in the party believed it was time to clear the air and try to regain a majority, and I was amongst them. I was very much a hawk on the issue, believing that the Ontario government needed a strong mandate in the face of the election of a separatist party in Quebec in 1976 and the prospect of a referendum on destroying the country. I also believed it was important for the national party and for Conservatives in other provinces who were down on their luck on occasion for this particular organization to survive and thrive. Keeping the keys to the Ontario store was one of the fundamental ways of surviving.

When the Liberals and the NDP combined to defeat a motion to change the percentage increases landlords could charge under the rent-control legislation, a motion the government took to be a matter of confidence, we hit the campaign trail. For me, this was an opportunity to see up close Bill Davis's unique mix of popular appeal, propriety, and closely controlled angst.

Just before the election, we travelled to the Quinte Fair in Belleville with the local federal member, Jack Ellis, and to visit farms and barns in the area. We stopped in at a speedway, and someone suggested it would be a great idea if the premier got into one of the cars and did a small spin around the track to say hi. He got in. The daredevil driver clearly had another view of what would please the crowd. Off he went, around and around, handling a couple of two-wheel spins and other popular manoeuvres. He was up. He was down. When the car got back to the reviewing stand, Davis's pipe was clenched so tightly in his mouth I was surprised his teeth hadn't gone through to his brain. He got out, looked at Jerry Lampert, the eastern Ontario organizer, and said, "That was very interesting."

Jerry said later, "I don't know about the premier, but I sure had to change my pants."

His admirable stoicism emerged frequently on trips to smaller centres via the many small airports that dot the Ontario landscape. A white-knuckle flyer, he would play cribbage on the plane so as not to think about crashing. During a particularly bumpy campaign flight to Timmins in an aging DC-3, we looked over to one wing of our ancient Millard Air aircraft to see it covered in leaking oil. I said to myself, "This is it. We're going to die on a DC-3 somewhere in the bush around Timmins. And just when he's running fifteen points ahead of the party."

Joined by Millard Air's similarly ancient stewardess, Grace, we began a chorus of "Nearer My God to Thee."

When the plane landed, the premier said, "Oh, Hughie. Do you think you could call headquarters and see if they might arrange another conveyance while we're in Timmins?"

"Yes, sir," I said. "I will do my best."

The flight worried me for another reason, as it seemed to be an omen of what might happen in the election. The sense of impending doom was intensified by the early response we had in Timmins, a seat the Grits had held in 1975 and a seat we weren't supposed to win, despite an excellent candidate in Alan Pope. Near the end of the campaign, a night rally was scheduled for eight o'clock at a school in Porcupine. At seven-thirty, the large hall was empty. But at ten to eight, we looked out the window and saw a huge throng of people marching on the school. The Polar Bear Express had come down through the riding, picking up people at every stop, because they knew that if they could get Alan elected they would have a bright, dynamic cabinet minister to represent them, which is, in fact, what transpired.

We won only seven more constituencies than we had in 1975,

taking 58 of the legislature's 125 seats. Many people thought the result was not worth the effort, but from my point of view, Stephen Lewis's career had been on a steep trajectory, with his approval rating so high that he was beginning to pull the NDP up to competitive levels. That had to be dealt with, and the election dealt with it. The election made Stuart Smith leader of the opposition and brought an end to Lewis's parliamentary career, which had the effect of extending the life of our government another eight years.

It was also an election that saw people like Bob Elgie elected in Toronto, who helped nuture the urban roots of the party and, as the minister responsible, brought in a new human rights code for Ontario, which did what was right to help people and thus broadened our base.

On election night, Davis committed himself to governing for a full four years, and he did so by getting support from the Liberals on some bills and from the New Democrats on others. The second minority was a full term in every sense of the word, with the premier still depending on a group of people who brought fresh insights, grass-roots experience, and unlimited competence, integrity, and conscientiousness to their tasks.

Eddie Goodman asked the questions that were on the streets but previously unheard in the precincts of government. Norm Atkins pressed for more organizational attention to detail and local realities. Recruits such as Michael Daniher in legislative planning and John Tory as principal secretary raised serious questions about legislative strategy and timing. There was little chance of reality being cushioned or diluted. Even Nick Lorito, Davis's long-term driver and often his toughest critic, would frequently start the nightly ride home to Brampton with, "So you think things went well in the House today. Let me tell you what I heard at the garage."

Some leaders lose their balance because a protective cocoon keeps them from street-level facts. In Bill Davis's case, the cocoon was made of glass that intensified what was going on and kept him awash in it. Ed Stewart kept the glass clean. Davis had the intuitive genius to assimilate it all and build a compelling political style that reflected not only reality but government at its most pragmatic, effective, and, in the end, trustworthy. Which is how one gets to be in the legislature for a quarter of a century and be premier for fourteen years.

The core notion was that civility in defence of right was no vice with Bill Davis, and nor was inclusion, even at some cost to ideological

Sadye Dankner weds Morris J. Segal in Montreal on
Christmas day, 1937.

The first year, with fraternal support:
Brian, the new arrival, Seymour.

Early canvassing and fireman's duties—rue Jeanne-Mance, Montreal. Unnamed campaign worker.

City-wide Public Speaking winner, 1966, and the only Union Nationale youth (Jeune Unioniste) and PC High School Federation member at Herzliah High, Montreal.

Successful candidate for student government vice-president, University of Ottawa, 1969.

On staff with the Reverend David MacDonald, MP for Egmont, P.E.I., in 1971, learning about potato blight, reefer cars, oyster bed leases, and carageenan as fast as possible (likely the only Herzliah graduate with expertise in any of these for all time).

Seeking the PC nomination, Ottawa Centre, 1972: visiting the Glebe Diner on Bank Street with Bill Willis, manager of Willis IGA.

1972 campaign ad.

Campaigning in the Rideau Gardens neighbourhood in the 1972 general election. I appear to be discussing a tree.

Joining Robert Stanfield's staff, November 1972.

Opening of the House of Commons after the 1972 election. Trudeau gets the elegant and erudite Gérard Pelletier (right); Stanfield is stuck with me.

Working with Claude Wagner on his first speech as foreign policy spokesman (on Vietnam and the peace process), 1972.

Campaigning with Bill Davis in the 1974 general election.

purity. Extremism in defence of an ideological view was never a virtue. Those were not tough rules, and they weren't excessive, but they determined how the man ran the store.

They also worked to support an important transition for me. The Davis style provided a great contrast in two ways of governing: the Diefenbaker approach of hyperbole, excess, and egocentricity versus the Davis approach of quiet incrementalism. More important, my time at Queen's Park gave me a glimpse into what the Conservative Party could be as a governing instrument. I had a good sense of what it was in opposition and what it could reflect and fight for. But in those days, the only long-term proof of what it could be in government existed in Ontario. We had a progressive healthcare system, a progressive education system, a social system advanced beyond those of most other provinces, industrial innovation and expansion, and a polyglot population, all things not generally identified with traditional conservatism. It was a fascinating example of the party's ability to be relevant.

It also said that there is more to competence and leadership in a political party than policy and power. Competence as defined in any contemporary sense through people like Bill Davis meant the ability to work with people, civility, campaign capacity, policy integrity, and links to the real world so the government could never be overtaken by civil servants, lobbyists or special interests. All those things are pretty fundamental, although they are not always pursued in the city of Ottawa by politicians of all affiliations.

5

MUFFLED DRUMS

I LEFT GOVERNMENT IN 1977. I needed a break and needed to get some real business experience. I had spent all my working days since leaving university in a member of Parliament's office, the federal leader of the opposition's office, running for Parliament, or serving the premier of Ontario. It struck me that conservatism was about society, not about government, and that I had better broaden my understanding of society and become a more rounded person, particularly in the context of understanding what goes on outside the world of politics.

John Cronyn, a director of John Labatt Ltd. of London, Ontario, invited me to consider joining the company. He had been very close to John Robarts and Darcy McKeough, and I knew him from Conservative politics. John had been a senior brewing engineer for a long time and had come up with the recipe for Labatt's 50, a significant event in the company's history. That assured him a role on the board of directors for many years after his formal retirement. Eddie Goodman was also a long-time director of the company and encouraged me to come on board.

I was hired as director of corporate and investor relations in the fall of 1977, reporting to Bruce Brighton, the senior vice-president of finance and administration, a strait-laced, hardworking, and determined financial man. An investment professional from a wealthy New Brunswick family, Frances Carmichael, a tough-minded investor, worked with me to teach me the ropes. The experience altered my view of the world.

London was a fascinating place to live. It had a tradition of being more centre-right than most Ontario communities. The Conservatives were far more right wing and, frankly, so were the Liberals. London was also a stratified community where who your grandfather was and where he was born mattered. Labatt's in the late 1970s, on the other hand, was a company aggressively pursuing a strategy of diversification and expansion. How hard you worked and how much of a contribution you made was far more important than who your grandfather was.

I had a chance to work directly with Peter Widdrington, the president of Labatt's, at a time when the company was making acquisitions in the wine and magazine businesses, disposing of assets in Brazil, starting up a major league baseball team in Toronto, and introducing new brands as part of the company's constant war with Molson's and others over national market share. It was a fascinating time. Bob Luba, who oversaw acquisitions and divestitures, and George Taylor, who was a rising star in finance, worked as integral parts of a management team I was proud to be on.

One role I found especially interesting was secretary to the board committee dealing with public and social responsibilities. On the committee sat Cronyn, Eddie Goodman, and Alec MacIntosh, a prominent Liberal lawyer. Quarterly, the committee asked questions about Labatt's community activities, its government relations, environmental record, support of charities, what it was doing to deal with employees' problems, what it was doing in training, and what kind of summer jobs it was providing across the country. Labatt's policy in those days was that 1.5 percent of its pre-tax profits had to go to charity, one of the highest commitments of any company in North America then or now.

This company took community and social responsibility seriously. It made the case that there was no conflict or contradiction between, on the one hand, a hard-driving company aimed at profit and a return for the shareholder and, on the other, a balanced and determined execution around issues of social responsibility. If there were no profits, there was no money with which to finance social responsibility, but at John Labatt the notion that social responsibility could be sacrificed to maximize profits was simply not on.

The Labatt's people gave me a broad scope. One week, I could be in Washington dealing with the State Department over whether baseball players from Cuba would be allowed to play with the Blue Jays. Another week, I could be meeting with a native group starting a broadcasting co-op in the north to which Labatt's was giving some money. It was a broad practice in the investor and corporate relations area for a company that had a big consumer franchise, had unionized employees in most provinces, and paid the highest industrial wage, bar none, in Newfoundland, New Brunswick, Nova Scotia, Saskatchewan, and Manitoba.

I also learned about the realities of how business is regulated in Canada, having to come to terms with living under a regulatory regime that, although some would argue it kept U.S. competition out, expressed the very worst of Confederation. Civil licensing matters remained with the provinces after 1867, and the only way a beer could be treated as a domestic beer by a province was if the brewery operated a plant in that province, the sole exception being Prince Edward Island. In bigger, more populated provinces, such as Ontario, Quebec, and B.C., the company had to have more than one plant. But even if the brewery were efficient to the point where the plants were running three shifts at 100 percent capacity, the truth was that one plant in Pennsylvania in a week's run could swamp Canadian production for a year, all because of the economies of scale allowed by the American market and because American breweries do not have the same constitutional burdens we do—a clear example of an arcane regulatory constraint putting Canadian jobs in peril.

During my time in London, I was not directly involved in either provincial or federal politics, although I kept myself informed on provincial affairs and kept a wary eye on the federal party as it headed towards an election under the new leader chosen in 1976, Joe Clark.

When Bob Stanfield was visited by leading members of the western caucus (also associated with the Diefenbaker caucus) after 1974 and told that the sooner he moved on, the better, my own conclusion, as a former candidate and as someone born and bred in Quebec but who had lived most of my active political life in Ontario, was that we needed a leader from Quebec. Addressing French Canada had clearly become a fundamental element of any leadership cycle. I believed for a host of reasons that the best prospect was Claude Wagner. For other Conservatives in 1976, the best prospect meant Brian Mulroney, whose support base from the west and many parts of urban Ontario was quite impressive. For others, the requirements of leadership meant something else entirely. Eddie Goodman supported Flora MacDonald, and Norm Atkins chose Joe Clark. (Bill Davis always let his people choose their own candidates.)

Joe Clark had won the leadership fair and square as the most appropriate option for Mulroney supporters who couldn't stand the thought of Claude Wagner winning and for some in the party who preferred not to have a French-Canadian leader at all. But the way Clark won became a burden that never left his shoulders. He was no one's first choice and not many people's second choice. He was everyone's third choice and to the surprise of many found himself in charge.

Abba Eban used to say about the Palestinians before the peace process, "They were a people who could not take yes for an answer." Joe Clark had that problem. He had been endorsed as party leader and had a chance to reach out to the other leadership candidates and build a coalition and a sense of unity, but he couldn't take yes for an answer. He was fundamentally insecure as leader and could never stop fighting that leadership campaign.

The Conservative Party is such a party of principle and strong opinions that it is traditionally factionalized, and the leader who doesn't broaden the tent at the moment of forming the new team is toast. The window of opportunity is not open for long. It is a measure of competence how quickly the leader opens it; the extent to which the leader delays is a precise indication of incompetence.

Claude Wagner was not an easy man to get along with. He could be imperious and aloof. But given how well he did at the convention, it would have been in Joe's interests to find a workable peace in the same way Bill Davis found a workable peace with his opponents. Rather than treat the people who had almost put Allan Lawrence over the top in 1971 as pariahs, Davis welcomed them into the tent within days. Only a few leaders in modern Conservative history other than Davis have managed that sort of thing well, including Sterling Lyon, Peter Lougheed, Richard Hatfield, and, eventually, Brian Mulroney. They reached out for the best of the brightest, brought them together, and didn't care where they had stood at the leadership convention (a gesture not repeated by Joe Clark, Frank Miller, or Kim Campbell, which speaks volumes).

Clark's insecurity prevented him reaching out to the people who had come closest to beating him. He was afraid to have them in the tent because he didn't trust them, yet those are the people who should be brought inside if for no other reason than to know where they are.

That Pierre Trudeau soon put Claude Wagner in the Senate provided another fascinating glimpse of how Trudeau understood the tensions of the Conservative Party. Clark was far more eager to recruit the remnants of the Ralliement des créditistes to the cause in Quebec and get them to come over one by one than to come to terms with Wagner in some way that could unite the party. Thus Clark further alienated the right wing of the party that Wagner had come to represent, even though moderates like me had supported Wagner because we saw him as humane, fiscally conservative, and responsible.

The lack of an immediate focus on unity was one sign of danger ahead for the party under Clark's leadership. There were many more. There was a wariness towards him even in his home base, largely because he had spent huge chunks of his life out of Alberta and had not achieved the measure of business or professional prominence Albertans often identify with their leadership.

As a Young Conservative, he had been a progressive, closely identified with the democratization of the party in 1966. But almost from the beginning of his leadership, he acquired Diefenbaker-like characteristics: remoteness, capriciousness, and unsteadiness of focus and judgement. All these simply added to the weakness of his leadership, beyond the contribution made by the manner of his election.

He had been steeped in the machinations of Bob Stanfield's office, where he had served for a time. He had worked for a summer at Camp Associates Advertising, preparing for the Fredericton policy conference in the early 1960s. He had sought provincial office. Yet his campaign for leader, his policy framework, and his style of leadership always had an awkwardness that succeeded in making both long-time partisans within the party and those who had never been partisan feel equally uncomfortable. This was an indecent burden for a thoroughly decent man who always tried to do the right thing.

He never built his own base in the party, beyond the narrow group who had been with him on the first ballot in 1976, and never seemed willing to return the loyalty the most loyal come to expect. He had a genuine dislike for the day-to-day realities of democratic politics, where those who seek positions of leadership and trust have to constantly reach out to those with whom they agree and with whom they disagree. Leaders have to shape, sustain, and advance affinities and consensus. Sustaining consensus amongst friends, allies, and those who share political affiliation is the fundamental priority. Fail at that, and you fail at sustaining the deep relationship essential if there is to be loyalty when the chips are down and the pressures most intense.

It was always apparent that Clark found the reaching-out part of the job difficult, perhaps even demeaning. It wasn't because he didn't understand its importance or relevance. God knows, he had seen it often enough in many places many times before. His approach seemed to reflect an unusual discomfort within the framework of the political family, as if tending to the family was beneath him or somehow improper. This ran contrary to the great humility and everyman quality with which he was viewed—and is largely still viewed—by the public and the media.

He was quick to avoid advice from Tories in government. Even before I left Queen's Park for Labatt's, I met with his campaign chairman, Lowell Murray, and chief of staff, Bill Neville, to discuss how the Ontario organization could help on the federal scene. The meeting did not go well, becoming, in fact, quite acrimonious.

There was some grumbling about Clark's leadership at the general meeting of the party in Quebec City in 1978, although nothing serious. I attended the meeting as part of the Ontario delegation with Bill Davis, and we all voted against a leadership review, even after Clark gave one of the great uninspiring speeches of our time. The meeting was a classic example of how he remained aloof from the process of making choices amongst people who had worked in the party for years. He acquiesced to MP Robert Coates being elected party president to appease caucus opponents, and discouraged others who might have broadened the base. He determined he would not be hostage to any particular group by, for example, developing a relationship with the Big Blue Machine. His discomfort with Peter Lougheed and his people was no less than it was with the group in Ontario.

I suspect no one would have known greater loneliness within the Conservative Party than Joe Clark. I also suspect that at no time in the party's history has the rank and file felt less close to their leader. Yet to be kept from the worst of its divisiveness, the Conservative Party needs to feel close to its leader. The rank and file had felt close to Bob Stanfield, despite the caucus problems Diefenbaker's people stirred up. The leader has to establish a measure of that intimacy, but

Joe never found a way to do it. It may not have been due to a lack of intensity or commitment on his part. His efforts may not have worked, although he certainly had staff who were able to make it happen if he would have let it happen.

During his leadership, he seemed focused on the tools of persuasion and the machinations of party administration and management. He could rarely disengage long enough to deal with people. He couldn't talk to the membership on the phone, spend time with them, have dinner with them, or drop in on them in a fashion that builds the kind of bond that partisans have the right to expect and that serves to sustain loyalty to the leader.

Successful politicians are the ones who can come to terms with their weaknesses and their strengths. They can magnify their strengths and use them whenever they can, but they make sure there is some way to compensate for their weaknesses. Joe Clark had many strengths: his frankness, his openness, honesty, and decency, his affection for small-town Canada, and his fundamental humanity on the large issues. But many people felt he could easily express his humanity in the abstract for those oppressed by apartheid, for example, but could never show any humanity personally through offering support to one of his advisers or friends who may have been ill or facing some burden. Such notions circulate pretty widely in a political family; they end up perceived as the truth, and that kept him from becoming a majority prime minister and kept him from staying prime minister.

The great tragedy is that Joe Clark is a bright, confident, able, thoughtful, and caring person. He has a tremendous commitment to the country. He sought to open the party in a host of ways, especially to young people and to women in a way that had never been done so effectively before. For all the people in the country who may have been offended by Maureen McTeer keeping her name, many young women opened up to the party for the first time because of her decision. He reflected an openness, freshness, and a new generation better than some others who sought the leadership, and he attracted some outstanding candidates to run for the team in the 1979 federal election.

Around the time of that election, with provincial energy negotiations coming up and the constitutional issue looming, Bill Davis had Hugh Macaulay, Ed Stewart, and Eddie Goodman join me for lunch to ask whether I might be interested in coming back to Queen's Park. I was enjoying the work at Labatt's, but figured when you get asked by your premier whether you can help, you had better think of a pretty powerful reason to say no. Donna had just finished her MBA at Western, so we returned to Toronto. Donna took a position at P.S. Ross, the consulting arm of Touche Ross. As a nurse, a nursing educator, and an MBA, she quickly made health-care her area of concentration, and I became secretary of the Policy and Priorities Board, at twenty-nine the youngest deputy minister ever appointed in Ontario.

I did not become involved in the federal election, but I soon witnessed first hand the uneasiness in Clark's relationship with Bill Davis and with old-time politicos of his generation. I saw Clark's discomfort with the instruments of power and the great distance between him and his caucus colleagues, not only at the best of times but at the worst of times.

Most Conservatives believed the party had a unique opportunity to win a majority in 1979 at a time when something might still be done about the massive escalation of the debt and the horrific downward economic spiral Trudeau had kick-started with his wild spending ways. The country was clearly fatigued with Trudeau and his various ministers who had left for unsavoury reasons, and his government had been deemed corrupt on quite solid and substantial grounds—the calling by a minister of a judge, huge untendered contracts and lease awards to friends of the party, the Hamilton dredging affair, Skyshops, unreceipted and unspecified mystery amounts collected for a swimming pool from sources unknown.

Leading up to the federal election, it was apparent that the people who had been involved in previous campaigns were going to be largely set aside. What usually happens in the Conservative Party when a leader doesn't want to be associated with any particular group is that the call goes out to Lowell Murray for help. Lowell has been a source of hard work, determination, and focus for most groups of the party. For Clark, he assembled a team who put together a workable campaign strategy with very effective communications—the late Nancy McLean, who did superb work on the film side, Peter Swain, who was doing the media buying for the federal party, Allan Gregg, and a few others.

But the people who had been successful for Davis in 1975 and 1977—Norm Atkins, Tom Scott, and others—weren't involved.

Davis was then midway through the second of his two minority governments and was becoming the Uncle Bill character. Most people liked him; his popularity was stable. But Clark made it clear that he didn't want to be in any way beholden to the premier or his people. Despite that stance and despite Bill Davis's own grave reservations about the leader, the premier was involved extensively in the last few weeks of the campaign, travelling on the bus throughout Ontario, making speeches and supportive comments, and doing all he could to encourage our people to help locally. But there was never any sense of closeness between the two leaders.

The Tories won fifty-seven seats in Ontario, up from twenty-five in 1974, but it wasn't enough to help Clark form a majority. Many Conservatives felt that his capricious demeanour in the TV debates with Trudeau and NDP leader Ed Broadbent, the sense of his being disconnected from the substance of the debate, the mood in the room, and the hollow, self-eviscerative laugh served to give the country the same kind of doubts about substance that had plagued some elements of the party for three years.

Canadians generally afford the Conservative Party a chance to govern only *in extremis* and only for the lack of any alternative. Canadians gave Clark a very modest mandate. He had no support to speak of in Quebec. His base was tied to urban Ontario, the Maritimes, and old Dief strongholds in the west. The fickle nature of this coalition would obviously pose problems were there not a sufficient period of performance to keep the coalition's sinews supple.

The warning signals appeared early on that a sufficient period might not transpire. Even during the campaign, Clark showed a tendency to enunciate a position before the consequences could be even partially divined. On election night, he took the position that he would govern as if he had a majority. The problem was that the people chose not to give him a majority. Bill Davis's position when he got a minority had been that he would govern as if he had a minority because if the people had wanted one party to be able to govern without compromise, they would have given him a majority. Saying "I'm going to govern as if I had a majority" limits one's options, yet it reflected Clark's belief, and the belief of others in his inner circle, that Canadians had voted for massive change. As it turned out, they hadn't.

The new administration met for an inordinately long time in Jasper to decide who would be in cabinet, how the civil service would be changed, and when the House would be called. It was an endless process that quickly dissipated all the energy and promise of the new team. By the time the House was called, Clark's honeymoon was over and the public's suspicion that there might be less than meets the eye to the new prime minister was greatly enhanced.

The cabinet also did not seem to have a sense that a minority government is an even more temporary trust than a majority electoral victory, which itself is only a temporary trust. They displayed a sense of self-righteousness. The notion that a minority government struggled from quarter to quarter and session to session was not part of their mindset.

David MacDonald had supported Flora and then Joe for the leadership and had been made a "superminister"—secretary of state, minister of communications, and secretary for social policy. As a member of Parliament since 1965, David had as a matter of course gone home every summer to hold constituency meetings. As a United Church minister, he had also run back to baptize, marry, and bury people. Even in the worst of the Trudeau sweeps, Islanders found it hard to vote against a guy who had just buried their dad or christened their child.

In the summer of 1979, I ran into him at the Vancouver airport. He looked pasty, almost grey. He had not been out in the sun at all.

I said, "Why aren't you in P.E.I.?"

He said, "I've got all these departments to learn, all these ministries. I'll be travelling around this summer getting briefed. I'll get home next summer."

I said, "David, what if there is no next summer?"

In my judgement, the new prime minister made a terrible mistake by not appointing Claude Wagner to the cabinet. Claude had been fighting leukaemia for some time, but was able to work. The MPs from Quebec—all two of them—got the call, as did two long-time senators from the province and a newly minted senator, Bob de Cotret, who lost the Ottawa Centre riding he had won in a 1978 by-election. But Joe believed Claude Wagner was part of the past, not the future. The day the cabinet was sworn in, Claude wasn't even there. He was dead about two weeks later.

Prime Minister Clark attended the funeral, as did Bill Davis, along with many, many, many people who walked with us in procession behind the hearse in the hot weather from the funeral home to a church that was jammed, the same church where Donna and I had attended the wedding of Claude's daughter a few months before. It was impossible not to get a sense of the enormous feeling for Wagner in Quebec society and to reflect upon how much of a linkage to a huge part of that society Clark had set aside. Had Claude been appointed to cabinet, he would have been buried as a Conservative federal cabinet minister with a massive public following in Quebec, something that does not happen very often. Avoiding that gesture spoke volumes for Clark's insensitivity. It wasn't mean or purposeful; I don't think it ever dawned on him that he was hurting people.

He displayed the same insensitivity towards the many people who worked to get him elected. When a leader comes through a successful tour of southwestern Ontario or Vancouver Island and hundreds of volunteers have worked their hearts out to make the success possible, a leader has to say thank you for their kindness and effort.

When in opposition, a leader who doesn't want to call or sign a note or photograph runs out of ways to say thank you. The vast majority of people in the party are there because they believe in what the party is about and believe in the larger family the Conservative Party is for them. Families should stay in touch with each other, send birthday cards, see how everybody is doing. That is not a lot to ask, but it was something Joe found extremely difficult to do.

Even as prime minister, he was troubled by the process. If someone said to Mike Pearson, "This weekend we're delivering to 24 Sussex 250 photographs and a special pen and on each photograph we want you to write something like, 'To Stan, for all your hard work in Muskoka. Many thanks, Lester B. Pearson,'" Pearson would not have fussed or complained. He would simply have done it. Joe Clark couldn't. He seemed to say, "Well, this is the prime minister of Canada. Maybe someday this will fall into the hands of the wrong sort of person." Fair enough. But a political party is a volunteer organization and all the volunteers who come through the door may not pass a boy scout test of morality on the abdication of self-interest. A signed photograph is not a passport or a letter of reference. It is simply a means of thanking someone for helping organize a meal. That kind of consideration becomes a function that is managed between the leader and his or her staff. It isn't easily done, but it is a requirement of leadership.

It seems paradoxical that Clark could not meet that requirement, having never engaged in anything but politics from the time he was a teenager, for if anyone should have the sensitivity and the common touch, it would be someone who had been in politics all his life. But someone who has never worked in the private sector or in a job where the main purpose of the exercise is for the company to survive, make a profit, meet the bills, and have enough money to hire people does not know what it means when someone working in a company says, "I'm going to take two months off and be a volunteer fundraiser for the campaign." It is impossible to appreciate the sacrifice a woman or man has made to do that, and that may keep the leader from understanding how much he or she should be thanking them at the end of the campaign.

It took months for those who volunteered for the 1979 election campaign to get thank-you notes from Clark. Many people are still waiting. The problem with not following through on such things is that when you get into the soup or face a convention deciding whether you should face a leadership race, all the people who worked in those campaigns and didn't get thanked will remember.

Brian Mulroney picked up support from sons and daughters of the party who had been there in all the bad years, just as he had. Mulroney knew who they were and knew Clark wasn't calling them, so he did. After the 1979 election he would call someone who had organized a great rally somewhere in New Brunswick and say, "I just want to tell you from one Conservative in Quebec, it was an uphill battle, you did a great job, and I just want to say thanks." He didn't do it in a self-seeking "build for the future" mode. He did it because as a volunteer in Quebec for so many years, he knew what it felt like not to be thanked. He knew what it felt like not to be thanked even while Liberals were imploring him to join up with them.

That attention to detail has a lot to do with building a sense of cohesion in the party. Clark's shortcoming in that area combined fatally both with his failure to build a personal constituency of any depth and with his government's lack of any cohesive conservatism of conviction. He was a progressive on social policies and a conservative on fiscal policies, but no social view aside from greater equity and opportunity permeated what he said or what his government did. There was no ringing theme in his administration except newness.

The "community of communities" view he advanced was, at best, an appeal for small-town virtues without the burden of a national will. That view became manifest in his efforts to deal with competing energy-price scenarios advanced by consuming provinces led by Bill Davis and producing provinces led by Peter Lougheed. That both were Conservatives was far less important to the argument than many contemporary historians believed.

I sat in on the pricing negotiations in Ottawa, went to Alberta with Ed Stewart to meet with counterparts in Lougheed's administration, and saw the way the federal government sought to manage the issue. From that vantage point, it became apparent that the feds had no policy on how energy markets should operate in this country. If Ottawa had had a policy tied to the marketplace making the key decisions, both provinces would have had to come to terms within that framework. The lack of that framework, or any other policy premise, made the federal government's burden one of finding some middle ground.

The trouble with that approach was that both Ontario and Alberta were operating from principled positions.

In Ontario, we took the view that the arbitrary line down the Ottawa Valley established by John Diefenbaker had forced provinces to the west of the line to always buy expensive oil and gas from Alberta, while provinces to the east could buy much less costly resources from Venezuela, the Middle East, Rotterdam, or wherever else they could get them cheaply. For generations, Ontarians had wilfully helped finance the expansion of western oil fields and gas reserves through those higher prices. Ontario took the view that its consumers, car drivers, and transportation industry had been heavy investors in the broadening of the west's traditional oil base and that, therefore, there should be a return on investment for Ontario taxpayers through a Canadian domestic price substantially below the soaring world price.

The premier of Alberta believed just as intensely that natural resources were clearly a provincial jurisdiction under the constitution and the province had a fiduciary responsibility to charge something approaching the world price to all consumers to protect future generations of Albertans.

There was no middle ground between two such positions unless the federal government had been elected on a clear mandate to achieve an energy market structure. Joe Clark's government had not, so it was trapped between two immovable forces and lacked the fortitude and policy focus to achieve a balanced solution.

The issue came to a head at the premiers' conference at Pointe-au-Pic, Quebec, in August 1979. The entire weekend was critical for the party in two ways. First, Ontario released a paper calling for two oil prices. Peter Lougheed was not happy. But in Ontario, we were a minority government, and consumer pressure on the pricing issue was put to us every day in the legislature. We had to respond.

Ontario's paper on energy pricing was scripted by people from Energy and Treasury, one of whom was one of the most brilliant and thoughtful public-policy people in the country, Les Horswill. Les had served as a researcher in Stanfield's office and was associated with the progressive wing of the party. He had been one of the many set adrift by Clark and, like many others, found his way to a provincial administration. It was an ironic twist how yet another person with whom Clark couldn't come to terms ended up in a role that was in the end unhealthy for Joe.

During the weekend, word also came that the Right Honourable John George Diefenbaker had died. Dief was to be seen to his final rest by a Progressive Conservative government, with David MacDonald, one of the "termites," overseeing the state ceremony. The funeral was to involve a train going from Ottawa to Saskatchewan with various of Diefenbaker's old retainers on board. This created something of a problem because there is a rule that there is to be no alcohol at state funerals. If Dief's cronies rode at the back of the train without any alcohol at all, several more bodies would have arrived in Saskatchewan. The government relented and alcohol was made available. Across the country the train went, pulling into places like Winnipeg at two o'clock in the morning, where out from the last car would come one Dief retainer or another in a state of modest disrepair to greet hundreds of people who had come to pay final tribute to the Chief.

The funeral marked the beginning of a great exorcism, banishing some of the anger of the past. It was an important passage that made it possible for old hatreds and continuing small-mindedness around the Diefenbaker–Camp battle of 1966 to die down.

Sean O'Sullivan, a former executive assistant to Dief and an MP who had resigned his seat to study for the priesthood, took upon himself the mission of gluing the pieces of the party together, a project he pursued in earnest until 1985. A lot of heat dissipated because of the humanity and gentle humour Sean brought to the task. One morning during a visit to New Brunswick to meet with Dalton Camp, Sean intently looked out across Grand Lake as Dalton made him coffee.

Dalton said, "What are you looking for?"

"The Soviet submarines," Sean said. "Dief told me they arrived every morning with instructions for you and your people."

As Sean began to face the burdens of leukaemia, he became more intense about reconciliation. That he would choose to do that in the way he did spoke for his fundamental humanity, but also revealed something about the Conservative Party. At its worst, it is a sentimental, grudge-carrying, fragmented family at war with itself. At its best, it's a fragmented, emotional, nostalgic family at peace with itself. That is a fundamental precondition, and, given that, the party is always a clear reflection of the country, embodying none of the artificial, corporate, top-down liberal harmony that says, "I know the vision, we're all united, and we're all marching together."

While Clark spent his brief few months in office, the party did not march together, coming to grief over the energy issue for lack of astute direction from the top. At one negotiating session between the federal minster of energy, Ray Hnatyshyn, and Ontario's minister, Bob Welch, the politicians could find some common ground, but the federal officials were not about to let that happen. I assumed they were Privy Council-directed, and therefore thought, perhaps wrongly, they were directed by the prime minister.

He was determined to show his toughness, but ironically the crisis was a coming together of two classic Clark weaknesses. First, the apparent lack of a cohesive policy framework and philosophical premise regarding what kind of Conservative he was. Second, his seeming unease at maintaining a sense of comfort with those who had been active in the party along with him and, while not leadership aspirants themselves, had important contributions to make.

His style of leadership reflected, no doubt unwittingly, a remote, *noblesse oblige* approach, disengaged from the unpleasant issues of patronage and the rest. Even in the areas of appointments his government was singularly incompetent. One did not have to be an old ward-heeling political pro to wonder about just how badly things were handled during the time Clark was in government.

He had been elected when Conservatives had been out of office more than sixteen years.

In defence of both Clark and his government, it was my sense that he was earnestly trying to provide a different style of leadership and government. He wanted to take a more hands-off approach to such issues as patronage appointments, a more sterile approach, to contrast with the excessive chumminess between elements of the Ottawa establishment and the Liberals who had ministered to them—and to themselves through them—for a quarter of a century. It is hard to fault his intent, but while he was seen by the public as so unassuming, he was viewed by some as the most vain and least flexible of all party leaders. Were that not the case, there were ample opportunities to change approaches, priorities, and style to address areas of difficulty and make progress against personal weaknesses. That never happened.

The lack of closeness meant that the benefits the party had gained in Ontario by managing through minorities after the 1975 and 1977 elections were lost to the federal government. There was advice widely available, but none was taken.

Clark made a commitment in the middle of the 1979 campaign about moving the embassy in Israel from Tel Aviv to Jerusalem. I believe it was Ron Atkey's view that such a commitment would help him win the Toronto riding of St. Paul's, as well as help other candidates in ridings with a substantial number of Jewish voters. Jimmy Carter had a similar view. But the policy was announced despite the advice of people in Ontario who had worked on such issues in the past and who cautioned both the leader and his advisers not to announce such a policy during the campaign. The commitment looked like and smelled like pandering on the eve of an election. If it looks like a duck and walks like a duck, chances are it is a duck.

We learned in Ontario that when you make mistakes in government, you should cut your losses. Admit you're wrong, say, "I'm sorry," end the discussion, take the heat, and move on. What you should not do is have the issue roll along in perpetuity to remind people about how bad your judgement might have been in the first place. After the election, some people put forward a suggestion that the way to bring the contentious issue to an end was to announce that Canada would build a consulate in Jerusalem. A large consular presence would not trouble the Arab states unduly nor violate any resolution of the United Nations.

Unfortunately, we heard a rumour that the under-secretary of state, Allan Gotlieb, encouraged the Arab ambassadors to go to 24 Sussex and complain, which they did. That, plus business pressure from companies doing work in the Arab world, forced Clark to appoint Bob Stanfield as sort of an ambassador plenipotentiary to the region, with a mandate to consult and report. This ensured that every time Stanfield's plane landed somewhere in the Middle East, the issue generated another news item.

The inability to take advice struck again when rumours emerged in October of a tax on gasoline to be introduced in John Crosbie's first budget. Consumers in Ontario were seeing prices jacked up by Alberta and perceived that increase as being the result of a lack of firmness on the part of the federal government. The administration's apparent lack of competence at a time of anxiety about oil scarcity had the effect of dropping the party's popularity in urban Ontario to the point where weighted national averages had the Liberals as much as ten points ahead and, in some cases, fifteen or twenty. A party can have a stunning campaign and not move seven points.

Disaster loomed if an election were forced, but Clark and his advisers could not believe that an election was in the offing. Trudeau was disengaged. He was packing his bags, wearing a beard, and not showing up in the House much, but the Liberal brain trust—Jim Coutts, Marty Goldfarb, and Keith Davey—said, "Hang in. This is going our way."

To be fair, the cabinet fixated on doing what was essential to reverse the massive deficit trend they had inherited from the Trudeau administration. Much of the motivation that went into the eighteen-cents-a-gallon Crosbie budget, and the determination of Clark and his ministers to stare down the opposition in the face of polls and parliamentary realities that made that task just about impossible, came from a resolute belief that if Conservatives did not confront that trend, whatever the political risk, their ability to be true to what the party stood for and to its fundamental mission would be forever impaired.

Davis aides and advisers, myself included, called members at the centre of the Clark administration before the vote, trying to prevent a loss in Parliament and the unavoidable election call that would result. We all met with the resolute response that the Clark government was determined to do what had to be done because they could not face themselves otherwise.

This was an admirable reflection of a profound tradeoff Conservatives often make when in office, navigating between the shoals of public opinion in support of a broader goal while trying to stand fast on a determined and principled course, whatever the charts might say. In the view of some, this is arrogance and self-righteous insensitivity to public concern and anxiety. To others, it is a stout and determined defence of principle, priority, and fundamental political philosophy.

But this was not a question of selling out principles. It was a question of deciding whether a federal Conservative government, committed to fiscal responsibility, was vital to the Canadian economic interest in 1980. If so, why give up the keys to the store? Don't impose an eighteen-cent-a-gallon tax right away. Try nine cents and see where the economy goes. There were many things that could have been done.

The Clark administration paid a huge price for its apparent obstinacy over the budget, a price many Conservatives believed should not have been paid. Many believed the party was simply trying to do what had to be done to rebuild the nation's finances. In the process, the wounds of the Diefenbaker–Coyne showdown and the currency crisis of seventeen years earlier were revisited, with the scar tissue being right well disturbed along the way.

The dissipation of the government's mandate, the failure to generate the numbers in the House, and the unnecessary defeat on the budget became a powerful signal to Conservatives across the country. It warned of the kind of folly that decent, kind, but unfocused leaders can get into if they don't understand the demands and necessities of leadership.

Here was a thoroughly modern man, progressive, articulate, relatively capable in French, with a bright, modern wife. He was thirty-six years old when he won the leadership, elected the youngest prime minister ever, with roots in the west, friends across Canada, and generally liked by the media (although ruthlessly crushed by the media when they smelled a lack of substance about him). Yet all had come to nought.

Some wondered whether Clark's defeat marked the end of a Conservative trend in the country. But Bill Davis soon won a majority, and so did Peter Lougheed in Alberta, Grant Devine in Saskatchewan, John Buccanan in Nova Scotia, and Richard Hatfield in New Brunswick. The Conservative cause was not only alive and well but was utterly disengaged from the Clark administration and the Clark leadership.

The roots of frustration the party sunk during that time implied that competence in administrative matters, in dealing with people, in persuasion skills, in English and French, and in addressing the needs of the party was vital for returning from the wilderness.

That leadership, despite Clark's best efforts, provided great decency and capacity, but also made the dynamics of an appropriate leadership profile for the future inevitable. Decency in defence of perceived incompetence and youth in defence of condescension, especially in the leader's relationship with the party, were no longer sustainable virtues. Sufficiency in Quebec, mobilizing the rank and file, and sustaining unity and loyalty in the caucus became *sine qua non*.

Tories had fought for likeable and decent leaders since 1967 to no avail. As the eighties began, the party had pretty much had it with being marginalized. The time for an all-pervasive competence at the helm had come.

6

FOR NATION AND ENTERPRISE

AT QUEEN'S PARK BETWEEN 1979 AND 1982, I focused largely on the constitutional front and the preparations for the provincial election expected in 1981, although within the government, we also began a fascinating process of expenditure management by global envelope. This involved shaping policy decisions based not on sectoral priorities in health or social services but rather on overall social and economic priorities, with a view about how limited government's role in that process could be. For me, the experience involved applying what I had done in the private sector and in the opposition in Ottawa to an entire province.

The interaction of these kinds of decisions and broader national issues such as the constitution and oil-price negotiations gave me an even stronger sense of how the Conservative Party at its best is an expression of differentiated interests across the country, as between Alberta and Ontario, for example, or New Brunswick and Manitoba. That gave me a further sense of the party as a public instrument rather than just a machine trying to get folks elected from time to time. It is a public instrument that has to reflect the views of the region from which its representatives come, even when those views vary from the corporate conservative premise. If that doesn't happen, the party is not doing its job properly. Its first job is to be an effective voice of the people, saying, "These are our principles and this is why we should be elected." Having been elected, the second job is reflecting those principles plus the concerns of the taxpayers the party is then working for.

Over the coming two years, Bill Davis was called upon to be an effective and principled voice for Ontario, a duty he discharged with his customary dignity, bringing together the notions of nation and enterprise that are the foundations of the conservative mission and the basis for any conservative success in this country.

Nation and enterprise reflect the distinctly Tory brand of conservatism that balances economic freedom with economic responsibility to all in society—and is very much at odds with the "I'm all right— why can't you all be like me?" neo-conservative bias.

Davis brought those notions together in a host of ways throughout his career. Building the largest non-denominational French-language school system outside France was nation and enterprise. Universal accessibility to post-secondary education, which was reflected in his term as minister of education and university affairs, was a coming together of nation and enterprise. The kids of the guys who had gone to war were now coming into the university marketplace in huge numbers, and Davis saw there were no facilities for them, so he built the facilities, and built them on the premise that anyone who had the marks to get in would find a place. Financial restraints would never stand in the way of one's education.

In social policy, the Guaranteed Income Supplement, or GAINS, was a way to ensure that Ontario seniors didn't live beneath the poverty line, and was another classic coming together of nation and enterprise. The creation of TVOntario as an educational broadcaster in the mainstream, and the creation of the Ontario Energy Corporation so that the vital energy interests of the people of Ontario could not be held hostage by OPEC, illustrated the same principle. I would argue that the purchase of a 25 percent share in Suncor was about nation and enterprise as well. On energy, he stoutly defended nuclear power, in minority and majority. In fact, a legislative committee chaired by former NDP leader Donald C. MacDonald passed Hydro's nuclear facilities. Their counsel, Alan Schwartz, had done an outstanding and thorough job.

Ontario would not now have a position in the transit technology business if Davis in the 70's had not created the Urban Transit Development Corporation, now owned by Bombardier and a successful privately run exporter of transit technology around the world. Many may still laugh about the Kraus-Maffi magnetic trains, but the hundreds of people who work at the CanCar Rail plant in Thunder Bay and the UTDC plant in Kingston don't think it's a laughing matter. It's why they're working. The people of Ontario invested heavily, and the continued jobs and the taxes collected are not an insignificant royalty. There might even have been a more direct royalty to Ontarians if the Peterson government, in my view, had not later given the company away for a mess of pottage.

In many respects, Davis was a visionary. Always, he was principled, even at some cost. He took the view that there was nothing wrong with having the Lord's Prayer in our classrooms. If people wanted to stand respectfully and not participate, that was fine. He didn't see that as exclusionary; he saw it as saying that there were some fundamental values in our society. He was dismissed as old-fashioned and ran into some heat from the multicultural hit squads, but he was right to do it, just as he was right to be concerned in 1974 with violence on television, appointing Liberal Judy LaMarsh to chair a commission on the issue twenty-five years before the present craze of concern.

But on no issue in the early 1980s did he take as much heat as for his support of Pierre Trudeau's efforts to patriate the constitution. After his re-election in February 1980, Trudeau's intense focus on the constitution became the dominant element in all the relationships between Ontario and the federal government.

With the referendum on negotiating sovereignty-association being held in Quebec in April 1980, Davis went there at the express request of Claude Ryan, the leader of the federalist forces. I had been working with Pierre Pettigrew, Ryan's executive assistant, on the timing of the visit and on what role Davis could play in the federalist campaign.

On his visit to Quebec, Davis made essentially two speeches: one to an anglophone audience and one to a francophone audience (he worked very hard on his French). The night before he gave the speeches, he went to Montreal for an evening at the St.-Denis Club, organized by Brian Mulroney, with business leaders, labour leaders, and others who could give him a feel for the province and where things stood.

The next morning, before the speeches, he met with the Conservatives who had been working on the No committee. The divisions between Jean Chrétien, Trudeau's point man in the campaign, and Claude Ryan were legion, deep, and problematic. The federalist forces in Quebec were divided and disorganized before Conservatives in the province joined the No committee. People like Rodrigue Pegeau, Richard Lelay, Brian Mulroney, Jean Peloquin, and others

brought the only real organizational competence to the No committee, and only then did Ryan's tour across the province and other
logistical issues begin to come together.

Davis's speeches were about the need for a more holistic approach
to constitutional change. He made a commitment that if Quebeckers
voted no and stayed within Canada, they should know that Ontario
also thought the federal government had to be changed and that
Ontarians were concerned about overlap and waste, excessive federal
powers, and federal institutions such as the Senate that didn't work
very well anymore.

The speeches received substantial and constructive notice in the
French press. As far as the media were concerned, Quebeckers
seemed quite delighted that Davis had spoken more French in con-
secutive pages of delivery on that trip than at any other time. The
toughest criticism came from *The Globe and Mail*, which decided that
his French wasn't up to standard.

The trip had two significant effects on the premier. First, he was
touched by the warmth he encountered amongst French-Canadians.
He had always unfairly laboured in John Robarts' shadow. Robarts
had gone to Quebec City, held one press gallery dinner, and become
the great hero and saviour of Confederation despite not doing all that
much. Bill Davis as minister of education had done all the tough slogging to build French-language schools across Ontario and help the
Quebec government construct the first department of education in
that province not run by the Church.

Second, the trip made him self-conscious about how his French
was viewed by the English-Canadian media. That self-consciousness
became one of the factors in his decision not to seek the leadership of
the federal party three years later.

The referendum was won—just—on assurances that people in
other parts of the country shared Quebec's desire for change,
promises made by people like Davis. Two months after the referendum, in June 1980, Trudeau launched his initiative on constitutional
change with a meeting of the premiers in Ottawa. It quickly became
apparent that there was no consensus around the table on what kind
of change was necessary, and that the process of reaching any kind of
conclusion by the end of 1980 or even into 1981 would be difficult.
The meeting decided that a group of ministers, including Tom
Wells and Roy McMurtry from Ontario, Roy Romanow from

Saskatchewan, and Jean Chrétien from Ottawa, would work at inter-governmental issues to try to find some solutions, which culminated in a meeting that September that began a long process of negotiations.

Davis supported Trudeau's efforts to bring the constitution home not because his constitutional plan was perfect but because Davis had promised Quebeckers he would support change. He wasn't going to let the fact that separatists were running the government of Quebec get in the way of keeping his promise.

More complex for Davis was the provincial election, called in March 1981. The major platform we ran on was called the BILD program, or Board of Industrial Leadership and Development, which was based on a series of tripartite partnerships for infrastructure investments. Such lever-aged partnerships are all the rage now but were then quite new.

BILD was developed over many months by outsiders and civil servants, plus such people as Tom Kierans, Brian Purchase, Les Horswill, Brian Davies, and Dunc Allan. The notion behind the program was simply that Ontario should have an economic development program different from Ottawa's approach to industrial policy, which for fifty years had involved supporting losers in ministers' ridings.

BILD was the ultimate coming together of province and enterprise because it spoke about Ontario's industrial, energy, social, technical, and agricultural self-sufficiency so as to give us the capacity not only to meet our own needs but also to export our excess in a way that generated value-added jobs and opportunities. The BILD approach was that there had to be investment from everyone involved: Ontario, the federal government, municipalities, and the private sector. This was about pooling our cash—about a billion dollars over five years, which wasn't a lot of money—to do things right. It was the notion of deal-ing with excellence in CAD/CAM design and in auto, agricultural, and electrical technology, broadening the energy grid and going ahead with the Darlington nuclear plant, increasing the focus on skills train-ing, and bridging the gap between what our schools were producing and what the industrial world required in its employees. These are all givens in today's marketplace, but they didn't exist then.

In the campaign, we didn't attack the enemy and we didn't make promises. Davis simply went around the province saying, "This is our program. This is how we will do it. We need a mandate from you to get it done." The program was in the public domain long before the election so the people could look at it and the press could tear it apart. It survived because it was a good piece of work. It has been the framework for modern industrial policy in Europe and elsewhere ever since and it constituted the next step for the province to define its role at the margins in an economy that, by and large, worked well without government intervention.

There was great pressure in the campaign on Davis to distance himself from Trudeau on the constitutional issue, but he hung in, basically supporting the notion of patriation and the notion of a Charter of Rights. When confronted, he always said, "Look, you know Pierre Trudeau and I disagree on many things, like the size of the deficit, the way he handled energy, and other issues. But we don't disagree on the need to have our own constitution, to bring it home, patriate it, and put the tools of our national development in our own country's hands." Of all the issues Davis fought on in his career, there was none he felt more duty-bound and strongly about than making it publicly clear to our friends in Quebec that promises made would be promises kept.

During the campaign, he addressed the campaign committee around the table at the Albany Club in Toronto. Some people on the committee were feeling quite uncomfortable about his support for Trudeau. There was some serious grumbling in the ranks. One of our challenges was that we always had a member of the federal Progressive Conservative caucus as part of the provincial campaign committee so that we could have some formal liaison. In 1981, the representative was Bill Jarvis, MP for Perth, in eastern Ontario, who reflected Joe Clark's bias on the constitutional issue. The tension between the federal and provincial wings of the party in 1981 was not unrelated to the tension between them during the 1980 federal election when Clark lost so many seats in Ontario primarily over the energy issue.

At the Albany Club, Davis answered a question with an impromptu speech in which he essentially said that he didn't view the federal government as nothing more than a travel agency for the provinces. He said this is a country, the country is larger than its parts, and everyone's opportunity is expanded because the country exists. He said we should not forget that, and that sometimes leaders had to take some risks. If as a premier and party leader he couldn't win an election by having those views, then he'd rather lose the election. Conservatives don't often say that.

A week and a half before voting day, he spoke at the Empire Club, where he again made a strong case for Canadians to come together on the issue. There was nothing in it for him. It would have been easy for him to attack Trudeau at that gathering, but he didn't because he wanted to make sure he won the election with a clear mandate on the issue. When he did win, *The Toronto Star*, which had supported Davis for one of the few times in his career, ran a four-colour picture of Bill and Kathy in front of a sea of Canadian and Ontario flags at a mall in Brampton, which was where we gathered on such auspicious occasions. The headline was "Davis Armed to Fight for Canada." He was armed with seventy seats, having crushed both the Liberals and the NDP, who between them had fifty-five.

The premier and I had an agreement that I would see him through the election and return soon thereafter to the private sector. I had been accepted for the mid-career Master of Public Administration (MPA) program at the Kennedy School of Government at Harvard. Donna and I had gone to Boston to find an apartment and were very much looking forward to spending a year in New England. But soon after the victory, Davis sat me down and said, "Trudeau's going ahead with this constitutional thing. With your background in the party, you have linkages with all the premiers, plus Ottawa. I really need you to stay."

It was a tough decision for Donna and me to make, but in the end, I decided Bill Davis had always been there for me and I could always do the course some other time. I also worried that if the constitutional process produced no progress, we could see the breakup of the country. The country is not a small part of my life. It's an obsession. I don't watch Canada Day celebrations on TV because my wife can't bear to see a grown man cry. I'm a hopeless romantic, sentimental fool when it comes to Canada. There it is. I told the premier I would stay. Harvard stood over the admission for a year, but by September 1982 the constitutional negotiations were just seriously beginning to roll. Harvard had other applicants and couldn't hold it over for another year, so the opportunity evaporated.

All through the spring of 1981, tensions over the constitutional issue rose right across the country as Trudeau insisted on patriation as the first step in constitutional renewal, with or without the agreement of the provinces. Davis and Hatfield supported that view, with the remaining premiers organizing themselves into what was soon dubbed the Gang of Eight (B.C., Alberta, Saskatchewan, Manitoba, Quebec, Nova Scotia, Newfoundland, and P.E.I.).

That didn't mean that Ontario was free from disputes with the national government, which were ongoing, although these related more to Ottawa's capacity for obtuse detachment from the real world.

The federal government had stayed out of the 1981 campaign. When asked by the press about federal involvement in the BILD program, the response, which was reasonable and appropriate, was, "It's not for us to comment. Provincial governments can get a mandate for these sorts of projects and we'll look at each one on its merits."

After winning the election, a group of us went to Ottawa to discuss specific projects such as the Quebec City–Windsor railbed corridor for a fast train, a roll-on-roll-off ferry for industrial and consumer use that would cross Lake Ontario from Oshawa to the U.S., the Chrysler and Massey-Ferguson bailout plans, and other infrastructure investments. We advanced the list to Ottawa at a meeting in the Privy Council Office with our deputies and their deputies. The Ontario people had their sleeves rolled up, ready to start dealing, and took an attitude of, "How do we do this? How do we do it efficiently? How do we save money? How do we get the private sector in? Let's get on with it."

Michael Pitfield lit up the biggest Monte Cristo I've ever seen and said, "Well, there is a more strategic question. The strategic question is, what does Ontario want to do when it grows up?"

Ed Stewart's eyes blazed. He said, "Get on with the goddamn job. Who has time for these conceptual games? I'll tell you who has time. The federal government of Canada. That's who has the goddamn time."

The Ontario civil service had able, tough-minded, bright people, but they were part of Ontario society and didn't see themselves as apart from it. In provincial government, the issue is: Are we going to build the highway? Is the sewage treatment plant going in? Do we have money for the school? Is the hospital going to get a magnetic resonance imaging machine? All practical, down-to-earth, make-the-place-run decisions. The federal government became so tied up in broad concepts that getting a yes, no, or maybe from these guys took a massive effort. It was thinking like that that produced huge mistakes like the National Energy Program, the Foreign Investment Review Agency, and the research-and-development tax incentives that became one of the great boondoggles of our time.

Even on smaller issues, federal officials provided endless evidence of bureaucracy gone mad. At a constitutional meeting in the fall of 1981, there was a washroom in the corridor outside the main conference room. When I went to the washroom wearing an Ontario badge, I was stopped by a federal security guard who said officiously, "This is a federal corridor."

I said, "Well, I wonder if I could have a provincial wizz in a federal washroom."

He said, "No. Your washroom is up by your office." The Ontario offices were on the next floor up. Getting there would have involved a fifteen-minute excursion, running through a gauntlet of the press in the process.

I went back to my seat in the conference room and passed a note to the premier. "I think you should know that all the provincial delegations are going to be getting antsier and antsier because the only washroom on this floor we don't have access to. They're going to be sent back by some idiotic federal official."

Davis passed a note to Donald Macdonald: "Do the provinces have the right to be in the bathrooms of the nation?"

Macdonald laughed and leaned over to the prime minister. Trudeau also laughed and indicated his answer was yes, so the matter was resolved, but that it would happen at all was both ludicrous and normal for Ottawa.

Throughout the eight months between the provincial election and the final negotiations, Davis stuck by Trudeau, never wavering in his belief in the essential rightness of the cause. Davis's relationship with Trudeau was correct. He almost developed a bit of a paternal feeling for him. It might strike some as strange, but he felt that the prime minister was probably lonely knocking around in that big, old house at 24 Sussex with no wife by his side. I suspect Trudeau probably had ways to fill his evenings, but that would not have occurred to someone from Davis's Methodist background. He always took Trudeau's calls and often gave him almost fatherly advice.

He also had quite a good relationship with René Lévesque. They respected and liked each other. Davis was also well liked and trusted by the other premiers, even though they disagreed with him. They knew he would never be duplicitous or violate a confidence.

A former Ontario public servant, Norman Spector, was the prime adviser to Bill Bennett, who was chairman of the first ministers' group during the process of conciliation. Bennett tried to be a constructive force in brokering some of the more glaring differences between his western associates and Ontario and New Brunswick. He didn't bring any strong biases to the process and, though he was ostensibly with the Gang of Eight, he was interested in a solution and kept a lot of doors open.

Within the Ontario cabinet, there was a dynamic between Davis, Roy McMurtry, and Tom Wells and the other ministers, who were never overly enthusiastic about patriation or a Charter of Rights. Traditionalists didn't like the imposition of court-made legislative decisions, but Davis was convinced that the politics of being opposed to a Charter would no longer work in modern Ontario. He believed government had to sustain its legitimacy on the issue. He also viewed the Charter not as something that increased the powers of one government at the expense of another but as something that increased the rights of the individual at the expense of all governments. He became quite a convert.

The opposite case was made most dramatically by Sterling Lyon in Manitoba, who was very much a traditionalist in terms of the need for Parliament and elected people to have paramountcy in the system. This was a position one could argue constructively in legislative debates, but it was a tough sell on the street, where Parliament is not always seen as an institution relevant to the people.

These months were not a good time for Davis's relationship with Joe Clark, although he respected what Joe was trying to do. Clark deserves great credit for fighting from opposition to ensure that patriation was done collectively, as was the custom in Canada, rather than by the strict reading of the law. He fought to improve the Charter of Rights at the same time as Davis and Hatfield battled alongside Trudeau and as Lyon fought to stop patriation altogether because he was opposed to the Charter. If there had not been those voices addressing the legitimate concerns of Canadians in that fashion and with that measure of pluralism, the country could not have achieved what it did achieve. The lesson learned later in the reaches of Charlottetown was that whenever there is too much unanimity and too much of a particular political class of a certain era saying that something is perfect, the average Canadian says, "There's something here I just don't like."

There was also a working relationship between Ed Stewart and Trudeau's secretary, Jim Coutts, which was quite constructive. It was hard to have a working relationship with Michael Pitfield, who was not an approachable person, but Coutts was down to earth. Ed's ability to send messages to Trudeau and receive messages for Davis made a big difference to the clarity of communication. This became important on such issues as minority rights, where Ontario supported minority-language education rights "where numbers warrant." In fact, it was at a tough unofficial meeting at the Park Plaza in Toronto where Eddie Goodman drew a line in the sand on this issue with Jim Coutts.

These words caused Trudeau great difficulty, but Davis was able to put his foot down and say, "I think sometimes the prime minister may underestimate how hard it is to sustain his position in the provincial Ontario caucus of the Conservative Party." That was the reality Davis had to live with, and "where numbers warrant" was one of those pragmatic saw-offs that was fundamental to making agreement possible.

Communication with other provincial governments was more of a problem. At a meeting with first ministers in the weeks leading up to the final talks, Davis and Hatfield were literally excluded from the room because they were urging moderation.

The day before the final talks began in November 1981, Davis and Trudeau met at 24 Sussex with plans to meet separately with Richard Hatfield later before the session began Monday morning. As the premier's associate secretary in cabinet for federal–provincial relations, I joined the meeting, along with Michael Kirby, who held the same position with Trudeau. Davis arrived in what he would consider casual Sunday garb: a hound's-tooth jacket, grey trousers, loafers, and a relaxed tie. Trudeau met him at the door in clogs, jeans, and a cable-knit sweater.

Trudeau was never very hospitable. It was not that he was inhospitable; it was simply that if ten premiers were sitting at his table, after dinner he would have a cigar box brought around with ten cigars in it. Not eleven. Ten. And the box would be locked afterwards.

As we sat there in the back room overlooking the Ottawa River, it took some time before Trudeau finally arranged to get us at least a cup of tea. Kirby and I took notes while the two first ministers chatted. The meeting began in the afternoon, and as the day faded, the room became darker and darker. By about seven o'clock, we were scribbling in the deepest gloom.

I finally said, "Prime Minister, I don't mean to be in any way disrespectful, and I know in Ottawa you're rather used to working in the dark, but could I turn on the light?"

"Oh, of course, Hugh, make yourself comfortable."

The Canada–Ontario–New Brunswick strategy was not to fracture the Gang of Eight or catch them in a web but merely to begin a dynamic process where Ontario would suggest some movement on minority-language education rights and New Brunswick would suggest splitting the package between patriation and the Charter so there could be some give-and-take. Davis, Hatfield, and Trudeau agreed that once that process began, there were all kinds of things Quebec could ask for to make its acceptance of patriation viable at home, such as a veto on cultural and linguistic rights or powers on education and immigration issues.

Ontario and others had no difficulty with putting such issues on the table and letting Quebec have an "out" from its political dilemma of being a separatist government at a federalist conference. The Parti Québécois had lost the referendum but had won a subsequent election, so Lévesque had a mandate to be a good premier but did not have a mandate to separate. He had become quite pragmatic. That he could come back from the meetings with powers that Quebec had never had before, all for the price of bringing the constitution home from *les anglais* in Westminster, should not be a particularly hard sell.

But as the negotiations got under way, Quebec never asked. This was a poker game in which Quebec left all kinds of chips on the table, solely because its representatives were so caught up in the Kafkaesque burden of being sovereigntists amongst the federalists. The job of a provincial first minister at such a meeting is to protect those powers he or she thinks the province needs for its own economic and social interests, to do what he or she thinks is right for the nation, and to get as much as possible for the province's own jurisdiction. Every province came to the table prepared to do that, except Quebec.

Lévesque's delegation could have won substantial language and jurisdictional gains for Quebec, but Minister of Finance Jacques Parizeau and the intergovernmental affairs minister, Claude Morin, the pipe-smoking intellectual touchstone on federal–provincial and sovereigntist issues, had no way of breaking out of their closed mindset. They appeared to freeze at the stick. The only betrayal of Quebec was by a Parti Québécois government that could not look beyond ideology.

Quebec was not isolated by the Gang of Eight. The very day Trudeau raised the possibility of a referendum on patriation and the Charter, Lévesque went for it quickly, deserting the Gang of Eight who were desperate to avoid a referendum. The last thing any of the remaining seven wanted was a referendum on the Charter of Rights in any of their provinces. Quebec turned its back on the gang because that got the sovereigntists back to their old game of having referendums and holding guns to people's heads.

The notion that there was some "night of the long knives" is one of the great convenient nationalist fictions for which there is absolutely no substantiation. Those who argue that Quebec was knifed in the back were either not there or incapable of seeing reality. A normally competent and able Quebec delegation completely came apart structurally when Lévesque deserted the Gang of Eight, fracturing the coalition.

In the afternoon of the last scheduled day of discussions, when it was apparent that the talks were going to fail because of the impossibility of meshing patriation, the Charter, and the amending formula to everyone's satisfaction, Trudeau said, "We haven't reached an agreement. Perhaps we should just call in the cameras and tell them we failed."

Peter Lougheed, who deserves great credit for his strategy, said, "Well, Prime Minister, if the purpose of calling in the cameras is to tell them we've failed, what's the rush? We can do that at four o'clock. We don't have to do that at two. Let's take a bit of a break and see what's going on."

During the break, all kinds of discussions transpired, including the famous meeting in the kitchen between Jean Chrétien, Roy McMurtry, and Roy Romanow, to which there was less than meets the eye but which soon became important to constitutional mythology.

Davis and Allan Blakeney discussed movement on several issues and agreed they would stay in contact through the evening and overnight as the back-and-forthing began over a "notwithstanding" clause and other possibilities to make the adoption of the Charter more palatable to the dissenting provinces.

Don Stevenson, Ontario's deputy minister of intergovernmental affairs, and Gary Posen, the director of policy for intergovernmental affairs, were out with the other provincial teams working on the draft proposal for the next morning. At no time was our provincial delegation instructed to exclude Quebec. Quebec sequestered itself. Michael Kirby came by our hotel suite to chat. Clearly, Trudeau was not happy with the "notwithstanding" clause, which would allow governments to override the Charter of Rights under specific circumstances. We sent him off with a stern message about where Davis stood on the issue.

As negotiations proceeded and we were moving towards eleven o'clock, Davis, Stevenson, Davis's OPP officer, Tom Wells, and I bunkered in to our suite to await developments. Nobody had worked harder on the file than Tom, a straight shooter and a man utterly without guile, who kept the process going endlessly, driven by his profound belief in the objectives of the exercise. He represented a multi-ethnic constituency (one of the first whose riding president was a Sikh) and knew the Charter of Rights was important and that both Ontario and a modern Conservative Party had to be on the right side of the issue.

Naturally, given a choice between fancy Four Seasons Hotel room service and locally delivered chicken balls with red sauce, Davis would go for the chicken balls every time. We had ordered in and were waiting for the food to arrive when I took a call from the prime minister's switchboard. I left Davis in his bedroom talking to Trudeau. He came out about twenty minutes later. We all wanted to ask him what he had said to Trudeau and where things stood. We also didn't want to ask him because we figured it was not necessarily our business.

Davis bit into an eggroll and said to Wells, "Tommy, I think we should know two things about this moment. First, the Chinese food is better in Brampton. Not as much ginger in the sauce. Second, look at our watches. It's about ten-forty. I think history may record that this thing started to go a bit better from this moment on."

He never divulged precisely what he said to Trudeau, but from later discussions, my sense is that he made it clear he thought the Gang of Eight had compromised enough around the "notwithstanding" clause, the Charter, and other outstanding issues, and that if Trudeau thought the compromise was not up to his standards, then Trudeau would likely be going to Westminster by himself. Davis was not prone to drawing lines in the sand, but this was a firm line that made quite a significant difference to the outcome of the talks.

The next morning, the agreement was reached in principle, although it had yet to be voiced around the table, and officials met all afternoon to niggle about details. The Ontario delegation gathered in the Conference Centre, with McMurtry and Wells in attendance, along with former deputy attorney-general Frank Callaghan, deputy treasurer Rendall Dick, and many other civil servants who had worked endless hours and had done an outstanding job, including deputy minister Don Stevenson, federal-provincial ADM Gary Posen, and Cabinet Office policy advisor Nancy Jamieson. Davis thanked them all for their tremendous hard work. This was the first time I had ever seen him emotional in public: he had tears in his eyes. He felt he had been part of something quite important and meaningful and that Ontario had done its job and had participated by keeping the patriation part of the argument alive and sustaining its legitimacy, then at the critical moment making sure that compromise could be achieved when compromise was truly possible.

We had brought home the constitution, entrenched the Charter of Rights, diminished the powers of government, and increased the powers of the individual and the disadvantaged. We had formed a basis for further discussions, because the agreement called for mandatory discussions on aboriginal issues. The final agreement had Conservative, Liberal, and NDP signatures on it. It had everyone's signature except René Lévesque's.

That he could have gone away from the table with far more than Quebec had ever before had, yet chose to leave with nothing, was an act of P.Q. negligence, almost criminal negligence in the political sense. The rights, prerogatives, and protections for the French language and culture that the Quebec government could have won in return for patriation would not have diminished the province's rights one bit. The P.Q. were simply frozen. Whether Claude Morin was part of this because he was, it later emerged, an informant for the RCMP, no one knows, but my bet is that he was doing what he thought was right to maintain the Parti Québécois' narrow partisan options.

Lévesque could have sold the "notwithstanding" clause, which meant that if any judge made a decision under the Charter that abrogated the collective rights of Quebec to protect its culture or language, Quebec could always pass a law in its own legislature that was "notwithstanding" the Charter of Rights, which the assembly, in fact, soon did. It was remarkable that while Quebec found a way to moderate the powers of the Charter, the separatists found a way to get no credit for it.

Everything Quebec did that last night was conscious and specific. They were in full command of all the details. Nothing was done behind their backs. I believe the Quebec delegation chose to cut itself off; its delegation had already withdrawn. They were already busy fashioning the mythology of failure at the table because they had to cover their own ideological shortsightedness (the game sovereigntists play on that score is essentially the same as that played by the person who shoots his parents, then shows up in court calling for clemency because he's an orphan).

That they would build up this canard of betrayal is not hard to understand. They had to cover for the fact that they had left on the table all these important instruments to serve the people of Quebec and to protect language and culture. It was easy for them to go back and say, "Because we are not part of the deal there should be no deal." Hence the unanimous resolution of the Quebec national assembly condemning the arrangement, and hence people like Lowell Murray voting in the Senate against the Constitution Act on the assumption that, whatever did or did not happen that night, Quebec should never be left out. The contrary argument is to say the country is doomed to never making constitutional progress because a separatist party in one province gets elected every ten years and there is no way that party will be part of any consensus, even if there is consensus among everyone else in the Dominion.

The work is dismissed today as that of "eleven men in suits," but it was seen then as being broad, inclusive, and important for establishing minority-language rights for francophones outside Quebec and for anglophones in Quebec. The first decisions that followed ratification were those of Mr. Justice Deschène relative to English-language education rights in Quebec and the legality of Bill 101. Thus the constitution began a constructive process of protecting minority rights.

For me as a Conservative, as for anyone who is in politics to make a constructive difference, this was an end point. Once we got through the negotiations, I decided there wasn't much I could be part of that would ever be as important. When my daughter, Jacqueline, was born in July of 1982, I also came to the conclusion there was nothing I could do in government as the hired help on the policy side that could ever be as interesting or as fascinating as my child. I had a duty as a parent to help ensure a level of income that could provide not only for my half of the marital partnership but for our daughter's future, and that could not be done within government. Though I had enjoyed my years of service at Queen's Park, I had a more fundamental responsibility to disengage from government and pursue family priorities in the private sector. So in November 1982, I had to leave politics aside as a luxury for others to pursue.

Unfortunately, in my view, the conclusion of the constitutional negotiations was also the point at which Davis began to wind down his involvement in politics and began to think about stepping aside to provide opportunities for other people. The passage of the Constitution Act in the Ontario legislature and the signing by the Queen the following spring had a significant outcome. The very first meeting of first ministers he had attended was in Victoria in 1971, where he had seen an agreement reached, only to see it collapse a few days later when Robert Bourassa and his cabinet withdrew their support. I felt that there was a sense on Davis's part that he had now come full circle. The job had been done to the extent it could be done with a separatist government in Quebec. From that moment on, his interest in politics began to wane.

This was not something I wanted to see. I felt he had a larger role to play. I wanted him to become prime minister of Canada. I believed that would bring to confederation the small-town decency and incrementalism of a politician I believed in profoundly.

His roots in the federal party went back a long way. Even though the federal party was often a significant burden to him, he never deserted it. When he first ran for election in Peel in 1959, John Diefenbaker, the prime minister, had just cancelled the Avro Arrow being designed by A.V. Row in Peel County in the Premier's riding hours before Davis hit the campaign trail, decimating middle-class Peel County in the process. Davis almost lost a safe Conservative seat because of it. In difficult elections, 1965 for example, he was out on the stump in Hamilton with Diefenbaker, who at the time was about as profoundly unpopular in Ontario as anyone could be.

It is often forgotten that there was a policy committee at the famous Montmorency Falls conference in 1967—at which Marcel Faribeault, concurrent with his position of prominence with Bob Stanfield as a leading candidate in Quebec, advanced the notion of "deux nations"—that was co-chaired by a young Conservative opposition leader from Alberta, Peter Lougheed, and the chubby minister of education from Ontario, William Davis.

Nor is it often noted that when Grant Devine, Lougheed, and other Conservative premiers ran for the first time, Ontario always sent help, encouragement, money, advisers, and organizers. In those long days when the party was nowhere nationally and there were almost no Progressive Conservative governments anywhere across the land, there was always Ontario, where the party had strong roots and was as tied to the urbane, progressive reality of economic and social life in Canada as any party was likely to be.

I believe he had some federal aspirations, although he seemed to be of two minds. There were times when he would see Stanfield not succeed at some initiative or see Trudeau make what could have been a successful conclusion to an issue difficult and divisive. At those times, he knew that his political persona and his general approach of bringing people together and finding middle ground would have been constructive for the country during a period of consolidation after Trudeau.

On the other hand, there were logistical matters he could never get his head around, such as the notion that a prime minister could not live in Brampton.

I once said to him, "You know, nothing would be more salutary for the country than to have a prime minister who does not live in public housing that the rest of the country thinks is excessively luxurious. Parliament meets too often, cabinet meets too often, the federal government's agenda is far too costly for this federation. You could be prime minister and live in Brampton, be in Ottawa a couple of days a week, get your business done, and get back to your riding."

I suspect he wanted to believe it but knew it couldn't happen. The idea of living in Ottawa was tough; all the pomp and officialdom surrounding a prime minister was foreign to his down-home style. I always had trouble imagining Davis surviving in or wanting to be part of a milieu so disconnected from reality. He often seemed to tilt away from a run at the leadership, but every kid playing bantam hockey thinks about playing at the Montreal Forum. The dream is never gone as long as you can skate and the Forum is still standing.

I urged him to enter the leadership race once Clark called a convention in 1983. I believe to this day that had Davis become leader of the federal party, he would have had great support in an election from the Maritimes, and passing support in Quebec (but no less than Chrétien had in the 1990s), and would have attracted his share in urban Vancouver and Winnipeg. Certainly, his plurality would have been no more devoid of western representation than Trudeau's was in 1972 and 1974.

The same is true of Peter Lougheed, who would have garnered a corporal's guard in Ontario (at least the twenty-five seats Stanfield got in his worst election), could have done well in Quebec because of the common alliance on so many issues between Alberta and Quebec, and would have cleaned up from Thunder Bay to the Pacific. The Grits would have largely kept the Maritimes, but a good chunk of Ontario and the Maritimes is not enough. Running Lougheed or Davis against John Turner, the party would have been all right.

But one of the rules of the road in the Conservative Party is that if you are an effective spokesman for a conservative view of a province's interest, you lose the right to be an effective federal leader. The enmities built in other parts of the country become so deep they make an entry into the federal arena a matter of serious controversy. Bill Davis knew that if he entered the race, Lougheed and Devine would have done everything in their power to stop him. Rather than heighten east–west tensions and cause a divisive convention, he put aside his aspirations, saying he had never done anything to divide the party and was not about to start now.

For Bill Davis to have kept his aspirations for the federal leadership in hand, he would have had to have been far more supportive of those who were against patriation than of those who were for it. But that position would have been phony as far as he was concerned and quite unacceptable politically, given the broad reach of the party and the party's mission in Ontario. Having made the stand that Ottawa shouldn't just be a travel agency for the provinces, he incurred the wrath of Conservative chieftains across the country in perpetuity. Elements of the federal party never forgave him. Many had never forgiven him for the battle with Clark over oil prices.

He knew viscerally that part of what he was surrendering in the effort to bring home the constitution and to make good on commitments he made to Quebec was any chance of future federal service. But he determined that to have fudged or hidden on those issues to sustain his own federal opportunity would have been to let down Ontario's intrinsic interests and Canada's interests. Bill Davis is a guy who sleeps quite well and, to this day, is at peace with himself, having done his very best for nation and enterprise.

7

ARMCHAIR STALWART

WHEN IT BECAME KNOWN that I was leaving government and going back to the private sector, I had an offer from a bank to be a vice-president of public affairs, one from a major consulting firm, one to be vice-president of development at a university, another from a large trust company, others from some American-owned advertising agencies in Canada, and one from Camp Associates. Sifting through them all, I concluded that wherever I went, some would say I was taking the position because of the "government business I could bring."

As Camp Associates already had government business—and had had government business since the late sixties—my arrival would not add $1.00 of government billing. I chose to join Advance Planning, the public-relations and public-affairs arm of Camp Advertising, a company I would end up buying some years later—with Dianne Axmith, Arnold Wicht, and John McIntyre, all of whom had long been associated with the firm—when Norm Atkins went to the Senate and Dalton Camp took a position in Prime Minister Mulroney's Privy Council Office. In fact, when I was campaign secretary in 1975, Dianne Axmith had been the main committee room manager, putting in endless hours despite a difficult pregnancy. We developed a friendship that will survive forever. When you look under party loyalty in any dictionary, you should find a picture of Dianne.

My mission in the company in 1982 was to help grow it. Over the next nine years, in collaboration with my outstanding partners, we made acquisitions in many areas of North America, including the

Northwest Territories and the west, buying a minority piece of an advertising company in, say, Yellowknife, to extend our reach and service capacity. We invested in publishing and direct-mail companies. We took a company earning about $9-million into the $40- to $60-million range in advertising and PR, while acquiring a minority interest in sport publishing companies growing in the $50-million range, with half of those revenues in the American market.

Through making acquisitions and dealing with investment bankers, banks, and other companies operating in various parts of Canada, I learned how business cultures differed across the country. I learned that taking a central-Canadian view of how the world should work is not only a conceit but simply misinformed. We would work with all kinds of clients: beer clients, wine clients, clients in the industrial sector, clients like Labatt's, Inco, and other broadly based companies. Sitting in focus groups with potential consumers, I could easily get a sense of how diverse this country is and how sensitivity to local circumstances is a fundamental of any national enterprise. To try to impose top-down decisions on a national enterprise is to negate the value of partners out in the field.

Almost as soon as I left government, I also began, quite by accident, something of a secondary career in the media. In 1982, Al McKay of TV stations CJOH in Ottawa and CKCO in Kitchener put together a province-wide network to cover the NDP provincial leadership convention and asked me to appear as a Conservative spokesperson to comment. When the Ontario Liberals held the convention that elected David Peterson, the stations mounted the same panel and got very good ratings, so good that CTV launched a national effort to cover the Tory leadership convention in 1983 and asked if I would be in the booth. I was a tacit supporter of Clark, bitterly disappointed that Davis hadn't entered the lists, so the booth was about as safe a place as I could find. It led to a CTV *Canada A.M.* panel position in the 1984 campaign.

That there was a convention at all came as something of a surprise. At the party's general meeting in 1983, 66 percent of the membership endorsed Joe Clark's leadership by voting against a leadership review. But Joe again couldn't take yes for an answer. When I heard the number, I was stunned that he decided to face a convention. Any Conservative who can get two-thirds approval from the party on any issue need only count his blessings.

To be fair, there had been a lot of hoopla before the meeting about how Stanfield used to get approval ratings in the nineties and that anything less than 70 percent would be problematic. But at that point, the party was ten to eleven points ahead of the Liberals. When Trudeau returned to office in 1980, he brought in austerity, focused on the constitution, and divided the country. Conservative support once hit 55 percent. It would not have been easy for Joe to proceed with 66 percent of the party's support, but after he became prime minister with a majority government, the number would not have mattered.

On the other hand, Clark had been sniped at mercilessly since 1980 by his caucus, by forces supporting putative leadership candidates, by the media, and by the bagmen because that setback had been such a reversal for the country's economic interests and for the party's claim to competence in public affairs. His pain was intense. He did not have a cadre of supporters across the party whose advice he had sought, because he had sought no advice. He did not have a cadre of people he had visited or with whom he had spoken regularly on the phone, because he avoided the telephone like it was radioactive waste. Feeling isolated, he wanted to put his leadership to the test. Having received the support of 66 percent of the party, he wanted the chance to come back and ask the members in convention to give him 51 percent.

I was a bit of a free agent in those days, but I went to the convention with the view that Davis might still be interested if a vacancy came up. I figured Clark's leadership was the one most likely to produce a vacancy fairly soon, so I supported Joe. I was also concerned that we would likely see a change in the Liberal leadership before the next election, and none of the other candidates, except for Brian Mulroney, had the capacity to broaden our base or reach in Quebec, which struck me as very important with the PQ still in power. I thought that Clark, because he had fought hard to make the patriation process as consensual as possible and had defended Quebec's interests with intensity, would be the least corrosive leader for us to have.

The convention brought together the propulsions, repulsions, forces, and pressures of two decades of exile. There was a tough fight in the trenches as Mulroney cobbled together a bit of a rainbow coalition. Davis loyalists like John Tory stayed faithful to their 1976 stand with Mulroney, reflecting their desire for an open-minded, urbane, and economically competent leader who would concede neither urban Ontario nor most of Quebec to the Liberals. Peter White, Conrad Black's colleague from the days of the Sherbrooke *Record* and the Union Nationale, rallied youthful support from some of the more conservative elements in the PCYF with the help of U.W.O. Young Conservative Tom Long. Michael Meighen, who had fought lonely battles in Quebec alongside Mulroney and who had always stood for socially progressive and fiscally conservative politics, helped lead a group of Mulroney friends nationwide, such as Frank Moores and John Lundregan of Newfoundland, Sandy Leblanc from New Brunswick, the business class of Quebec and Toronto, Janis Johnson and Duncan Jessiman in Manitoba, Lee Richardson in Alberta, and Lyle Knott in British Columbia. They shaped a coalition that was not so much anti-Clark as anti-exile.

In the end, John Crosbie and Mike Wilson, who both did respectably well on the first ballot, seemed to conclude, "We've had this Clark phenomenon too long. Rather than a source of leadership or direction, it's becoming a problem in and of itself. The problem has to be fixed." The Crosbies and Wilsons decided, either by sitting still or by going over to Mulroney, as Wilson did, that it was time for a change. The move was a response to a seven-year relationship with Joe that revealed that the qualities of leadership showed no chance of improving. The normal growing into the job a leader requires, the enhanced facility with the instruments of leadership, simply were not there.

On the last ballot, Mulroney became the party's choice, helped by a coalition ultimately embracing Maritime Red Tories, Bay Street conservatism, the western populism and neo-conservativism of the recently PC Peter Pocklington, and Mike Wilson's grass-roots Ontario.

Clark's support fragmented as he alienated the Davis organization, elements of Bay Street, the Lougheed people, and parts of the Atlantic PC core. All these could feel comfortable with Mulroney. Diefenbaker acolytes in the west and many who had fought alongside Dalton Camp to democratize the party could feel comfortable with him too. Many in the press tried to portray this as a sign that Mulroney was vacuous and without sufficient policy principle to alienate anyone. These would have been (and often were) the same journalists who portrayed him as too much a soft Red Tory on some days and too much a neanderthal of the right on others. They all missed the point.

This convention was not about the policy biases candidates brought to the leadership. It was about the competence they brought to the task of leadership and its many exigencies, from articulating policies and shaping an organization to using the media to advance the cause. It was about who could produce unity and cohesiveness. Above all, it was about who could make the party and its policies understood, respected, and assessed fairly in flawless English and French, reflecting not the jowly fuzziness of divisions past but a genuine focus on the task ahead.

Mulroney had been a volunteer organizer, fundraiser, and party worker for decades as an aide to Alvin Hamilton in the Diefenbaker government, a supporter (with Lowell Murray and Joe Clark) of Davie Fulton for leader in 1967, a combatant in the wars to build a beachhead in Quebec—on some days, he *was* the beachhead—and a facilitator who brought Dalton Camp and Frank Moores together to help Frank make his exit from Newfoundland politics.

I had known him over the years and had great respect for him as an organizer, but had no relationship with him per se. I didn't know much about his personal life or the people he had gone to school with at St. Francis Xavier University. I knew only that in my years with Stanfield, he was always there when we went to Quebec raise money, help find a candidate, do a bit of organizing, or help rally the troops. In my years with Davis, Mulroney was always helpful whenever the premier had to deal with Quebec issues and had offered particularly helpful advice leading up to the 1980 referendum.

Occasionally when he was in Toronto for meetings of various corporate boards while I was on Premier Davis's staff, we would have lunch at the King Edward Hotel and chat, sharing perspectives on politics in Quebec, the country, and the party. While friendly enough, there was a pro-forma "touching base" element to the meetings not lost on either of us. The relationship was correct, cordial, but remote. There could be no backgrounds more dissimilar than those of an Irish Catholic with a French-Canadian mother from Quebec's north shore and the grandson of Austrian and Russian immigrants to working-class Montreal. To many of the established elites in the party, we would have been just about as distasteful.

Brian Mulroney was a scrapper. If he wasn't, he would not have been able to feed his family when his father passed away, build his law practice, run the labour-relations-sensitive Iron Ore Company, help keep the Conservative Party alive during the dark days of Liberal hegemony, run for leader, or become prime minister. All the frustrations the rank and file had gone through in 1968, 1972, 1974, 1979, and 1980 became part and parcel of his instincts. He was a child of the party, as battle-scarred as any, but with the resolve to do what was needed to articulate a Tory vision and display the frank pragmatism needed to execute a winning campaign. He simply would not let ghosts and old divisions intrude.

Having worked in the vineyards for decades, he knew instinctively how the strange Conservative factional chart worked. He knew how it portrayed the torn fabric of the party and hindered its electoral chances. So within hours of winning the leadership, Mulroney opened the tent wide to all who could or would help. Just about all my friends who supported other candidates were warmly invited into the tent for the coming election campaign. Harry Near, Norman Atkins, and Bill Neville, all Clark supporters, were welcomed. Norm was appointed campaign chair.

My distance from many other Mulroney operatives and my business responsibilities kept me a modest distance from the federal campaign of 1984. The only role I played was, with others, to help prepare Mulroney for the TV debates, for which, in my view, he needed no preparation. I went to Stornoway to offer what advice I could. He was energized, calm, well briefed, and focused. He had measured John Turner and sensed quite correctly that the Liberal leader would not engage fully even when required. He had the measure of both debates well calibrated in his mind, as if he had been preparing himself for this moment since his college days. Those of us who went to brief him arrived at least twenty years too late.

His outstanding performance in the debate destroyed the Liberal lead. Liberal myths shattered overnight; the Big Red Machine in Quebec was as hollow as a pumpkin on Hallowe'en. Turner, the Bay Street candidate, reverted after a couple of weeks to an orthodox Trudeau Liberalism utterly opposed to the billing that had won him both the leadership and his early lead over the Tories. Canadians had no idea whether Turner was lying when he'd been on Bay Street or now that he was ensconced in Ottawa as prime minister or, worse, whether he believed he was telling the truth from both locations and couldn't distinguish between the two. Either way, the competence factor that had so far always sustained the Liberals as the natural governing party evaporated. The thoroughly decent Turner was poorly served.

The wildly successful Conservative campaign, policy platform, and, above all, competent leader produced a historic majority for the party, historic not only in its dimensions and total popular vote, but for the utter collapse of the Liberal Party's stranglehold on French-speaking seats.

In Ottawa at the end of 1984 there was a national Conservative government, with strong representation from every region, facing a Liberal opposition, just ahead of the NDP, reduced to a core of seats in urban Montreal and Toronto, a smattering in the Maritimes, and Lloyd Axworthy in Winnipeg.

I had been on the CTV *Canada A.M.* panel during the election campaign with Thomas Axworthy and Stephen Lewis; Gerry Caplan would sit in on occasion when Stephen couldn't be there. On the night of the great Tory sweep, Tom was genuinely sad to see his party face such a significant setback. Understanding his sorrow as any Tory would, I tried to cheer him up. I said, "This is a great night for us, but John Turner has held his head up respectably. He's run his campaign. They will be an effective opposition. They do have control of the Senate and they'll be back."

To myself, I said, "Boy, this is a good example of how the world turns, because there will be a night four years from now, maybe eight if we're lucky, when the cycle will turn."

Trouble began almost immediately for the new government. The number of Tories swept into office, especially from Quebec, soon became a burden. The party had not recruited in the salons of Outremont or Westmount or on the Grande-Allée in Quebec City, where few had much time for us. We'd recruited where we could—at CEGEPS and small businesses, at local clubs, and among local lawyers, entrepreneurs, community workers, and so on. The inexperience and insensitivity among a small number to the differences between parish-pump politics in old Union Nationale Quebec and more appropriate ethical requirements caused some grief to Mulroney in the next four years.

More important was the difficulty of a government coming to office with a profound agenda that, if just one-quarter successful, would fundamentally change the way Ottawa operated, how much money it had to spend, and how it taxed Canadians. It would change the structure of social programs and the structure of our international relationships. Hints of all this could have been found in policy documents, Mulroney's speeches, and the concerns raised by Conservatives in the three years before 1984. But Ottawa—official, permanent Ottawa and the permanent press core that covered it—never accepted that fundamental change was possible or that the conviction to achieve it could be real.

This cynicism wasn't premised on a belief that the Tories were lying. Cynicism about what Liberals stopped believing when they moved from Trudeau's left-wing biases to Turner's biases of the right, and then, to protect their core, zigged back to left-wing Liberal orthodoxy, was simply transposed to the Tories. That cynicism meant that when the government actually began to move in some truly conservative directions to redefine how Ottawa might be run and relate to the provinces and how our relationships abroad might be restructured, there was an immediate backlash that threw the administration off course.

In forming his team, Mulroney had to be careful not to choose individuals too identified with the Lougheed or Davis cadres. To do so would break the commitment he had with all elements to avoid the factionalism that was so damaging to the party's long-term interest. Some who joined his office were new to politics, many were new to Ottawa, and most were new to government. Nowhere on his staff could anyone be found who had served as a deputy minister in another administration, Conservative or otherwise.

The normal relationship between the media and the public service involves a series of networks where public servants float balloons or raise issues that journalists then use to develop stories or thematic commentaries, which then produce responses by people in opposition or the government. These responses produce a fresh range of story opportunities, often beginning with unnamed sources or spokespeople who prefer to be unidentified. There is nothing wrong with any of this. It is part of the back-and-forth of democracy. But it was quite new to the team that hit the beach running with Mulroney when he formed his first cabinet.

It is a watchword of politics that the first team to hit the beach usually takes the highest casualties, particularly when an administration of another affiliation has been in place for a long time and has a network of supporters and links to the public service and the press. This was true of those who came to Ottawa with Trudeau and those who served in Allan Blakeney's first administration. It was, sadly, true of many of those who answered the call in the first year of the Mulroney decade.

Mulroney treated the senior public service with a measure of respect and civility that some in the party found puzzling, but he was quickly dismissed anyway by many at the assistant deputy minister level and among the New Edinburgh and other Glebe centres of Liberal self-righteousness as simply not up to the intellectual standards of Trudeau, the gentlemanly standards of Stanfield, or the decency standards of Clark. (They always prefer Tories who are beatable.)

The press chose to become the official opposition, enhanced by the almost instant chatter amongst Liberals about Turner's leadership. Chrétien forces and others began to gnaw away at Turner's credibility, creating a sense that the Liberal Party, rather than having conserved a beachhead, was in a state of decline. The media moved quickly to stories of whether the Liberals could survive, whether the NDP might become the official opposition, and whether we would be into a British-style conservative-versus-labour parliamentary duality. These stories were as meaningless then as the stories about the end of the Conservative Party are now, but they provided a framework in which the press found it legitimate to become the opposition. Were I in their shoes, I doubt I could have resisted the temptation myself.

The early resistance of the bureaucracy was easy to spot. Stories in the newspapers were clearly worded by bureaucrats sending out the message that some initiative was giving up the national government's "right to decide." In fact, the national government never had the data to decide anything. They may have had data in the years leading up to and through World War II, but thereafter, Ottawa created an artificial reality about Canada that constituted a policy context unrelated to the real world.

In the first years of the administration, I saw Conservative ministers trying to change things and defend the need for change. The backwash from the central bureaucracy was constant. This was no longer an abstract issue about how best to articulate policy. This was now about their jobs and was, therefore, serious. If more powers devolved to the provinces or levels of government even closer to the folks, eventually there would be less need for senior bureaucrats to do conceptual work in Ottawa, a place where four hundred people have the rank and status of ADM. What are they doing? Where are they going? What are they running?

My private-sector experience made me much more intolerant of the structure. I never developed any animosity about the people. Most were outstanding, hardworking people wanting to make a difference in the right sort of way, but they were caught up in a system not of their making. The system evolved after the war from the liberal consensus that said, "We got all our people together, we raised all this money, and we beat Hitler, which seemed like a pretty difficult task. If we can do that, why can't we solve the housing problem? Why can't we put all our money together and develop a program to deal with poverty? Why can't we address homelessness or financial insecurity for old people?"

The drift of public policy—in Canada, the United States, and Great Britain—between 1945 and about 1982 was essentially that there was no problem that could not be solved with another program. The so-called spending power that Ottawa sought to preserve was tied to Ottawa's fundamental belief that spending power was the core instrument for bringing real solutions to people far away. In fact, it may have been the worst instrument at their disposal, and its use impoverished future generations.

Adding to the government's woes in its early days was the response when it tried to address what is now viewed as a consensus priority, namely whether well-to-do senior citizens should receive quite as much financial support from the state. In this effort on social-spending reform, Mike Wilson was left to die on the vine. He and others on the centre right of cabinet were deserted by their own rank and file (particularly in parts of rural eastern Ontario, Quebec, and the Maritimes), by the Business Council on National Issues, the Chamber of Commerce, many of the banks, and others who joined the opposition parties and much of the media to oppose fundamental change.

It is not surprising that a party that came to office for the first time after almost twenty-five years would be thrown off track by the desertion of centre-right business interests and by a massive attack from the established pro–social spending forces on the left, in the media, and elsewhere. What is surprising is that it wasn't thrown off track on more issues.

I watched all this from a distance. After the election, the Lewis-Axworthy-Segal panel became a regular Thursday-morning CTV event, becoming TV's response to the very popular panel on Peter Gzowski's *Morningside* radio program. As the government struggled to fulfil its mandate for change, I had no difficulty defending the Tories on TV once a week or in speeches across the country. My partisan affliction didn't lead me to conclude that the government was without failure, excess, misjudgement, or glaring inadequacy, but I was quite comfortable comparing its efforts to what we had lived with during the Trudeau years.

The original panel ended when Brian Mulroney, in an act of raw partisan patronage, appointed Lewis, the former NDP leader, ambassador to the United Nations, which brought Gerry Caplan permanently on board. When Tom Axworthy went to Montreal to work with the CRB Foundation and teach at Harvard, Michael Kirby, who had entered the Senate just before the 1984 federal election, took his place.

The various hosts we had over the better part of the next decade—Pamela Wallin, Linda McLennan, Nancy Wilson—each understood that her job was to ask perceptive journalistic questions and keep the panel from running away with itself. Each did a very good job.

The show produced some fascinating effects. First, it identified me as a Conservative across the country. I couldn't go anywhere without people stopping to express their views. Another fascinating thing was that people felt they knew me personally. In airports, on planes, and on the streets, people would say, "Hi, Hugh," and talk as if they had known me for years. On the odd occasion, a very attractive young woman would say, "I wake up with you every Thursday morning." Being a Bill Davis Conservative, I'd turn beet red and be stunned into silence.

In the mid-eighties, I was in Swift Current at a provincial policy meeting when a gentleman came over and said, "You don't know me, but I run the Transport City Truck Stop on the Trans-Canada Highway just outside town. Thursday morning's one of my best mornings. They all stop to watch the panel and they order a second cup of coffee so they can fight over what you guys said."

I could only think, "Many politicians work their whole life in Ottawa and no one knows who they are outside their own constituency. How fortunate I am. How privileged."

During the next panel discussion, I said, "Look, Kirby, that may be the sort of ivory tower thing you guys get into in the Senate. But I'll tell you, at the Transport City Truck Stop out by Swift Current this morning, people are asking themselves whether or not it's time to cut government waste."

Michael and Gerry looked at me as if to say, "What?"

I heard through the grapevine and by letter that it was quite a morning at the Transport City Truck Stop.

Despite what many believed, none of us was an official delegate of our parties. CTV simply invited us to be there because the network felt our backgrounds were relevant to their programming goals. We usually defended our parties' positions, yet there were often times when that was not possible. We dealt with serious issues, but never in a way that was unpleasant or with the kind of intensity seen on *The Capitol Hill Gang* or other programs in the U.S. One of the producers once said, "Remember this about your audience. Half are asleep, the other half are naked. So don't take yourself too seriously."

The panel forced me each week to reflect as an outsider upon the government's policies, mistakes, and problems. Early on, I decided I would not call Ottawa for briefings on issues. Knowing the facts from the government side would be a substantial handicap. The only way to come at it would be to form my own conclusions as a relatively detached but interested partisan and come up with my own answers. Many mornings, I would stand in the shower before going to the studio and say to myself, "What in the name of God am I going to say in defence of that?" By the time I towelled off and got dressed, I could come up with one or two notions.

My role on TV produced a series of invitations to speak at party events across the country. I did fundraisers in Saskatchewan, British Columbia, Ontario, the Maritimes, and even Alberta. Classically, I'd find myself out in the country at a Conservative meeting while we were low in the polls. Grant Devine in Saskatchewan or Gary Filmon in Manitoba would introduce me as "the happy warrior," saying, "When we're feeling about as low as we can feel and when we're getting thrashed by the press, we all know that if we can make it to Thursday morning, Hugh Segal will have something to say that will make us feel better about our policy, our party, and our government."

That perception became firmly rooted. After a while, I began to see my position on the panel as a responsibility not to be taken lightly. I could never take myself too seriously, but the responsibility of trying to find a way to give Conservatives some heart, even when the going was tough, was serious indeed.

I enjoyed discharging that responsibility very much, although the party wasn't always so happy. When we had a partisan dog-fight on an issue, CTV would get complaints from the public, but all three of us would get calls from our partisans saying, "Great stuff! You sure stuck it to them." When we explored an issue where there wasn't much partisan distinction—abortion, euthanasia, the constitution, or foreign policy—and so could have a more thoughtful discussion, ratings would go up the following week and CTV would get calls from the public saying, "Gee, that's great. Can I get a tape?" Those were the times when we would get the most criticism from our partisans, saying, "You're being too much of a statesman. You should've thropped him on the schnoz when he said that stuff." This revealed the classic barrier between partisan expectation and the fact that, aside from the 2 percent of the population who have party cards, the vast majority of Canadians see politics as a process they're not a part of.

As the government fell in the polls between 1984 and 1988 and the sense of inevitable defeat grew, I found it easy to mount a spirited defence by calling upon the historic rechargeable batteries that came from periods of isolation and opposition, all the way back to my suspension from Bible class over the Diefenbaker decals. For a Happy Warrior, this was the best of all worlds: a party in government being treated with less legitimacy than it had in opposition because it dared to believe in radical change. The tougher the odds, the more isolated the party, and the more the media, business, and bureaucratic elites beat up on Conservatives, the more I enjoyed the fight.

The experience brought home to me the fundamental truth that Conservatives are popular when they're in opposition because that is when they legitimize the way the system operates. When in government, they are the butt of consistent attack because they are usually questioning something fundamental about how things are done.

As the government headed towards an election in 1988, it became clear that the chosen ground for battle would be profoundly fundamental change. Many forget that the free trade issue pre-dated Mulroney. The Trudeau-appointed Royal Commission on Economic Union and Development Prospects for Canada, headed by Donald Macdonald, enthusiastically recommended a free trade agreement with the United States to secure within the global trading community the most important market for Canadian goods, services, and resources.

For Mulroney, free trade became a crusade. He saw it was a vehicle of change and a point in history when the Conservative Party could achieve with and for Canada an instrument of economic advancement for future generations.

Many saw Mulroney's pursuit of the FTA as a supplication to American economic might and a sell-out of our economic, social, and cultural policies. I thought the agreement was a straight-line projection from the anti-reciprocity, pro–national policy stance taken by John A. This might strike legions of anti-American and anti–free trade advocates as the most hideous of perversities, but the truth is that the mission of the Conservative Party has always been to defend our common nationality and independence from the capricious, rapacious Manifest Destiny conceits of our American friends.

The Americans have many compelling qualities and are probably, within reason, the best neighbours we could possibly want. But it has always been the role of the party to advocate whatever policies are necessary to ensure the survival of our economic interests. The most substantial threat to those interests in the mid- and latter 1980s was the vehemence of American protectionism in Congress that targeted everything from steel to shingles to fish to women's dresses. It was pervasive, it had legislative clout, and it was politically popular. It had largely Democratic adherents, but there was tacit Republican support in Senate circles.

The relationship between Mulroney, Ronald Reagan, and Margaret Thatcher, and their common pursuit of many goals—global reduction of trade barriers, free movement of goods, services, and capital across borders, strengthening Western defence to deter Soviet adventurism—produced a rare window of opportunity. Canadians could limit the fickle use of American trade sanctions, thereby protecting Canadian jobs and economic interests.

Mulroney's defence of free trade in caucus, in cabinet, and to the party rank and file allowed the government to move beyond the setbacks in social spending, the deficit, and the ethical mishaps of caucus members and begin to fashion a new and distinctly un-Tory coalition.

The 1988 election campaign began well enough, with the government even leading in the polls. But victory turned into a close-run thing. I volunteered on the Conservative campaign, developing communications, advertising, and debate strategy. Before the leaders' debate, Lowell Murray and I were the last two political people to advise the prime minister. Then we left him in the hands of two civil servants, Paul Tellier and Derek Burney. I don't know the advice they gave, but it's my suspicion that with the polls high, an anticipated win in excess of two hundred seats, and the Liberal campaign stalled, they encouraged him not to lower himself and dirty his hands.

Mulroney was suffering from a bad cold that night and, I heard later, was taking antibiotics. Many people expected John Turner to just show up with an iron lung and bleed, but he did more than that. He put in a surprisingly pugilistic performance, and the tide quickly began to run out on free trade. Suddenly, we were in free-fall, dropping fourteen points. The Liberals made much of unfounded allegations that health-care and social programs were in jeopardy if the FTA came to pass. The Liberals' advertising agency, Vickers and Benson, created an outstanding television ad showing the border between Canada and the United States being gradually erased.

But Turner championed the anti–free trade position without covering his flank either about where he had been on the issue while on Bay Street or about the Liberal allegations over social services. Our advertising strategy had to change direction, with our priority being to get the border-erasing ad off the air because it was so damned effective.

Soon after the debate, I had essentially my first fundamental, if brief, political discussion with Mulroney. He took me aside and said, "I know what happened in the debate and I know who has to fix it. It's me. I'm going to hit the road and I'm going to campaign like hell until your stuff hits the air."

He campaigned his heart out, doing a run up and down B.C. and throughout Ontario and Quebec, taking Turner to task and seeding the clouds with questions about the fall-out from Turner's anti–free trade position on autoworkers, the lumber industry, steel, aluminum, fish, manufacturing, high technology, and pharmaceuticals.

I worked with Tom Scott of Foster Advertising, Lowell Murray, Allan Gregg, Rich Willis, and Bill Liaskas to craft sharp and specific responses in tough TV ads to collapse the bridge between the free trade issue and Turner's credibility. With the help of production wiz Carmel Prudhomme, who may be the best in the busines anywhere, Scott, who was in charge, produced a masterly ad that saw Conservatives drawing the line at Liberal misrepresentation. The line was drawn across the belly of North America, right where the border had been erased by the Vickers and Benson Liberal ad.

We created other ads from newsclips that went to the core of Turner's credibility. In one, Emmett Hall, godfather of medicare, destroyed the notion that health care was at risk. In another, free trade's negotiator, Simon Reisman, once John Turner's deputy of finance, made the point that anyone who said that this deal constituted a sell-out was simply not telling the truth.

It was a tough fight. We ran the "redrawing the line" ad intensely for several days. An established rule of advertising is that if there are two ads contrapuntal to each other, if you run your own ad with sufficient frequency, every time the enemy ad is seen, more and more viewers will think of your ad and the effect of the enemy ad will be nullified. The strategic response of the enemy is usually to pull their spot. With heavy weights on our ad, we tried to get the Grits to blink. They obliged: they pulled their wonderfully effective "erasing" ad and replaced it with ineffective ads about soccer balls. They soon lost their post-debate lead, and the momentum came back our way.

A campaign with a double momentum shift is extremely rare. What held it together was not the advertising campaign but the sheer strength and will of the prime minister. We wouldn't have made it without his tenacity. He fought back with an intensity and focus we shall not soon see again. Don Mazankowski, deputy prime minister and minister of agriculture, did yeoman's service in rural Canada. Barbara McDougall fought the battle with great courage and effect in a troubled Toronto. Mike Wilson and Joe Clark engaged at critical points to sustain the argument. Bernard Valcourt almost single-handedly, with John Crosbie, saved ten seats in the Maritimes, despite a despicable Liberal scare campaign. But it was Mulroney's single-mindedness that won the day.

Being close to the campaign, I know that some counselled surrender or modest mitigation when the issue was joined and the heat intensified. Succumbing to that counsel would have spelled the end of the campaign, the government, and Canada's opportunity. But politics on the tough issues is about the courage to do what is right for the nation's interest. Mulroney persisted and prevailed.

The pro–free trade stance muted the effect of the Reform Party in the west and allowed Quebec and Alberta to produce a solid Conservative majority. In Ontario, superb organization and hard work by people like Bill Macalear, Glen Wright, and Ed Arundel allowed 40 percent of the vote to produce a six-seat plurality over the Liberals, despite an equal percentage of popular votes.

Traditionally, our coalition has been made up of rural and small-town voters from eastern Ontario, a few on Bay Street, suburban voters who see their middle-class economic interests best defended by our party, a determined Maritime constituency, and the old anti-Trudeau forces on the Prairies and in B.C. Some stood with us because they resented the National Energy Program or the Official Languages Act or because they came from bedrock Tory stock defined more by religion, geography, and empire than by economics, demographics, or education.

In 1988, free trade divided voters along very distinct lines. Those who felt vulnerable and uncertain about what free trade might mean for them worked against the party. In many traditionally Tory constituencies, we lost disproportionately amongst senior citizens, dairy farmers, and others. These voters were amply replaced by young people who felt confident about their skills and their capacity to compete, better-educated voters, wealthier voters, and voters in wealthier sub-urbs. They added to solid votes within the oil and beef industries, in provinces with a strong southern orientation, like British Columbia, and massively in Quebec.

It was quite an interesting election when the Tories lost the riding of Leeds in eastern Ontario, which we had held for more than twenty years, and won in Outremont, a seat we had never held because of its upper-crust French-Canadian Liberal tradition.

The changing coalition represented a broadening reach of the party and the imposition of a greater framework of ideology on political debate, but it came after an incredible job-creating boom from 1985 to 1987 that bolstered confidence, produced record stock-market advances, increased the net worth of hundreds of thousands of Canadians through real-estate appreciation, and generated a sense of economic well-being unrivalled in our post-war history. A coalition fashioned then could not be expected to survive during the more difficult economic times that would surely come.

Free trade agreements don't prevent recessions, and neither do they undo the fiscal burdens of previous administrations or the need for arti-ficially high interest rates or currency values. Unfortunately, all these things reduced Canadians' capacity to sense just how big the export opportunity was and how many jobs it could generate. The depth of the worldwide recession robbed the government of a window in its second mandate during which a clear case might have been made on the wise and stout defence of national interests that free trade provided. The shutting of that window and the failure to make the case not only eroded the government's support but, when combined with the joys of the GST, deeply fragmented the Conservative coalition.

The significance of the goods and services tax is far greater than its effect on the popularity of the government or the efficiency of the tax system. As a policy, it was the manifestation of all the motivations, strengths, and weaknesses Conservatives face on fiscal policy while in office. Conservatives have a legitimate anxiety about how spendthrift Liberals and socialists are when in government. The anxiety about waste, out-of-control spending, and usurious tax levels always produces in incoming Conservative administrations a desire to confront and overcome these issues, not only to demonstrate the party's fiscal respon-sibility but to ensure that history will record the sense of responsibility with other people's money that Tories truly believe they have.

It was intrinsically Tory to want to replace a job-destroying 13 percent manufacturing sales tax, however invisible and politically non-corrosive, with a tax that was above board and tied to consumption as opposed to production. It was intrinsically Tory to want that tax to be out in the open for all to see so that future governments could not fiddle with it unseen and could be held accountable for how the money was collected and spent.

The finance department tried to advance the notion of a consumption tax in the last days of the Trudeau government and met with a jaded response in the early days of the Conservative regime. But then Finance found itself in a context where it could gain from all the fiscal frustrations amongst centre-right conservatives. It could parade an instrument that would respond to that angst, giving cabinet a way to make up for all the frustrations Finance itself had caused.

The likelihood of morale being dashed in a governing cabinet, caucus, and party is extremely potent when the cabinet is trying to reduce the gap between expenditures and revenue by reducing costs and not raising taxes. If it reduces costs and significantly narrows the gap by cutting spending (and surviving the political heat), it can find its fiscal situation deteriorating rather than improving if the revenue projection is off by 10 or 15 percent in the ensuing quarters of the fiscal year—and the department of finance has not been within 10 percent on its revenue forecast for the past quarter of a century.

The Mulroney administration faced this circumstance from 1987 right through to the imposition of the GST in 1990-91. Centre-right Conservatives, deeply troubled by the debt and deficit, increased the pressure immensely. The Mulroney administration took the operating costs of government, net of debt interest, from an annual $12-billion deficit in '85 to a $16-billion surplus by 1991. But increasing interest rates on the '68–'84 debt inherited from Trudeau wiped away the benefits of these gains. Spending fell to levels well below inflation, but rising debt-servicing costs provided the opposition on both the left and right with ample opportunity to point to a worsening cumulative debt, with great political effect.

For many in the Maritimes and Quebec who voted Conservative in 1984 and 1988, reducing the size and cost of government was not at the top of their list of priorities. This produced stresses and strains in a government that believed itself prudent and responsible. All these forces came together to produce a stew within which the GST did extremely well as a focused and, unfortunately, all too understandable instrument to indicate the government's resolve to reform the tax system. The fact that even the party's traditional constituencies in medium and small businesses were deeply opposed to the tax did not serve as a danger beacon, but rather encouraged Conservatives to believe they were putting the public interest and fiscal reform ahead of political opportunity.

The will to be fiscally responsible, frustrated in the past, made the government determined to face down any and all who were contrary-minded within or without the Conservative family. Part of the dynamic around the GST, abetted by the intense fight from Liberal senators, was that sense that this was a partisan watershed where the party had to indicate its resolve. Just as Mike Wilson and others had hung tough during the difficult days of Meech and Oka, Mulroney and his Quebec caucus felt they had to stand with Mike Wilson, minister of finance, notwithstanding concerns about the department of finance and the high-interest-rate policies of the Bank of Canada.

These were shoals Conservatives remembered from the Diefenbaker–Coyne affair. The memory of those who had been there—like Mulroney had as an aide to Alvin Hamilton—could not have sanctioned a reversal on fiscal policy that might have forced a tougher stance by the Bank of Canada and produced a confrontation between the government and the Bank. The demons of history, the need for unity above all else, and the deep and debilitating fiscal anxiety typifying Conservative failures in 1962 all conspired to allow Finance to find ready warriors for the GST.

What seemed not to count at all was that the tax was inefficient (replacing a relatively small number of tax-collection locations at large companies for the Manufacturing Sales Tax with a huge proliferation of inefficient retail tax-collection locations), would dislocate what was left of the Tory core constituency across the country, and would depend upon a harmonization with the provinces that no rational assessment of federal–provincial relations could ever predict. This was, perhaps, more apparent on the outside than the inside.

Mulroney must have known how damaging the GST would be for both him and the party, but in the end he must have concluded he had precious little choice. The tax would bring Canada into compliance with most nations of the free world and massively assist exports, none of which could matter a hoot before the next election. To the public, it became a symbol of a self-righteous arrogance and insensitivity so profound, intense, and broad as to make it difficult for more than half the population to consider voting Conservative again as long as the leadership of Mulroney, Wilson, and Deputy Prime Minister Donald Mazankowski was in place.

As a Tory, I found that conclusion unfair and insensitive to politicians trying to do what was best for the country's desperate fiscal situation; as a student of politics, I found it not only predictable and unavoidable but, without question, terminal.

The dimmed prospects for a third mandate only added to my sense of unease about the government in the early nineties. More problematic was the fall-out from the failure of the agreements reached at Meech Lake to end honourably the estrangement of Quebec from the Canadian constitutional family. In the heat of nationalistic fervour generated by the collapse of the second Meech Lake accord, Premier Robert Bourassa decided that Quebec would hold a referendum on sovereignty—or new federal proposals—in the fall of 1992, just months before the Tories would inevitably face the electorate one more time.

Although Brian Mulroney was certainly the most effective Conservative prime minister of the century, it seemed beyond the capacity of anyone on the planet to successfully juggle the Quebec question, the fiscal situation, government reform, caucus unity, and a host of other issues. The notion that I might go to Ottawa in 1991 to help him do it emerged from discussions he had with various people, not all known to me even today. I heard nothing from the PMO or the prime minister until his executive assistant, Rick Morgan, informed me I should be in Ottawa on a Sunday in late May to meet with the prime minister. Apparently, he wanted my help specifically to strengthen the team that would remove the bullet of the Quebec referendum from the country's future and maintain party unity through the process.

About two weeks before Morgan's call, I detected smoke signals from my old friend Harry Near, old Davis collaborator John Tory, Mulroney's campaign chair, Bill Fox, a former *Toronto Star* bureau chief and Mulroney press secretary, and some fellow ex-Stanfield staffers like Graham Scott that something was afoot. Bill Fox, who had served as communications director in Mulroney's first years as prime minister, was someone who had set aside a distinguished journalistic career with *The Toronto Star* and Southam as bureau chief in Washington and Ottawa, and in foreign correspondence, to serve the PM and the party. His counsel, as one who had made that sacrifice, was especially important to me.

I heard from Eddie Goodman earlier that week. His advice was not to do it. "I like Mulroney," he said, "and he's about as courageous a prime minister as we've ever had and then some. But the glue is too deep. I'm not sure you can help. I mean, wanting to help, sure, that's loyalty and patriotism talking. Thinking you could make a difference, that may just be conceit." Considering these words came from someone who, after having his tank shot out from under him in Normandy, snuck out of a hospital to rejoin the front lines because he felt his unit needed him, I reckoned there was no more lovable expert around on either patriotism or conceit.

I wasn't going to get excited or change my plans on the basis of rumour anyway. If something was going to happen, I'd believe it when it did happen. I had already ruined one summer dealing with a putative call. The tip-off that the whole notion might be real came when Bill Davis spoke with me in May 1991. He tried in his characteristic fashion to warn me about what was coming.

He said, "You know, Hughie, I don't want to be too blunt about this sort of thing and I'm not suggesting the two issues are related, but you remember when you had that admission to the Kennedy School of Government and I prevailed upon you, while I didn't want to, but felt I had to, back in 1981, to help with the constitution for that one year more and we agreed then that you would do that for Ontario and its belief in Canada? I can't be certain, and perhaps wouldn't be if I could, but you and Donna should not be surprised if, and one never knows how this sort of thing may develop, but in the event you are asked to give perhaps a bit of a helping hand up there on the bridge because the ship of state, well, with the referendum scheduled for the fall, you know he may not be perfect, but as a prime minister, I think Brian has genuinely tried to do the right thing, especially on free trade and the constitution, which is not to say that mistakes were not made, but you and I know that if they don't restart the constitutional process or if the caucus comes apart, then the country will come apart and, frankly, I don't want to put too much of a burden on you but, well, if you do not help, that is if you are asked, you may always feel badly because there is only one Canada and, now this may sound a tad like a former Ontario premier speaking, but it is a great country and one worth preserving for, I guess, your children and my grandchildren— and you know, you should really have more than one, I had five, I did my part—but it would be a lot less constructive in terms of their futures if that 1992 matter were not in some way sorted out and, frankly, there's no one who has a better chance of keeping it together than Brian and so, you know, if you could see your way clear, it would be good for the prime minister and the party although probably disruptive to your own life, even though it's not as if you're fifty, you're just forty, so there would be time to make up any economic loss, although I know that would not be your first concern, but Kathleen and I were talking and we can understand how that might trouble a young man with a young family, but in the end the best thing for them is a strong Canada and I think you will be asked to help and I hope you would not rule it out right away without thinking about it and, you know, I would not want to impose any pressure, but I can't think of anyone who might be able to help more directly in that regard, especially in terms of the dynamics and the politics, than, well, I don't want to be flattering, but I think you know where I'm headed."

Bill Davis does not get more concise. This was as close to a direct order as I had received from him since we first met. He does not impose on his friends lightly, especially since leaving public life, but as a former boss, mentor, and friend, he was sure prepared to impose on me now.

The meeting with Mulroney at 24 Sussex soon transpired, followed by a breakfast meeting with chief of staff Norman Spector that could not have been more friendly. Norman had attended the same high school I did in Montreal, although two years ahead of me, which, as an adolescent, is like being on a different continent. We had vague memories of each other from those days, but had no further contact until the late seventies and early eighties, when I was on Davis's staff and he was director of telecommunications policy in Ontario's department of transportation and communications.

Our *modus operandi* was easily agreed to. As senior policy adviser, I would work on the constitutional file with him, try to repoliticize the prime minister's schedule to connect with the country, and generally take on issues of domestic policy.

I began my transition from private life to government service comfortable with the two things that mattered most: one, the intent, purpose, and realism of the prime minister, and two, the desire of his chief of staff to be constructive and helpful. One could not ask for better points of departure than that.

8

ANSWERING THE CALL

DURING JUNE AND JULY 1991, I divested my commercial holdings under the direction of the assistant deputy registrar-general and arranged my affairs. I also consulted with the prime minister's staff and members of caucus and cabinet about how they saw the political situation, what the major challenges were, and what the primary focus of my mission should be. Naturally, my approach was to reflect the prime minister's policy priorities: first, the country and its preservation at all costs, second, the party and its legitimate partisan interests, and last, his own interest as a party leader going through a period of significant difficulty.

I appeared on my final *Canada A.M.* at the end of July, then went downtown to tend to some personal business. I was stopped in the Toronto-Dominion Tower by a corporate-looking guy who said good-naturedly, "I understand why you would serve on the bridge of the *Titanic*, being the loyalist that you are. But I can't imagine why you would arrange to have yourself dropped on the deck after it hit the iceberg." This was a point to which there was no rational response.

Arriving in Ottawa in August was like landing on another planet, the most striking sensation being the degree to which Ottawa is a one-industry town. One of the great joys of politics in cities like Toronto, Kingston, Montreal, or Calgary is that while you may be chief of staff to the premier or secretary of the cabinet, there are a host of other positions in the city—in the arts, academe, business, or sports—that are of far greater significance than your own or, for that matter, that of your boss. This provides a healthy leavening of the tendency found in all bureaucracies for those at the centre to take themselves far too seriously.

There is no such leavening in Ottawa. A sense of self-importance pervades the city. When a deputy minister walks into a restaurant in Ottawa, bowing and scraping by the restaurant staff and more junior civil servants and the throwing of rose petals pass for normal practice. The puffed-up delusions of the diplomatic, bureaucratic, and political players are enhanced by the massive concentration of journalists for whom Ottawa is the best domestic posting and allegedly the one of greatest importance. Preserving the importance of Ottawa and the centrality to society of every nuance, activity, rumour, press conference, or relationship are fundamental to a journalist's survival. Add in the then-unpierced insulation of Ottawa from the normal economic to and fro of the country and you have a world unto itself, completely disengaged from the life and times of Canadians who are, after all, paying the bills.

It is a town where Conservatives are always outsiders. Those who focused their dislike of Mulroney on Ottawa may not have sensed the irony that no prime minister did more to shake up traditional Ottawa and wrench it into the modern world than he did. He received the antipathy not only of everyone opposed to fundamental change in our economic or trading relationships but of all the established interests in Ottawa who had survived just fine in this self-nominated centre of the universe. I did not have a sense of many allies when I arrived in town.

Tory forces in Ottawa, with a few exceptions, seemed genuinely pleased at my arrival, and many went out of their way to be helpful and hospitable. I even heard from Liberals, including the leader, Jean Chrétien, whose family had grown up with Donna's mother's family in Shawinigan and who had always been very friendly and generous.

Newspaper stories created expectations that this recruit had the capacity to turn around the government's situation. I did my best to diminish those expectations, not only in self-defence but because I knew that whenever the media pendulum swings for any individual, intense natural forces soon swing it against that person with a velocity substantially greater and an effect that is far more corrosive.

I had to make a decision about where I would live. Donna's career kept her in Toronto, Jacqueline was enrolled in a school she enjoyed, and Donna had no desire to live in Ottawa's fishbowl, especially as my evenings would not be my own. It made no sense to disrupt their lives for what was basically a two-year assignment. Many aides live in hotels, take flats or apartments, or bunk in with others doing similar work. I thought an empty apartment, a hotel room, or sharing space with fellow ministerial chiefs would be a mistake, so I bunked in with a group of senators I had known for some time: former party president Nate Nurgitz from Manitoba; Con Di Nino from Toronto, the first senator of Italian extraction ever appointed as a Conservative; and Michael Meighen, recently appointed from Toronto, senior partner of Meighen Demers, former national president of the party. Both Michael and Nate had been close friends for years.

The Senate sat only from Tuesday to Thursday, so members were unlikely to stay in Ottawa more than two nights a week. I had a room with a lock on it and a secure scramble phone, provided by the Privy Council, and some camaraderie on nights when one feels very far from home and alone. From this sanctuary, I took some initial soundings on my primary areas of focus: the constitutional issue, the relationship with the party, and the policy relationship with the bureaucracy.

I had no more sense of how things would develop on the constitutional file over the next year and a half than anyone else. But I did know that between Ottawa, the provinces and territories, and natives, achieving a measure of trust and common cause and reducing the heat and tension around the process would be both fundamental and almost impossible.

I knew that Lucien Bouchard's decision to destroy the Conservative Party in Quebec—a party that had nurtured him, advanced him, financed him, and made him prominent—would put the management of the Quebec caucus under an intense microscope. It would require a full and focused commitment on the part of the prime minister if the government were to stay together long enough to help keep the country together. I knew that while caucus cohesion would always be a challenge, the caucus had shown loyalty and commitment to Mulroney during some pretty dark days, partly because many of them would not have been elected without him in 1984 and 1988. They were also loyal because of the frankness and clarity he brought to sharing problems. He forged an intense, personal link with almost every member.

My experience in Ontario was that a good public service with commitment, determination, competence, loyalty, and enthusiasm will occupy any vacuum created by a lack of political focus. So I knew that unless the government set an aggressive policy agenda, gave direction to the public service, and made the constitution part of a larger context, the public service would precisely define fiscal and economic constraints and bolster their definitions with wildly inaccurate forecasts. These would constrain cabinet's opportunities to the point where there could be no initiatives, no reform, and no substantive change.

Since John A., few prime ministers in our peacetime history have imposed upon the bureaucracy as many ideas from the policy beliefs of the elected government as Brian Mulroney. Privatizations, tax reform, the western and Atlantic energy accords, Meech I, Meech II, free trade, changing our military commitments abroad, engagement in the Gulf War, the South African stance, the Haiti initiative, joining the Organization of American States, and broadening our participation in more peace-keeping theatres had all been imposed upon the bureaucracy. Each induced a response that constrained opportunities and policies elsewhere.

This was not because the bureaucracy was in any way disloyal or purposefully dysfunctional. It was simply because the bureaucracy is nothing more than a large organization of people trying to work with existing resources within existing time frames to achieve specified goals. When broad and massively uprooting goals are imposed upon the system, the system's ability to maintain the intellectual or fiscal resources necessary to fuel other initiatives is constrained.

Many of the Mulroney administration's initiatives were quite contrary to what Ottawa was used to. My sense was that getting the system to respond would be difficult, despite the best efforts of many public servants whose ability, loyalty, and judgement were beyond question by any political party. I knew the prime minister would work day and night and that he had in his cabinet many who had the ability and strength to help.

He was not a leader like many others. He had strong views about almost everything and believed that any failure of will on his part to ensure that matters were addressed forthrightly would have catastrophic results for the government and the party. He believed that if he had a view about matters of detail regarding how a speech might read, what a policy should be, how a policy might be implemented, or how an event might transpire, he had a duty to put those views into the system and assess the response before making a final decision. He became quite certain in his years in government that the only mistake was not having a view. If you did not have a view, the system, reflective as it was of disparate interests, bureaucratic inertia, and regional or other agendas, would have its own view and that view, accountable to no one in particular, especially the people, would prevail.

He had confronted the system with his views on free trade and NAFTA, and with his strong belief that if Conservatives were not treated as "somebodies" by a Conservative government, they would never count. He had lived too long in Quebec, where being a Conservative didn't count for much and where being on the outside looking in was a permanent way of life. What some dismissed as an imperial prime ministership was really an expression of the need to make sure party members believed their leader to be important. That would make their association and involvement with him, the party, the government, and the national interest of great importance to each and every one of them. Failure to sustain that link would produce the divisive viral infections that had enfeebled Conservative caucuses and leaders in the past.

My first chance to see him up close after joining his staff was at the general meeting of the party a few weeks later. This was the first gathering of the clan since the 1988 election and since the all-time low of 9 percent in the polls had been reached.

As usual, *The Toronto Star* began beating the bush for delegates who might be unhappy, disgruntled, or in any way troubled by the leadership, hoping to fan whatever sparks they could find—or conjure some into existence. A year earlier, the *Star* constructed one of those "you can't get there from here" questions for David McFadden, a former president of the Ontario party and former candidate for the legislature. In response, he allowed that if the numbers didn't improve before the election, the leader might want to consider his options. That's the sort of innocence the *Star* has dined out on for years. Poor old McFadden never had a chance. The impact of the *Star* story was to create the impression that he was a great disloyalist when the truth was anything but.

More than twenty-five hundred delegates converged upon Toronto in August of '91 for the general meeting held in the Metro Convention Centre. The requisite demonstrators were out and the requisite massive coverage of their activities dominated the media when Mulroney arrived.

A fellow named John Clark, a well-known organizer of anti-poverty groups, squads opposed to racism, environmental desolation, and the like, had put together a new organization for the event. His troupe of the day was an anti-poverty outfit focused on housing. They constructed a village of about ten tents, none higher than four feet, within view of the CN Tower. This produced cameramen on their hands and knees searching for camera angles that would make the tents look larger and more numerous. Through the magic of the media, viewers had a sense of a sea of tents spreading from the CN Tower right through to Etobicoke, all in defiance of the Conservative Party and in personal opposition to the dastardly Mulroney.

Many in the media admitted afterwards that their coverage was a touch overdone. Many failed to understand the degree to which their excess galvanized the delegates who had paid their own way to come to town as volunteers for all the right reasons. The delegates saw the small gathering of tents and they saw the TV coverage. They had ample evidence, uninfluenced by Mulroney's rhetoric or their own bias, of how the media could hijack any event, amplify dissent to the point of absurdity, and magnify the anti-government, anti-party, and anti-Mulroney sentiment in the land. This produced, beyond the normal affection for a leader who had brought them to power twice with historic majorities, an outpouring of confidence and affection I had never seen before.

Mulroney performed as well for the party as the party performed for him. It voted massively in favour of a resolution recognizing Quebec's right to self-determination, firmly removing the party from any association with the federalist dictat so much a part of the Trudeau legacy. It even voted in support of turbans in the RCMP, not as massively, but with a plurality respectable enough to dilute the efforts of any who wanted to put the party on the wrong side of the tolerance issue.

On one day, Mulroney gave fifteen speeches, to the caucus of each province, riding memberships, riding presidents, local MPs, defeated candidates, candidates for the coming election, fundraising committees, PCYF, the PC Women's Federation, and on and on, campaigning with an intensity and level of connection with the crowd that was stunning. I knew from hard experience how hard it was to hold this party together. I had never seen the effort so close up. It was awesome.

Many of the press came with the view that this meeting would be the party's undoing. There would be disloyalty in the ranks and major defections, a coming apart of the Tory coalition under the relentless pressure of polls that said more than 90 percent of Canadians had no intention of voting for Progressive Conservatives ever again. But none of that happened. Pierrette Venne of the Quebec caucus left to join the Bloc Québécois, but other members of the Quebec caucus, encouraged and buoyed by the respect for Quebec shown by the membership, hung fast.

There was a new openness to the party, a frankness and honesty born in part out of respect for the leader's determination to carry on and out of the common alliance one always feels when surrounded by adversity and hostility. For the first time in party history, policy resolutions were voted on publicly and electronically, with results projected instantly on a large screen for all to see. Bill Fox had coordinated a host broadcaster function that became gavel-to-gavel coverage to all parts of the country. The protesters outside, maintaining a regular chant on this issue or that in a contrived process of instant dissent, helped the party immensely.

I had my first opportunity to spend more than ten minutes with both Mulroneys. I came away with an impression that would not leave me in all my months of service. Here was a man at peace with himself and in harmony with his family. He was determined to get the bullet out of Quebec's revolver, build the party's popularity, and maximize the party's options for the next election. Someone who refuses to be discouraged at 9 percent is not likely ever to be discouraged. When physical and mental strengths can be poised to produce the kind of exertion I saw that weekend, there could be no question about his motivation or his certainty about the nobility of the cause.

Was he without ego in the exercise of his duties? Of course not. Could he have survived under that pressure with any less ego? I'm not sure. The loud criticism in some quarters, as distinguished from the legitimate criticism he probably deserved no more or less than any other prime minister, sometimes produced an excessive response that he and others would regret. But survival under that kind of pressure and maintaining a sense of balance, humour, and humanity are not easy. It requires a measure of will and determination to persevere rarely found elsewhere.

As the meeting wound up on Sunday, I left a few hours early to make what was left of visitors' day at Jacqueline's summer camp in eastern Ontario. On the flight to Kingston, I reflected on what I'd seen and what it meant as I began my term of service.

The hostility of the press was intense, but it wasn't unified. The Quebec press treated Mulroney with respect and even some affection.

The English press, with a few exceptions, reflected the biases in English-Canadian polls. The caucus remained united, but would require constant attention, the lack of which could be disastrous. The Quebec caucus was more volatile than others and was still getting used to Benoît Bouchard as head honcho, especially while others like Marcel Masse sought to maintain a separate, more nationalist constituency within it. The prime minister had a set of themes he felt comfortable with, and which would bear repeating often, related to what the government had achieved, what the challenge was, and who and what the enemies of progress were.

I was quickly connected to the massive paper flow that comes daily into the PMO from the Privy Council Office, embassies, foreign leaders, and, above all, the people of Canada, the caucus, and the cabinet. To protect the office from that kind of problem, I hired Mark McQueen, an able assistant to Mary Collins, associate minister of defense, as my executive assistant. His relentless defense of the PMO against accidental paper flow—and general defense of the public interest—made my time use as efficient as possible.(What struck me as an overwhelming problem was the degree to which the flow seemed unrelated to the focus of the administration.) I was afforded access to all cabinet committees and the senior bureaucracy, who, by and large, were helpful.

Talking with members of the staff, I found a high level of professionalism and a determination to help Mulroney reconstruct the constitutional and national agendas. The office was made up of people who had served in party ranks for many years, like the deputy chief of staff, Marjory LeBreton, and those who had come from the private sector or elsewhere in government. Rick Morgan and Paul Smith—one from a distinguished political family in Quebec and the other from St. Boniface—were outstanding managing that difficult executive assistant's role. Maria Grant was part of a determined scheduling and tour team that included Scott Munnoch and Susan Ellacot. As a special assistant in the office who not only coordinated Mrs. Mulroney's schedule but also helped shape overall priorities, Bonnie Brownlee had experience, reaching back to Mulroney's Opposition days, that was especially important. Lawrence O'Neil and Camille Guilbeault handled caucus relations. On lend lease from the civil service—specifically from External Affairs—were Robert Grauer, who acted as deputy chief of staff and who died of a heart attack in early 1992, and Mark Entwistle, who was a professional and superb deputy press secretary when I arrived.

The notion in the press that the way the PMO operates changes because the personality of Stanley Hartt may be different from that of Bernard Roy, Derek Burney, Norman Spector, or Hugh Segal is fiction. What matters is the purpose of the prime minister and the degree to which he or she determines that certain priorities are pursued, although a good chief of staff can make the case for a shift when circumstances change.

Norman Spector was carrying an unbelievable load. He was the key intellectual manager of a bureaucratic process aimed at producing a constitutional paper by September 1991 that would begin a national debate in yet another round of constitutional review, picking up the pieces left by provincial failures to ratify the thrice-agreed-to Meech Lake accord. This was neither Norman's preference nor Mulroney's. But with Robert Bourassa's decision to have a referendum in Quebec on sovereignty, the government couldn't stand back and see that referendum go forward without a firm federal position.

Norman had to deal with all the other responsibilities imposed upon the PMO, plus shepherd this constitutional process within the bureaucracy. He was also the main link between the PMO and Joe Clark's cabinet committee on the constitution, established when Mulroney appointed Clark to tend the constitutional issue some weeks before my arrival. Norman found himself with an acute burden of tasks for which there were insufficient hours in any day even for a relatively spartan bachelor like him. He therefore managed the office in a fashion that liberated time for the constitutional dossier.

I saw the strengths of the PMO as an intellectual attention to detail, a sensitivity to caucus and individual cabinet concerns however trivial, a devotion to ensuring that the prime minister was always prepared, an intense belief in his re-electability and the importance of the task he was pursuing, and a genuine affection for Mulroney and his family.

I felt that many good people at the intermediate level felt out of the loop. They were trying to do their best, but often with half the information they needed. I didn't think this was so much an issue of trust on the part of the chief as a time-management issue. In that respect, I felt the office could be changed, and I did this when I became chief of staff in January 1992.

I sensed a defensiveness and a too readily spiked anger about the press, premised on the notion that the press had a duty to help the prime minister do his job and get the message out. I had quite the opposite bias, having long set aside the notion that the press had any-thing to do with conveying information. It is about interpretation and is hostage to every journalist's biases and personal background.

My conclusion from reviewing the media was that the core prob-lem Mulroney had was not his policies and programs, nor even the nation's deep economic difficulties, but the perception of his motiva-tion. Party research indicated that on issue after issue, Canadians agreed with the government's agenda, but by 1991 they had great dif-ficulty with the prime minister himself. Based on the papers they read and the TV they watched, they concluded that even when he did something they believed to be right, he was doing it for reasons that related to some interest other than their own.

It struck me that the party's problems were the result of Mulroney's having become a target of every public angst, frustration, and suffer-ing. Well aware of what the establishment, media, and civil service forces had said about Stanfield and Clark, I discounted much of the intensity and excess. Besides, to be a Conservative is to know what it's like to be dismissed, misrepresented, and marginalized, especially at the federal level. But I felt that the sourness and condescension of the Ottawa press corps were so distorting the view of the prime minister's motivation that the most appropriate way to deal with it was to get him out of Ottawa to listen to Canadians, express his views, engage on issues, and let them glimpse what his motivation truly was. My propo-sition was not terribly insightful, but it was pragmatic and to the point.

My role was to make sure the pressures of the constitution, run-ning the store in Ottawa, and handling the intense foreign-policy burden at the prime ministerial level did not create a schedule that had Mulroney dealing almost exclusively with ministers, caucus members, staff, and senior bureaucrats, keeping him away from the country, the people, the press, and local communities. I partially suc-ceeded and largely failed.

I had no sense of how the domestic agenda interacted with the prime minister as foreign-policy maker and as Canada's key link to other nations, but I found out rather quickly. Aside from many other endearing qualities, all three of my senatorial roommates were unre-pentant jocks. Sports fanaticism has never been one of my most com-pelling attributes. Beyond the Montreal Canadiens and the University of Ottawa football team, I'm not sure that any team in any league in any sport can really be taken seriously. To survive this crowd, I took to watching Global TV's late-night *Sportsline*, which was about as good a discussion of the week's sporting events as one might get. This was the barest necessity to survive coffee in the morning or the odd evening chat with my friends. On Sunday, August 18, while I was working through an immense in-basket and catching up on the latest scores, the show was interrupted by a report of rumours of a *coup d'état* in the U.S.S.R.

My first thought was, "That's interesting. I wonder if anyone at the office cares." I quickly realized that this was the sort of thing the prime minister might just want to know about. He had told me that all he expected from his staff was that they never assume he knew anything until they themselves had spoken with him. He made it clear that if I thought something was important enough for him to know even in the middle of the night, he would never be troubled if I woke him up.

It was after midnight when I saw the news, but I had no direct access to the prime minister at that point. Protocol demanded that, as a senior adviser, I call the chief of staff or, if I couldn't find him, the clerk of the Privy Council. Norman's answering machine duly took my message, and I heard back from him minutes later. He wasn't aware of the coup either and had heard nothing from External Affairs. He called the prime minister.

Unhappily, our ambassador, who had put off a leave on many occasions, had left Moscow just a few days earlier for a bicycle trip through Belgium. Equally unhappily, the under-secretary of state was in Italy on business and the minister of external affairs was taking a few days off at her summer retreat on Nova Scotia's south shore. A briefing for the prime minister was arranged for early the next morning.

The meeting was an eye-opener. In came the acting under-secretary, the head of the Canadian Security and Intelligence Service, the chief of the defence staff, plus the senior desk officer from External on both Russian and European affairs, all primed to brief Mulroney on everything they knew. I had been in the office early reading the wire copy from the foreign news services plus the overnight reports from other parts of the world. As the group droned on, I realized that what they were offering was little more than a distillation of these sources, which the prime minister himself would have read by six o'clock that morning.

Then Mulroney proceeded to brief them! Mulroney had been on the phone overnight to Eastern Europe, London, and Paris and to

George Bush in Washington. He had got through to people he had met on visits to Russia and had put together a compilation of who was who and what was what, all with far greater detail than the information offered by those around the table. I was elated at his capacity for hard work and "stick-to-itness" and troubled by the systemic response, which, while within the bounds of relevance, was nowhere near the level of acuity a prime minister has the right to expect.

Mulroney made it perfectly clear that Canada would stand four-square behind Gorbachev, that the safety of Gorbachev and his family was a prerequisite to any relationships in the future, and that there would be no official recognition of the coup. Full stop.

I then learned another lesson about government. The prime minister might articulate foreign policy and lay out fundamental principles, but there was always another view at External reflecting the department's "maintenance bias" about our world relationships. The general bias of people who perform diplomacy as a career is that a nation's best interests are maintained when all options are open. Statements of principle or preference for one side or another have a tendency to limit options, diminish relationships, and produce problems for the future. Avoiding such unpleasant things generally increases one's options, and that, after all, has to be in the national interest.

Tensions between External and the prime minister had developed over the years. In the early days, Joe Clark's position as minister was very much on the outside of day-to-day domestic affairs, and both Clark and Mulroney gave themselves a fair bit of room to manoeuvre. On the Middle East, Clark, burned badly on the issue when he was prime minister, felt most comfortable with the consistent, determined, even-handedness that allowed him, on the pretext of keeping options open, to unwittingly make enemies of both Arabs and Jews. Mulroney was more pro-Israeli and was prepared to get involved in the odd dust-up. Second, a strong line of thinking inside External was opposed to free trade and in favour of a multilateral and sectoral approach. Although they had lost that fight, the war was not over. An incipient anti-Americanism was alive and well in the department, something that Mulroney's determination to stand firm with Canada's allies only aggravated.

While coming to terms with all this, I made my first mistake. I assumed that, with Mulroney having expressed to the press clear support for Gorbachev and a clear distaste for the conspirators, the mere transmission of his text to External would ensure that the briefing offered to the minister, Barbara McDougall, would be consistent with the lines he had laid out. What I should have done was invite myself to the briefing so she and her staff would be well aware of what he had said and why.

She was badly advised and unwittingly committed a serious blunder by indicating that, after all, one had to keep an open mind about coup plotters and perhaps there might be some basis for normalizing relationships. This was consistent with the thought in the department, but totally at odds with the prime minister. The press pounced on the discrepancy in a fashion that would have cost another minister her job. But Mulroney's frustration was muted by his genuine affection for and faith in the minister and his belief that she was ill served by the department.

The critical lesson I learned would be instructive over the next few months: Never assume anything about the delivery of a message on a matter of policy unless you deliver it yourself. I also learned that in terms of civil service agendas, the Mulroney government was many things in Ottawa, but it was certainly not in control.

At a briefing on other matters at 24 Sussex shortly after the coup, I expressed my amazement at how Mulroney had defined the issues and approaches by his phone calls throughout the world the night of the event. Relaxing in his den, he put his feet up, had a sip of coffee and a bite of cookie, and said, "You know, one of the things the most extreme Canadian nationalists fail to realize is that while we may believe Canada is the most important place in the world, as it is for us and our children, there's an entire world out there that doesn't share that view. Oh, they like us well enough. They think we're decent and helpful, by and large, and we're listened to on occasion. But I'll tell you, Hugh, that's not because of who we are or where we stand or the geopolitical framework. That's because of how hard we work to make sure we get noticed. That's what few people understand about the job a Canadian prime minister has."

I said, "But isn't that what our involvement in the UN and NATO and *la francophonie* and all those institutions is all about? I mean, we only establish our credibility because of our presence in those organizations, so we find a way to get consulted in the process."

He looked at me with a look he often used when he was about to pierce a tired cliché. "That's actually 100 percent wrong. There are all kinds of countries in *la francophonie* and the Commonwealth and the UN and NATO that do not get consulted by the United States on policy in the Mideast or Central America. There are all kinds of countries in NATO and the UN that the Russians don't call on when they're trying to shape a Western response to their situation. Our membership gets us no leverage and no particular place at the table. Our membership has to be personified in a way where other countries with the economic power to have an impact on our quality of life want to deal with Canada because they believe the country and its leadership can make a contribution."

"In other words, it comes down to interpersonal relations."

"Absolutely. Without that, we just don't count, certainly not in terms we would like to count."

The core of his approach was building relationships that could transcend the bureaucratic difficulties and false struggles that the permanent practitioners of international relations sometimes create for reasons best understood by themselves.

I saw evidence of this at a dinner at 24 Sussex for Boris Yeltsin in February 1992, a month after I succeeded Norman Spector as chief of staff. It was a working dinner with a full delegation of Russian ministers matched by an equal group of ministers on our side. Yeltsin and his delegation were about to fly back to Moscow after having spent a couple of days in Washington. Since Yeltsin's elevation, Canada had, on a per capita basis, led all countries except Germany in the commitment of trade credits and financial support for the new Russian federation. Yeltsin had made that point in the United States and elsewhere, and was beginning to show frustration with the slow pace of Western support.

Extra security was apparent as I arrived at 24 Sussex on a typically bitter cold Ottawa Saturday night. Not only were there extra police, but an RCMP helicopter circled the house doing a searchlight check of the cliffs leading down the bluff of the Ottawa River. The plan called for Mulroney and Yeltsin to arrive at 24 for a brief reception, have a working dinner, then go to the rotunda of Parliament to give a joint press conference and sign a series of bilateral agreements on cultural, economic, and trade issues.

My brief chat in the upstairs den of 24 with Paul Hinebecker, the foreign-policy adviser in the Privy Council Office, was interrupted by a phone call informing him that when shown the draft agreement on the flight from Washington, Yeltsin had indicated some difficulty with two or three sections. This produced a modest diplomatic panic at the Russian desk at External and in the Russian Embassy. With translation problems and no understanding about the president's problems with the text, the risk of a slight setback in Canadian–Russian relations loomed large. The prime minister was made aware of all this as he waited on the tarmac at Uplands Airport.

As the discussion went back and forth in the dining room, I slipped out two or three times to see how the sort-out was going, only to be met with ever more bleak expressions by Hinebecker. We were clearly headed towards an evening with no progress made and no agreement to be signed.

Then I saw how careful planning by Mulroney could contribute to solving a sticky diplomatic problem. It was Yeltsin's birthday, and with the dessert in came a cake with "Happy Birthday, Mr. President" inscribed in Russian. Its arrival softened the evening to the point that Yeltsin sliced the cake before plates had arrived, forcing Mulroney to accept a slice in his hands. The suggestion thereafter that both sides proceed with the signing and that any imperfections be addressed when they next met went down as easily as the cake. A mini-crisis was averted.

Mulroney's personal approach to foreign policy was tremendously effective for Canada on many issues and with many countries, but was open to wilful misrepresentation when it came to our closest ally. Despite the still widely believed fiction, the fact is that Mulroney did not seek to endear the country or himself to the Americans. Quite the opposite. On visits to the United States, he spoke clearly about excesses in U.S. foreign policy and clashed more than once in public with American trade policy. But in the end, he believed sincerely that in the broader framework, Canada and the United States, the NATO allies, and the UN had more to gain from an alliance than they would by picking at each other or by the pettiness of drawing artificial lines in the sand the way Trudeau did for almost sixteen years, thereby excluding Canada from any important role in the multilateral issues that defined the geopolitical realities of his time.

Mulroney differed substantively with the Americans on a host of foreign-policy issues, from the Middle East to aid to Russia, from sanctions against South Africa to policy on Central America, Cuba, Yugoslavia, China, and Haiti. Those positions were often set aside by many in the Canadian media, but they were important, as people like Nelson Mandela, Daniel Ortega, and Father Aristide would testify.

The acid-rain treaty between Canada and the U.S., which went against the grain of many long-entrenched members of the Congress and sceptics in the Reagan and Bush administrations, spoke eloquently to the progress that could be made if Canada stuck to its guns and defended its interests. On larger questions of global peace and strategy, including the Gulf War, Mulroney stood with the Americans because he genuinely believed they were, on balance, a force for good in the world. Compared to other powerful military nations, they had been generally benign and constructive in their use of military capacity.

For every Canadian who is convinced that Brian Mulroney sold out to the Americans by negotiating free trade, there are tens of thousands of Americans—in lumber, high-tech, autos, beef, shakes and shingles, steel, transportation, and financial services—who are convinced Reagan and Bush sold out to Mulroney. That the public perception is otherwise is due to the constant and consistent attacks on Mulroney personally and as the personification of his government, all of which emerged from the climate of sourness and a mutual distrust I found when I got to Ottawa. I spent much of my time in the capital trying to understand the reasons behind the media becoming Mulroney's nemesis. I am trying to understand them still.

Watching from afar between 1984 and 1991, I felt the entire Mulroney government was simply too much in the media. The prime minister seemed too eager to catch every grenade the opposition or the press heaved over to the government side of the House. Keeping the caucus encouraged and in good cheer during the tough times produced on TV a sense of rococo defiance or partisan excess that collapsed Tory numbers between elections. At election time, that same fighting spirit brought home the electoral bacon.

When I got to Ottawa, I asked Mulroney ever so gently whether being on television so much and associating personally with every hot potato were truly in his best interest. The answer I received at Harrington Lake one afternoon in August brought back all my memories of the Stanfield and Clark years.

He said, "Do you think it was my first choice to be out front and centre on the GST? That was Finance's formulation. Do you think I want to be on TV every night dealing with the constitution? Don't you think I know how it helps the Mulroney-haters and the opponents of the government? But the truth is, there has to be absolute consistency between what I say in caucus on Wednesday mornings and what I'm seen to say in public in defence of our program and our ministers. Silence from me will let Lucien [Bouchard] or Preston [Manning] start picking away at our caucus one by one. We can't hold the government unless we hold the caucus. The caucus did in Stanfield and it did in Clark. It's the Conservative virus and it's inter-generational. My own popularity is a small price to pay for caucus unity, holding the government, and pulling the federalist option together so we won't see a pro-sovereignty vote in Quebec. That's my first responsibility."

Early in my term at the PMO, I had lunch with a senior network bureau chief in Ottawa. I moaned about how sour I found the mood towards all governments, not just Mulroney's, and wondered whether my companion could give me, a new arrival in town, some insights.

The bureau chief's response opened a new door in my understanding of the media. The gist was that people during the recession were down on government, politicians, and bureaucrats, and that defined the market. In editorial choices for, for example, the national supper-hour newscasts, stories that made fun of or underlined government incompetence or misadventure would get the nod. Viewership had to be sustained. Markets for supper-hour viewers were competitive, and "good news" stories could lose market share. High market share produced better advertising revenues, hence the tilt towards "bad government" stories. It wasn't that reporters were directed to have an anti-government slant against the Mulroney, Rae, or Romanow governments. It was simply that of ten editorial ideas raised in morning discussions, those with a negative slant had more yank. I stopped asking questions at that point. I wanted to keep down lunch.

As I drove back to Parliament Hill, I reflected on the inexorable economics of it all. The bureau chief was simply reflecting a hard economic truth. The hope of someone being in government or politics for the right reasons, or that an intrinsically fair process would determine overall coverage, is not only hopelessly naive but likely unfair and unreasonable.

But that still could not explain the personal vilification of the prime minister on grounds that went beyond anything seen in this country before. Part of that had to do with the perception sunk in concrete during the early days that ethical concerns were not uppermost in the minds of some of the caucus. To this day, the francophone press are far less interested in, or convinced of, the alleged corruption in the early years of the Mulroney government because they put it in a historical context with previous Liberal administrations, which were demonstrably worse.

When the Liberals were in control of the patronage machine, the equivalent today of $250-million of advertising spending was split between four companies. In the heyday of the Mulroney government, the equivalent of $150-million in advertising was divided among a hundred and ten companies. During the days of the Trudeau government, one Liberal president of a Quebec ad agency came to Ottawa in his gold Bentley to meet with civil servants about advertising contracts. Conservatives didn't come close to that kind of arrogance, yet were seen to be excessive.

I could only conclude that the real problem was one of style. Mulroney won the party leadership by embodying the essence of a winner. Here was a guy who could actually walk and talk at the same time, who was fluently bilingual to the point that when he spoke French, listeners did not know he had any English roots and when he spoke English they had no idea he had French-Canadian roots. He spoke to the party's desperate desire to have a winner. He reflected and embodied it in the context of the 1980s. The eighties were a period of excess, but within that context he wasn't excessive.

A lawyer from the boonies, he had worked his way through Laval and St. FX to become one of the great labour lawyers in Montreal. He had become part of the upper echelon of legal and business people in the city and lived the lifestyle a prominent lawyer or CEO of a large company would routinely have. The notion that when he came to Ottawa, he would start buying his suits at a discount house was ludicrous. In his world, people of substance dress like people of substance: fashionably and well. Why would they not?

The fact that Ottawa is a sort of rumpled, civil-servanty place, with Mike Pearson making a virtue of managing to get through the 1967 Centennial celebrations on one pair of striped pants, speaks to the virtues of Mike Pearson's Methodist background. But that was not relevant in Quebec even when Pearson was prime minister. It certainly wasn't relevant some twenty years later when Mulroney appeared on the scene. That he was found wanting for stylistic reasons was a sign of how insular Rockcliffe, New Edinburgh, and Ottawa had become and how disconnected civil servants had become from fashionable business and entertainment circles in other parts of North America.

Part of what fed the anxiety about stylistic issues was that even the best journalists in this country are chronically underpaid. The sight of a swell of Conservatives, including the well-dressed prime minister and his well-dressed wife, along with businesspeople, well-paid young executive assistants, and lobbyists also moving in high-priced circles, all congregating at some event, infuriated those who might gladly wear the same pair of corduroys to the press gallery three months straight. The issue in the city soon became not who was doing good, but who was doing well.

The press never came close to reporting the reality that was clearly visible every day to those without blinders. Unlike many self-obsessed professionals, Mulroney was a strong family man, very focused on his children and his wife. It was a rare day indeed when one of his sons, his daughter, or Mila didn't call about midafternoon or show up because they had a guest or classmate they were bringing to the House or because there was a family event that night and they had to pick up dad. He was extremely devout about those kinds of events. He wouldn't miss any judo matches involving his youngest son, Nicolas, or any of Mark's hockey games. Many fathers (often absent themselves) dismissed it as just for show. But after he showed up for the third, fourth, and fifth games, other fathers started showing up too.

Spending time with his family was a lifeline for him, a way of keeping sane and of putting in genuine perspective yesterday's nasty editorial in the *Citizen*, some shrill attack in the House, or an act of treachery by Lucien Bouchard.

The degree to which he could be solicitous when there was any kind of family event to celebrate or any kind of family misfortune was overwhelming. If he heard about a birth or death or illness, he would pick up the phone and call to express his best wishes or his condolences, sometimes reaching people in the hospital on the first day after a baby was born or people at home getting ready for a funeral. He had a wonderful Irish capacity never to be intimidated by another person's misfortune and to be untroubled by death or wakes or suffering. He always wanted to reach out, if for no other reason than to bring a little encouragement into that person's life. It didn't matter who the people were. They were of all political stripes or no political stripe at all. If they were down on their luck, he wanted to help, and not in some kind of magisterial, prime ministerial way. Nor was it methodical or cunning. He was extremely genuine. This was simply who and what he was, whether as a student, lawyer, business executive, or politician. That it was also his genius politically was a bonus.

He was so solicitous that some in the civil service perceived this genius as a potential problem. As he headed to Manitoba to meet with the premier and speak at a fundraiser in the winter of 1991–92, concerns were raised about a possible meeting with David Milgaard's mother, who had been running a campaign to have her son's conviction for murder reviewed and to secure his release from prison. The advice from the department of justice and people in Winnipeg was, "The prime minister must not touch this issue. It's not what prime ministers do. There is a judicial system and there is a process that's being reviewed. He must not go near it." At the pre-Manitoba briefing, I expressed this view to him firmly.

Thankfully, he did not bump into Mrs. Milgaard in the halls of the hotel or at other venues. But as he left his hotel in a snowstorm for the airport, there she was planted firmly outside with a sign reading, "Prime Minister. My son is sick and needs help." Mulroney stopped the car and went over to talk to her.

I received reports from our advance man in the field and immediately thought, "Great. Now we're going to be running the prime minister's court of appeal." I raised him on the phone and diplomatically expressed my anxiety.

He said, "Hughie, she's a mother. She's standing in the snow with a sign that says her son is sick. I've never driven by a person like that in my life. Why would I do it as prime minister?" I had no answer. He said, "I didn't undertake to do anything with respect to the guilt or innocence of her son. I merely said I'd ask the solicitor-general to find out whether or not it's true he's sick."

It turned out Milgaard actually was not well, so he was moved to a better facility and given medical care. That he was later freed and given a chance at a fresh life is worthy of note.

Often, Mulroney would call people in the outside world who would rank as his severest enemies to offer an encouraging word in the face of personal challenge. He always made the distinction between the roles people played in their public life—as, say, leader of the opposition, head of the Assembly of First Nations, or a premier hostile on some issue—and that individual's personal life. It didn't matter what the individual's most recent attack on the government had been. He would always separate the issues, displaying a compassion that was rarely reciprocated.

As far as the Canadian people were concerned, this was one of the best-kept secrets in the world. Only on the day he announced his departure from public life did people like Audrey McLaughlin rise in the House to talk about the many personal kindnesses she knew he had shown other MPs, and particularly the late Pauline Jewett.

I thought long and hard and discussed with others on staff about how to soften the vitriolic, personal nastiness so often directed towards him. In the end, I came to the conclusion that the gestures he made in private were extended for the right reasons. To try to make hay out of them would have been to destroy their sincerity and integrity, which he would not have permitted anyway, and, on balance, would have been quite wrong.

The sourness in the Ottawa press gallery produced low-level sustained fire aimed even at this particular grace and kindness. Just a night or so before the beginning of the discussions to bring Quebec back to the constitutional table in the late summer of 1992, Mulroney invited out to Harrington Lake a few people who had had a pretty difficult year on the personal front. Charles Lynch, a pillar of the gallery who had outlived a host of prime ministers and was now fighting a brave battle against cancer, his spouse, and journalist Don Newman and his spouse, who had suffered the tragic loss of a child a few weeks earlier, joined one or two others (myself not included) for a quiet evening so the Mulroneys could provide some encouragement and at least a touch of cheer. The choice of the night resulted simply from schedules that made it possible for all couples to be present.

Sure enough, three days later, that humane undertaking was portrayed as an attempt to influence the media before constitutional negotiations began. At that point, I concluded that the will to distort and vilify was so intense amongst some in the press that any effort to present them with the facts would be the ultimate waste of time and soul.

9

DEBILITATING WAR

IT IS NOT UNUSUAL IN THE ANNALS of military or political history for those who focus on winning a particular war or debate at just about all costs to not only prevail in the war or win the debate but to spend their own life force in the process.

Part of what hollowed out the party's policy core during the two years before the leadership convention to replace Brian Mulroney was the intense struggle to reconstruct a constitutional agenda so as to keep Quebec from holding a sovereignty-only referendum in October 1992, as promised by Premier Robert Bourassa. When he made that decision after Meech, the pro-independence forces in Quebec could count on popular support of more than 60 percent. Although there were brief respites and other events, domestic and international, they all occupied a sort of background space to the threat of national disintegration.

Confederation itself was just one of a series of preliminary steps in the nation-building understandings between heads of governments of various political parties that produced a nation on the northern half of the continent without bloodshed or civil war. Few nations in the world can claim such peaceful evolution. It was achieved because many potentially divisive issues were sunk in the unifying glue of ambiguity, living in a grey area from which came forth agendas for disputes from 1867 on.

In the early 1970s in Victoria, first ministers reached a constitutional agreement that would have passed but for Quebec's decision to disengage after the fact. The 1982 negotiation after Quebeckers rebuffed sovereignty in the 1980 referendum produced an agreement Quebec did not sign, since no separatist government could sign any federal agreement. This all led inexorably to a fresh constitutional process that could resolve Quebec's status.

There are two corrosive lies about why the Meech Lake negotiations even took place. The first, that Quebec was knifed in the back, I have dealt with earlier. The other lie, prominent in the Liberal salons of the University of Toronto, Outremont, and Rosedale, is that Brian Mulroney exploited the nationalist sentiment to include Quebec nationalists in his 1984 sweep.

Once again, the facts are otherwise. The one Mulroney speech on the constitution during that campaign was little more than a vague commitment to allow Quebec to address its genuine concerns with some confidence and respect. Any analysis that ties the Quebec PC vote in 1984 to the constitution is perverse.

The Parti Québécois was in power in Quebec while Canada languished under the federal Liberals until 1984 and continued in office until defeated by Bourassa in 1985. Some months after Bourassa's election, Quebec attorney-general Gilles Rémillard put out Quebec's reduced list of five points essential for the province to sign the constitution. There was no response from the new Tory government in Ottawa. Later that year, a premiers' conference in Edmonton—no federals present—called on Ottawa to act. No response. Some months later, Jean Chrétien gave an interview in the French press calling on Ottawa to begin a process of negotiation. Michael Pitfield, an independent senator and former clerk of Trudeau's Privy Council, warned in an interview that Ottawa's failure to act would allow the forces of separatism to reconsolidate and threaten the union. Ottawa still did nothing for almost a year.

But setting those pressures aside would probably have produced a Parti Québécois back in power after one Bourassa term and would have sent a message to the premiers that the government cared more about its economic priorities and ideological biases than about unity. Sending such a message would have been inimical to everything Brian Mulroney campaigned on when he sought the leadership and sought a mandate from Canadians to work with the provinces on economic and social issues in 1984.

He was a Tory Everyman. Every time John Diefenbaker battled a bureaucracy that seemed insensitive to any part of Canada beyond Rockcliffe Park, every time Bob Stanfield tried to find a bridge between Quebec and the rest of the country and oppose the excessive centralization and derisiveness of Pierre Trudeau towards Quebec, every time Joe Clark stood in the House or Lowell Murray in the Senate to oppose patriation without provincial consent, they fed a Tory tradition no successful Conservative leader could evade. Brian Mulroney translated that tradition into electoral success, but also into a duty to address the constitutional issue once and for all, but only after it was pushed and pressed upon him well into his first term.

The summer before my arrival in Ottawa, watching the Meech Lake agreement being reached and then collapsing taught me that the processes that led to the successful 1982 agreement would have to be fundamentally changed. Some believe Meech foundered because Mulroney used the "rolling the dice" metaphor in a relaxed, if ill-advised, interview with *The Globe and Mail*. Some believe that it was the process that was problematic: the eleven-men-in-suits angst.

My own assessment was that the amendment formula imposed by the 1982 agreement created time lags that meant the ratification of any constitutional agreement could be interrupted by at least one, two, or maybe even three new federal and provincial governments, given our electoral cycle, creating almost insuperable odds.

Clyde Wells reneged on his commitment by not allowing a vote in Newfoundland, despite his signature on an agreement to the contrary. Frank McKenna started the ball rolling by using Meech to campaign against Richard Hatfield. Gary Filmon found himself in a minority government facing a Chrétien Liberal in Sharon Carstairs who was opposed to the agreement and who reflected the Manitoba backlash to Bourassa's decision on minority English-language rights and Bill 101 during the ordeal. But if Wells, McKenna, and Carstairs had not been actors in the process, others would have been. To personalize what happened at Meech is to give up the capacity to make progress.

The collapse of the agreements meant the process had to be taken up again at some point. There were and are many who do not believe Quebeckers will ever freely vote to leave the union. They often encourage other Canadians to play chicken with the threat, being intolerant of Quebec's legitimate aspirations. But that had a somewhat hollow insouciance when played against the backdrop of a provincial statutory date of October 26, 1992, for a Quebec sovereignty referendum. Whatever motivated Bourassa to set that date, the fact that he did was the dominant political reality the federal government faced in 1991, at a time when support for independence in Quebec was well over 60 percent.

When I arrived in Ottawa, I found no great enthusiasm or fascination within the ranks of the Mulroney government for a constitutional agenda, nor did I find the prime minister enthusiastic. There was simply a sense that the government of Canada had no choice but to remain engaged until the file was closed and the nation sustained. It often felt right to advocate disengagement from the constitutional agenda. It's boring and vexing to most Canadians and far too complex to be easily understood. But the hard truth is that a monster was unleashed the night in October 1970 when Trudeau imposed the War Measures Act. Every generation of politicians from that day forward has had to address the monster. The cost of the engagement was going up, the risks were higher, and the patience and tolerance of Canadians and Quebeckers were steadily diluted.

This would allow no Canadian prime minister the indulgence of folding his arms and letting Quebec go ahead with a referendum on sovereignty only, especially one who brought his party to power by breaking the Liberal stranglehold on French-speaking seats throughout Canada. That abdication would be a recipe for the fracture of the country and a massive increase in the personal costs all Canadians would face day to day, leaving aside the tragedy of the loss of a country like Canada.

I found a clear understanding that failing to achieve some consensus before the referendum would be to abdicate the responsibility every government has to keep the union together and sustain the nation during its watch. Bringing Quebec to the table and knitting Confederation more closely together was a key part of the Conservative platform of 1988. No mandate was ever sought and none given to preside over Quebec's unilateral declaration of independence by virtue of a provincial referendum. Some parliamentary consensus had to be reached, the public had to be consulted, the provinces and aboriginal and territorial leaders had to be involved, and the separatist pressures in Quebec and Parliament had to be managed.

Long before my arrival, Norman Spector and Paul Tellier, the clerk of the Privy Council, had done an unbelievable amount of work to reconstruct a constitutional agenda, rebuild a basis for negotiation and discussion, and ensure a process to maximize the country's ability to find some solution other than the one that would inevitably result from a Quebec-only referendum. Both focused intensely on the detail and strategic process by which the provinces could be engaged, the process begun, and the bullet removed from the revolver pointed at the country's heart. They worried about the stances we might take on various issues as a government, the requirements of Quebec and other parts of the country, and the anti-French purport of much of what Preston Manning was up to, implicitly if not explicitly.

I took a different approach, focusing less on the substance and far more on the mood and the options Canadians would have as a result of the efforts of the prime minister and cabinet.

Many expressed to me concern about Mulroney's decision, some months before my arrival, to ask Joe Clark to head the constitutional process. My own anxiety about Clark, based on his relationship with the party, almost kept me out of Ottawa. Whether or not a senior minister got along with me didn't matter much. Certainly my view of Clark mattered even less. But if I was unable to work with Joe, especially on the constitutional file, it would be better for my position to be filled by someone who could.

Clark had been given the baton by the prime minister and would, as a process-driven person, use the exigencies of the process to influence the content and substance, as opposed to the other way around. I had a sense that his approach risked disaster for the country because of its erratic nature. Yet, in the end, the prime minister and his cabinet and staff would have to mop up whatever mess resulted. I buried my anxiety in the same way one sets aside a capricious but noticeable chest pain in the sincere hope it will not come back. Sadly, that political angina would be a frequent visitor, with greater and greater intensity, during the coming twenty months.

On August 22, 1991, I attended my first meeting with Mulroney, Tellier, Spector, Jocelyn Bourgon, the deputy for federal–provincial relations, and Clark, along with his executive assistant, on lend lease from external, the unflappable Jim Judd. The purpose was to look at how the cabinet committee on national unity could prepare, assess, and elaborate the government's constitutional document by early fall. The document would form the basis for parliamentary review, negotiation, and the completion of national proposals that could be used either to derail the Quebec referendum or provide federal alternatives.

As I prepared for the meeting, I recalled sitting months earlier in the CTV studio high up in the rafters of the Saddledome in Calgary

during the Liberal convention that chose Jean Chrétien as leader. I saw
Clyde Wells embrace Chrétien and thought of the premier of Quebec
attempting to keep his province within Confederation and maintain
Quebeckers' self-respect after what the government of Newfoundland
had done. I knew from confidential reports just how difficult
Bourassa's task was, both to keep his cabinet and caucus together
and to maintain something other than a straight-for-sovereignty
nationalist posture. The contrivance of the Wells forces, Trudeau
forces, and Carstairs-Chrétien forces to derail Meech was clearly a big
part of the pressure he faced.

In my first few weeks in Ottawa, I also picked up just how much
pressure Brian Mulroney was under in managing his caucus and
maintaining the cohesiveness and unity necessary to rebuild a constitutional framework. I heard that several Quebec ministers had already
quietly complained about the way Clark was running his cabinet
committee: it lacked organizational focus, documents to consider, and
any sense of direction. I heard representations from English-Canadian
ministers who thought they were being marginalized and not allowed
to play in any strategic sense around the table. I had no views on this
myself. I hadn't attended a meeting chaired by Clark and had no idea
what the dynamic was. But I knew from my days at Queen's Park
that ministers not in a position of primacy over a process will on
occasion be unhappy with how it is run.

I carried all that in my head as I entered the meeting in the prime
minister's boardroom in the Langevin Block. The meeting was significant less for any specifics than for the sense that emerged from it. I
came away knowing Mulroney was committed to a process that had a
beginning, a middle, an end, and a bottom line. The middle would
involve abundant opportunity for consultation with cabinet, caucus,
Parliament, the provinces, and natives. That was the only way to
ensure an integrated perspective on how the future of the country
might best be reflected in the federal proposals.

I had a sense that Tellier was grounded in a determined pragmatism, so no proposals would go forward that were not practicable,
affordable, sustainable, and protective of the broad national jurisdiction Privy Council clerks are sworn to preserve. I had a sense from
Spector that his critical priority was simply bringing the file to a close,
finding a way to make sure the process produced a clear yes or no
decision from the country in a way that let the country get on with

dealing with the results or moving on because the problem had been resolved. Madame Bourgon was a new quantity to me, but I was impressed with her sense of provincial sensitivities to some of the ideas being kicked around, such as those on the committee between, for example, Benoît Bouchard on behalf of Quebec and Perrin Beatty on behalf of Ontario. Her sensitivity was much more highly developed than I expected from an "apolitical" political servant.

The surprise was the mindset of Joe Clark. He was clearly troubled by the approach implicit in the Michael Kirby memo of 1981, written when he was senior adviser on the constitution to Trudeau, which layed out a strategic approach to the negotiations and to Trudeau's unilateral approach. Clark had opposed it vigorously. His general view, articulated afterwards, seemed to be that any strategy or any planning process—even a critical path that would see a certain amount of work done within a certain time to be referred to cabinet on certain dates and then taken forward for refinement through broad or quiet consultation with the provinces and other interest groups— would, by its very definition, constitute bad faith with all participants. I tried to understand this mindset then and often thereafter. It was honest and no doubt awash in good faith, but I had great difficulty accepting it. Clark had determined that Meech Lake had stalled because of a fundamental lack of legitimacy and inclusiveness to the negotiations. He had a sense that any strategic plan, however flexible, was a threat to the legitimacy of the government's activities and would destroy its credibility. The only acceptable plan, therefore, was no plan. This position was, in my view, pure folly.

It was far too soon in my relationship with Clark to raise any concerns. At that first meeting, it would have been impertinent and disrespectful. But I became profoundly troubled. The political angina became a bit more regular and pronounced.

The document that Clark's cabinet committee produced in the fall of 1991 was sent to the premiers and the parliamentary constitutional committee. The constitutional road show then began in earnest. Months of meetings sponsored by non-partisan organizations across the land, the work of the Spicer Commission, and the hearings by the parliamentary committee chaired first by Dobie-Castonguay and then by Beaudoin-Dobie meant that any Canadian with even the slightest interest in matters constitutional had the chance to be heard. In the entire history of Canada's politics, there had never been a more wide-open, inclusive process. Both Clark and Mulroney deserve credit for this.

During those months, many in the cabinet quietly expressed to me the view that Clark's religious avoidance of any organized plan was a simple framework for capricious improvisation so that little could happen without him being in the centre of it. I doubt this was his intent; my suspicion is that he truly felt he was handling the assignment the only way he knew how and in the best way for the country. And, as he was the designated minister, there was little that could be done.

The collapse of the parliamentary committee and the rapid construction of constitutional conferences to fill the void reflected the heroic efforts of Mulroney, Tellier, and Spector to keep the process moving despite Clark's stop-and-start, yank-and-pull oscillations.

The battle to keep the country together and keep Clark from accidentally destroying caucus or cabinet unity as he free-associated his way around the country, redefining his mission every day, consumed more and more of the prime minister's time and energy. The party's history made it impossible, or at least improbable, that Mulroney could remove Clark or recast his role. Despite past differences, the two had developed a *modus vivendi* that had an elegance about it. Mulroney was unfailingly courteous and generous, defending Clark in caucus and cabinet. Clark, to my knowledge, never spoke ill of the prime minister in private or in public. Some might have worried that Clark's oscillations were part of a wilful insubordination. I prayed that was not the case, and knew there was little one could do if it were.

It was left to Mulroney to play the diplomat in caucus, between premiers, and in cabinet when any particular Clark improvisation proved explosive, and very few of his improvisations failed to generate at least some collateral damage. The irony is that because of the high regard with which he was held and the strong sense that he had no Michael Kirby–style scenario, he sustained the trust of most of the participants outside the government, especially Premiers Gary Filmon, Mike Harcourt, and Bob Rae, and the aboriginal leadership. Building trust is far more easily achieved if it is an all-consuming goal rather than the means to a goal.

The apparent disregard for any strategic approach also endeared him to many in the media. They knew there was no strategic framework from which they were being excluded, because there simply was none. The press also saw his operation as without guile, which was essentially correct, and the entire exercise benefited from that. His relationship with the opposition parties was also essentially constructive, which was an immeasurable asset.

The largest gulf between Clark and the rest of cabinet developed over the possibility of an agreement that could in the end make everyone happy. Having seen Meech Lake collapse, ministers from all regions were justifiably sceptical that an agreement could be drafted that satisfied all parties without being either so diluted or so vague as to make its execution or defence in a referendum next to impossible. Yet Clark always seemed determined to produce an all-signed and sealed agreement at almost any cost, no matter what the content.

This approach was hard on Ontario ministers, who didn't want to see national authority in key regulatory and policy areas so weakened that the national will ceased to exist. It was tough on Paul Tellier and Norman Spector, who sought a cohesive plan in which the cabinet could be left with some strategic choices to protect the national interest. For caucus, the notion of an agreement at all costs was troublesome because it would play into the hands of regional voices that argued this government had no bottom line.

In my view, Clark was wed to any process that kept premiers engaged. In Alberta and Quebec, suspicion and anxiety about his chartless thrusts increased by the day. Few journalists zeroed in on the lack of constitutional vision or core values, other than Lysiane Gagnon of Montreal's *La Presse* and *The Globe*. The "loyal soldier" posture, more apparent on the outside than on the inside of government, provided a protective patina shielding Clark from critical analysis. But the strategic incoherence coming from him multiplied by a factor of ten the problems Brian Mulroney, Benoît Bouchard, Don Mazankowski, John Crosbie, Michael Wilson, Barbara McDougall, and Kim Campbell had to face.

Clark's focus on process *über alles* led back to the "community of communities" idea that had helped unravel his government, attributing to Ottawa little more than the role of transfer agent, social-service guarantor, and travel agency for the provinces. This was David Crombie's town-hall-meetingism writ large across a diffuse, underpopulated nation. More negotiations, more people at the table, more process, and fewer results sustained a communitarian optimism that never anticipated the nation having the capacity to actually resolve a dispute.

The lack of belief in a results-oriented strategy also betrayed Clark's diffidence towards Quebec, Ontario, and Alberta, which were more Mulroney's power base than his. Some decentralization was and remains consistent with conservative principles, but no apparent philosophical vision underpinned Clark's constitutional view. Peace in our time, cooperation, and community were all descriptive values, but the vision was less than apparent.

After meeting with nine premiers and territorial and native leaders in the spring to discuss the proposals produced by the endless consultation, the same group met for days in Ottawa under Clark's chairmanship, leading up to an agreement reached on July 7 while the prime minister was in Europe at a G7 meeting. The agreements reached in Ottawa—on the Senate, distinct society, the House of Commons, the social charter, and aboriginal self-government— reflected Clark's descriptive values, especially appeasement.

This agreement shook the government. Clearly, the premiers, by reserving the right to present the proposals in provincial referendums, were not signing on to the agreement in any committed way. The terms of aboriginal self-government would be problematic at best. There was also a risk of a Conservative government being part of an agreement that isolated Quebec. At the first cabinet meeting after July 7 without specifying who said what to whom, there was in my view only feeble explanation or support for Clark's agreement. It was left to Mulroney, who had his own severe doubts, to defend Clark.

The nature of the agreements also made a national referendum unavoidable. Some still believe a referendum was a Mulroney contrivance, but they ignore reality. British Columbia, Alberta, Saskatchewan, Manitoba, and Newfoundland all had legislative or political commitments precluding any ratification before a vote or other local consultation. Quebec had a referendum date set. Ontario, the Territories, New Brunswick, Nova Scotia, and Prince Edward Island couldn't be the only provinces left out of the mix when it came to public consultation. Although not conceiving the notion, Mulroney was not opposed to it either. In January 1992, when he made a speech in which the referendum surfaced, I expressed my traditional anxiety about any use of referendums on matters of substance beyond an election itself.

He said, "I don't believe this country is so fragile that putting an honest question and having it honestly answered will threaten the union. If anything, it may strengthen the union and help lance the boil."

Through the summer, Mulroney fought to strengthen the union by finding a way to bring Bourassa to the table and to undo the damage done by the July 7 agreement. He battled, coaxed, and cajoled premiers, territorial leaders, and aboriginal leaders day after day for weeks to produce the agreement reached in substance in Ottawa that was taken to Charlottetown for final approval.

There is nothing worse than reconvening all those who have just agreed to a hypothetical deal to ensure that the precise wording is correct. There are hundreds of ifs, ands, and buts, and the maybes mushroom in every civil service department, premier's entourage, and aboriginal group's team of legal counsel. The media, to the extent they could, would fan any apparent differences, creating fresh pressures on this already pressured lot. So the feel at Charlottetown was essentially edgy.

It had been an especially difficult few weeks for the two senior federal public officials on the file, Jocelyn Bourgon and Suzanne Hurtubise, the senior associate deputy. They had been involved in the back-and-forth discussions with the provinces and territories, endless briefings of the cabinet and caucus, and working with Joe Clark. Any of these tasks would be a full-time job for a small army. I came to depend on Suzanne for an absolutely clean and frank read of the worst and best of any situation. They were the only officials in the room when the premiers, territorial leaders, aboriginal leaders, and the prime minister met day after day in Ottawa. They had the absolute trust of the prime minister and earned the trust of all others at the table. They were also the only officials in the room at Charlottetown, except for P.E.I. premier Joe Ghiz's adviser on federal–provincial affairs, Gerry Steele. The rest of us awaited dispatches.

The delegation from Quebec was in a state of utter agitation. We suspected the old civil service forces that had conspired to keep the PQ government from getting an outstanding agreement for Quebec in 1982 were very much at work here. Diane Whilhemene and André Tremblay seemed perpetually depressed, agitated, or both. Clearly, the more nationalistic side of the delegation wanted more than this particular negotiation could ever produce.

John Parisella, Bourassa's chief of staff, provided a calming, stabilizing influence. While a confirmed federalist, he had a strong commitment to making sure Quebec had the *instruments du société* essential to preserve a thriving social, economic, and cultural reality for French-speaking Quebec within Canada and North America. As he tried from his end to manage the pressures created by the Marcel Masse–Gilles Rémillard alliance that sought to radicalize the Quebec cabinet while weakening the federal position, I could share the burden with him from the federal end. We often joked that our respective roles alternated between fireman, backstop, and doorstop.

Far more important than the relationship between the hired help or the bureaucratic armies was the relationship between Bourassa and Mulroney. I found this out in November 1991, when, alone among Mulroney's advisers and still very much the new boy on the team, I had taken the view that if the rumours about his being offered the job of UN secretary-general were true, he should give it serious consideration.

I said, "If you accept that gratitude is the least likely emotion to be expressed at election time, especially after a grinding recession, and if you remember that the good voters of Britain gunned down Winston Churchill in 1945, there are likely to be zero electoral benefits in '92 or '93 for free trade, the GST, the Gulf War, or two constitutional agreements. And you would, Prime Minister, be an outstanding secretary-general."

He didn't respond directly at the time. But after he decided to set aside the proposal—which I thought must have come from the Americans and the British—he said, "How the hell could I have done that, Hugh, when most of the cabinet, including Maz and Benoît, said it would be next to impossible to keep the caucus together or get any kind of agreement on the constitution were I to leave? Besides, look at Bourassa. The man had life-threatening cancer and had every reason to leave, but he hung in. He put off treatment because he didn't want to leave the province during Oka, then he stayed on after and between treatments to bring some closure to the Meech process. My taking a UN appointment would be disloyal to the caucus and cabinet and especially to people like Bourassa, who are staying to find a way to keep the country together."

At Charlottetown, this relationship was particularly important. Time and again, members of the Quebec delegation would say things to the press or send issues into the room aimed at moving Bourassa away from the agreement in principle reached the previous week. Time and again the relationship held.

In a post-session briefing at the end of the first day, when more difficulties had been raised than progress made, Mulroney looked tired and drawn. An official asked if the gap between aboriginals and Quebec could be bridged. The prime minister said, "No one is working harder on it than Joe," trying once again to compliment his constitutional affairs minister. "And no one is trusted more on this than Bob Rae. They're both doing all they can."

The Mulroney–Rae relationship, despite many ideological disagreements and personality differences, blossomed around national unity. The relationship was essential to making the negotiations work. It struck me that it was a contemporary reflection of the Davis–Trudeau relationship ten years earlier, also between profoundly different political personalities and also vital to the success of the process.

After the core difficulties were worked out and an agreement assumed, Mulroney met with all the senior policy people and other staff in the federal delegation's room before going down to address the press and the country. He said, "The process looked and felt impossible a few months ago. None of you ever gave up. Joe Clark never gave up. Benoît Bouchard never gave up. You worked nights and weekends and early mornings. You worked without sleep and you didn't see your families for long times at a stretch. I want to say thank you on my own behalf, on behalf of my fellow ministers, and on behalf of the people of Canada. They will likely never know how hard you worked or how important it was to have this process succeed so that federalists in Quebec and the Canada they believed in wouldn't be hung out to dry. Whatever happens from this day forward, you have my undying gratitude, forever. This is a great country, and every prime minister faces the challenge of keeping it together in one form or another. If we get through this one and we proceed somehow to the country on a broader agreement, then we will have sustained the nation for a bright future. Each of you has earned the profound gratitude of all those who believe in that future."

There was a lot of emotion in the room. Since my eyes fill up at Bell Telephone commercials, I was lucky to keep even a modest measure of control. Some in the room had gone three days with less than six hours sleep. Some, like Suzanne and Jocelyn, had been going at that pace almost twelve full months.

As we went down to the press room to address the country, I bumped into the distinguished historian and Trudeau apologist Michael Bliss, who was there as an expert commentator, likely for the CBC. Bliss extended his hand and said, much to my surprise, "You guys seem to have done a good job." I shook his hand and wished him well. But I sensed he would, in the end, be wherever Trudeau was, and I knew Trudeau would never sanction any agreement beyond the one he almost failed to cobble together because of his own arrogance in 1981.

Premier Davis and Kathleen get the world's ugliest puppy (Blue); Santa Claus is Fred Ross. The tams say "Go Blue" and are from the University of Michigan—Kathleen's and Ed Stewart's alma mater (no partisanship intended).

With Davis at the 1976 Davis leadership convention. I am supporting Wagner. Davis is believed to be supporting at least two candidates.

The Day to Day Minority Government Team (keeping it alive, day by day). *Standing, left to right:* Jim Mackenzie, assistant to Bob Welch; House Leader Bob Welch; Dr. E. Emslie Stewart, secretary to the cabinet, deputy minister to the premier, treasurer of the National Scottish Trust, and determined nonpartisan; legislative assistant in sports jacket (lost by my wife after I wore it in Paris); Brian Shannon, assistant to the premier. *In front:* William Grenville (there are still some farmers in Brampton) Davis, premier from 1971 to 1985.

At the Opening of the Ontario House, with Donna, 1979.

The other gang of four: Mr. Davis, Jacqueline (age six weeks), Donna, and Richard Hatfield, at Robertson's Point, New Brunswick, 1982.

Winnipeg, 1983: at the launch of *No Small Measure: The Progressive Conservatives and the Constitution*. *Left to right*: press secretary to Premier Davis Dennis Massicotte, co-author Senator Nate Nurgitz, Premier Lyon, Premier Davis, and the other co-author—all wearing Clark buttons.

Senior Adviser to the Prime Minister, 1991, with Chief of Staff Norman Spector and the prime minister in the Langevin Block.

Trudging up the hill in winter 1992 to an all-day cabinet meeting at Meech Lake.

With House Leader Harvie Andre and the prime minister before Question Period, winter 1992.

Goodwill visit to the Enemy Head Office: a visit to *The Toronto Star* editorial board, with editor and soon-to-be publisher John Honderich and the prime minister.

With Don Mazankowski on the tarmac at Lloydminster for the last rally of the Yes campaign for the Charlottetown accord referendum.

At the last cabinet meeting I attended, in the final week of April 1993, I am sitting next to Marcel Massé, former clerk of the New Brunswick cabinet, fomer head of CIDA, new deputy minister for Intergovernmental Affairs, and, in the tradition of nonpartisan civil service in Ottawa, about two days away from announcing his candidacy for a Liberal nomination in the rock-solid Liberal seat of Hull.

Meeting with the press after the prime minister has announced his intention to retire from public life.

Author with Donna, Jacqueline, and Angel at home, Kingston, November 1995.

As we left for the airport, a good-sized crowd outside the Prince Edward Hotel cheered and waved signs thanking all inside for their successful work. This seemed to energize Mulroney, who had also had very little sleep, at least for the moment. As we drove to the airport, he was uncharacteristically detached, not the usual inveterate cheerleader who always bucked up others.

He said, "Well, what do you think?"

I said, "If it was this hard to get all the federalists together on an agreement, imagine the referendum."

"We're going to have to try, Hugh."

"It's going to be like open-heart surgery without an anaesthetic."

"But at least we start with a patient very much alive."

"Yes, sir. But will anyone ever thank you for that?"

"Look out the window when we're flying home. Thanks is not what this is about."

The battle plan for winning the referendum developed within a framework defined by two crushing burdens. First, all the leaders had agreed at their last meeting in Charlottetown that there would be a national structure, operating independently of governments in each jurisdiction, with a cross-representation in the Yes committees of all political parties. This grew out of the tiptoe-through-the-tulips, non-strategic approach Clark took to the July 7 meeting and Mulroney's restructuring of a workable agreement that neither isolated Quebec nor eradicated all national government. Both were premised on an endless search for collegiality. Everyone was consulted *ad nauseam*. No opposition spokesperson, provincial official, or native subaltern escaped. But as the referendum approached, this collegiality became a serious organizational burden.

Mulroney was not insensitive to this reality. He simply felt it would be counterproductive and divisive to have an agreement like Charlottetown achieved through the cooperation of provincial premiers and opposition leaders of all political stripes and then, under the provisions of the referendum legislation, have Yes committees divided by partisanship.

Nationally and in the provinces, the horizontal framework meant that people who had never worked together before—in fact, who had always worked in opposition to each other—had to cobble together cohesive strategic and tactical structures. They had to execute at the local level without stumbling over each other, while bridging huge cultural divides between the way the parties operated in each province and territory. There was an implicit responsibility to achieve cohesiveness, unity, cooperation, joint strategy, and joint implementation.

Yes committees across the country tried almost overnight to establish these norms, meld operating styles combining party biases and prejudices, and merge advertising agencies and local and community groups. The imposition of a horizontal decision-making framework on what had to be, if successful, a vertical strategic and tactical structure for a referendum was fatal.

All the No side had to do was sow doubts about the contents of the accord. The more disorganized they were and the less organized they appeared, the more credibility and legitimacy the media gave them. CTV decided, quite capriciously, to sprinkle equally over a range of time periods the paid and free-time commercials and announcements available to all the No and Yes committees, rather than cluster the free-time ads in free-time broadcasts. With that, the network destroyed the purchasing and advertising power of the Yes committees who had worked out cohesive, strategic, and communication frameworks. With one decision, the network destroyed the communication salience of those who were paying CTV for advertising (their customers) and gave equal salience to those who weren't. This served to ensure that those with large budgets had no more representation during prime or other targeted times than those with almost no budget at all. This may have been a great blow for equity and fairness, but it tilted the media towards the guerrilla tactics, all quite legal and understandable, of the many No committees.

Equally burdensome to the framework was the agreement that there would be broad consultation on the content of the question. Representatives from the territories and provinces, other political parties, and aboriginal leaders met with me one afternoon over corned beef sandwiches in the Langevin Block. I had asked Bill Fox on a volunteer basis to present historical research on referenda. It showed that the Yes side always fights a losing war of attrition in any referendum on any issue at any time. That has been the case in every Western nation since World War II.

The data on framing the question were clear. If the key five elements of the agreement were presented—in a question such as "Recently the provinces, aboriginal leaders, the Territories, and the federal government concluded an agreement at Charlottetown with the following elements: a reformed Senate, recognition of the distinct society of Quebec, enhanced representation for the West and Quebec in the House of Commons, aboriginal self-government, etc. Do you approve?"—most voters would find something on the list with which they disagreed, but would also find one or two things about which they felt positive. This would have the effect of increasing the vote for the Yes side by at least 20 percent and in some regions by 30 percent.

The representatives might have been impressed with the research showing that a question that arrayed the specific elements would do massively better than one that simply referred to the accord without specifying its contents. But the research didn't matter one bit. When they returned to their home bases, the message they received from Bourassa, Rae, Chrétien, and others was that the question was to be precisely one line, with the elements of the accord not specified, and asking whether people agreed or disagreed that an agreement be completed on that basis.

To this day I find it hard to understand why. There was a sense that laying out the options, particularly in Quebec, would make the matter too complex. This was simply Bourassa underestimating the sophistication of Quebec voters, a mistake he had made before. For Rae and Chrétien, it's likely they believed a simple question would have citizens believe they were affirming the country rather than choosing items on a menu, although the proponents of a question arraying the contents never contemplated anything other than a cumulative yes or no at the end.

The Prime Minister asked that Harry Near represent the Conservative Party on the national Yes committee. Perhaps the finest operational planner and tactician in the party, Harry had volunteered in more campaigns than any other Conservative in the country of his age and agreed to volunteer for this effort too. The Prime Minister also asked for Bill Fox to come on board. He had provided some of the most insightful and thoughtful communications counsel to corporate clients across the country. He also agreed to volunteer. I was delighted they had accepted—although I knew it was not in their business interests. The Liberal Party made Gordon Ashworth available on a relatively full-time basis. Les Campbell, the chief of staff in Audrey McLaughlin's office, represented the NDP.

Volunteers worked day and night, aided by a strategic group that gathered several mornings a week. Sharon Vance, a senior New

Democrat, and Gerry Caplan represented the NDP. Jodi White, a former Clark chief of staff, Harry, Bill, and I were there regularly for the Conservatives; Gordon Ashworth, Mike Robinson, a treasurer of the Liberal Party, and Eddie Goldenberg from Jean Chrétien's office were there for the Liberals. The aboriginal leadership was invited to send a representative, but declined.

The national Yes strategy group, chaired by a prominent John Turner Liberal, Torrence Wylie, tried to define a broad strategy and address tactical imperatives. A national Yes committee leadership made up of individuals like former Liberal cabinet minister Iona Campagnolo, Ted Newel, a senior business leader, Michelle Bastarache, a prominent Liberal from New Brunswick, former UN ambassador and Liberal Yves Fortier from Montreal, well-known NDP journalist June Callwood, and Mary Simon of the Inuit Tapirisat, among others, provided national focus and direction for committee activities. The group, pulling together people who had worked against each other most of their lives, and putting together a relatively apolitical, non-partisan national leadership not used to the day-to-day ups and downs of a political struggle, established an immense and undeniably vulnerable target for the guerrilla, community-based No committees.

The Yes committee sought to coordinate schedules. Conservative ministers and the prime minister shared their schedules with the committee, as did the NDP and many premiers, although we're still waiting for Chrétien and his front bench to file their travel schedules for the period. The guerrilla side for the No merely pointed to areas that were grey, weak, or, in their view, inappropriate, always raising doubt.

The Yes committee sought to coordinate statements made by aboriginal leaders, provincial premiers, and opposing party leaders, and shape a joint strategy that was complementary rather than contradictory. People for the No merely stirred up anti-Quebec sentiments in British Columbia and anti-aboriginal sentiments in Quebec, without any measure of accountability or structural constraint.

The media justifiably felt they had a duty to cover all sides equally and fairly, so they worked up a digest of everything being said and reported it nightly or hourly. The media mindset was focused by the early appearance of a Goliath caught up in his own sandal straps versus a series of small and sprightly Davids all firing their slingshots with some clarity and precision.

In Quebec, there was the soothing dishonesty of the Bloc Québécois and the Parti Québécois going from riding to riding and town to town saying that a No was merely a No for this accord and implied no endorsement of sovereignty or independence or any denunciation of Canada (although they would say immediately afterwards that the result showed that sovereignty was the only option). In this opposition, they were sustained by the wilful, nasty, self-serving, egotistical support of Pierre Trudeau, who conspired to make the debate in Quebec appear a foregone conclusion, with everyone sleepwalking to a massive No. For Trudeau, any constitutional agreement except his own is utterly unacceptable. It was only after his intervention at the Maison d'Egg Roll in Montreal that the numbers in English Canada began to turn decidedly against the Yes side. Only then did the numbers in Quebec begin to move more dramatically against Yes as well.

This was the old Trudeau calculus that had been so effective—namely, to first appear to English Canada as a French-Canadian leader who would diminish, deride, and otherwise make fun of French-Canadian aspirations. When numbers in English Canada move in support of that kind of jingoism, the numbers in Quebec move in response. This was true in the election of 1968, during the imposition of the War Measures Act in 1970, during Meech, and during Charlottetown.

Trudeau's intervention liberated people like Preston Manning to oppose the accord without the slightest worry of being seen as insensitive or unfeeling towards Quebec or aboriginals; after all, a former prime minister from Quebec was leading the negative charge. This also made it easy to capitalize on anti-aboriginal or anti-French anxiety.

Mulroney's spirited intervention in Sherbrooke, in which he tore up a list of the gains Quebec—and all other provinces—would have and could lose, was meant in part to jar Quebeckers out of the narcotic-like trance imposed by the largely pro-independence media and the No side. Our pollsters and local Conservatives advised Mulroney that the time had come to raise the temperature. The relative final strength of the Yes side in Quebec—compared, say, to Alberta, where Yes was crushed—indicates he was more right than wrong.

On the last weekend of the campaign, there was a huge rally in Lloydminster, a community straddling the Saskatchewan-Alberta border. Don Mazankowski and the local MP, Bill McKnight, joined native leaders and municipal and cultural groups for an old-fashioned high-school gym rally for Canada. By that point, the writing was on the wall. Some took encouragement from the large undecided vote in many parts of the country, but it was apparent that the No side would triumph, sustained by the hypocritical arguments made by the separatists in Quebec, their Reform allies in the West, and Pierre Trudeau, Michael Bliss, and the Trudeau centralist network in English Canada.

All who spoke, including Brian Mulroney, made emotional and compelling speeches. There was barely a dry eye at this gathering of local folks who were far less part of any elite than Pierre Trudeau or that wealthy scion of Quebec business, Jacques Parizeau. Most people in the hall had far less done for them by the state, wealthy parents, or taxpayers. They were there to express solidarity with Quebec and with the notion of a Canada based on less power at the centre, more local authority, less debt, a more democratic Senate, and a recognition of fair-minded realities such as the distinct nature of Quebec and the inherent right of aboriginal peoples to self-government. This was the kind of Canada they could rejoice in.

Standing at the back of the crowd, listening and looking at the faces, I thought about how comfortable Bob Stanfield would have been with these people making this case in this way at this time. I watched the prime minister walk into the hall and be introduced in an emotional, non-partisan, and stirring speech by Roy Romanow, who had been there in 1982 when Quebec, hamstrung by separatist theology, had abdicated its responsibility and who was now here, somewhat hoarse of voice, to give an outstanding speech in support of Charlottetown and of the multi-party, multicultural, multi-interest coalition he had come to only after careful consideration.

New Democrats and Tories have much that divides them in economic agendas and preferences. But on the core issues surrounding Canada and its survival, there is more of substance uniting mainstream New Democrats and mainstream Tories who believe in nation. Bob Rae had been a participant in the process both before the July 7 landmine and after. There would not have been a Charlottetown accord without his commitment, tolerance, and judgement.

That Liberals from New Brunswick, Newfoundland, P.E.I., and Quebec and socialists from British Columbia, Saskatchewan, and Ontario could join with Conservatives in Nova Scotia, Alberta, and federally to achieve this kind of agreement in concert with aboriginal leadership and the Territories spoke to the emergent consensus about what was wrong with Confederation and what could be fixed.

A reluctant constitutional warrior from the outset, Mulroney found himself staring at the defeat of Charlottetown just hours away. But on the flight back from Lloydminster, he was relaxed, pensive, and not without humour.

I offered him my resignation. A senior political adviser should be prepared to walk the plank when a political campaign for which he was as responsible as any has not gone well. I would do it with pride because I believed in the effort. Win or lose, I believed the referendum served as an important time bridge for the country to reflect on what subsequent moves made the most sense. The prime minister would need some months to stabilize the party and assess its prospects. I also believed my resignation would ensure that no volunteers in the cause carried any blame. As chief of staff I was on the payroll. So many others who had served were volunteers, and I felt I had a duty to protect them. He was quick to reject the idea.

I was feeling rather despondent, but he said something I found quite comforting. He looked at me a little wistfully, cup of coffee in hand, and said, "You know, Hughie, most prime ministers have had to face this kind of crisis, whether it's over the Winnipeg General Strike or conscription or Louis Riel. It comes with the turf. It's important that you fight for what you believe in and try to achieve as much of that as possible. But what's even more important is that you find a way for the country to pass judgement in a way that produces no recrimination. There'll be recrimination against politicians and parties and premiers and prime ministers, and that comes with the turf too. But it's important that there's no recrimination between English- and French-Canadians in this sort of process. Whatever happens, it will be Canadians themselves who are deciding and it'll be a decision Canadians themselves will have to live with. There'll be no reason for one part of the country to be hateful about another part of the country. They may all decide to hate me, but that's all right. It's a small price to pay to keep the country alive and be able to hand it on."

A good-sized group of volunteers from Yes headquarters and the local committee came out to cheer Mulroney's arrival in Ottawa. It was a last emotional show of spirit that few present will ever forget.

The results, though disappointing, offered glimpses of optimism and some political justice. The massive Yes vote in Newfoundland seemed to be a clear indication to Clyde Wells where the people stood both on Meech and Charlottetown. The support of New Brunswick and Prince Edward Island and the close win in Ontario were encouraging, if only to the extent that they reflected where those who traditionally voted on the moderate side were on the proposition. That a larger percentage of Quebeckers voted yes than was the case in British Columbia, Alberta, Saskatchewan, or Manitoba spoke eloquently to the difficulty separatists will have in taking the province out of Confederation. Quebec voters' commitment to bringing Quebec into the family with honesty, frankness, and pride was higher than many cared to admit. Post-referendum support for independence in Quebec collapsed by 50 percent.

The referendum settled some things for the future, including perhaps the one *de facto* Mulroney constitutional amendment that may well protect future generations of Canadians from endless constitutional fiddling and niggling, namely that no major change to the Constitution can now be made without a referendum.

The result might also occasion Canadians to face a horrible truth. The interests of those opposed to a solution are far more personal than the interest we all share in a constructive resolution of the issue. The marginal benefit we would all enjoy in our day-to-day lives from sorting out the matter is far less than the loss facing many groups. If the Confederation issue is put to bed once and for all, separatist and nationalist forces in Quebec, Trudeau's cadre of supporters, the Reform Party, organizations devoted to preserving the utterly unthreatened English language, sub-groups within the aboriginal community, and large parts of the federal bureaucracy would lose much leverage. The forces determined to keep the union on the precipice of dissolution are far better organized, focused, and determined and have many more personal and career interests to advance than those who share a common marginal benefit in the union being strengthened and the crisis going away.

Whether out of a search for fairness or the simple need to find point and counterpoint on every issue, the media's ability to balance the common interest is diluted by their responsibility, which democracy inherently demands, to be fair to those who take a contrary view. Almost unwittingly, the media become opponents to any solution, not because of any conspiracy but because the systemic needs of news coverage or balanced commentary magnify the concerns of those with a determined interest in a crisis.

This is not good news, nor is it a complaint. It is simply reality. The people who wish to work together to keep the country together on a basis that makes sense must be frank with themselves about the systemic and visceral opposition the nature of our society will produce and the significance that opposition will always acquire.

None of this can diminish the tremendous hit the Conservative Party took the night of October 26, 1992. In most constituencies in English Canada and throughout Quebec, Conservatives received no support from Liberals in local Yes committee activities. New Democrats, labour councils, and aboriginal groups did their best and in many constituencies, worked extremely hard with Conservative colleagues. Liberals in Quebec and throughout the country, federal Liberals specifically, were nowhere to be seen. This may have reflected the ambivalence within the party about an accord that would reduce the power of the central government and bureaucracy. But whatever their rationale, honourable or otherwise, the Liberal organization remained disengaged from the battle. With the exception of very few MPs, they spilled no blood locally across the country. In Kingston and the Islands, Tories like John Gale, Sally Barnes, Hugh Smith, John Chown, Wally Viner, Ray Hessian, Blair McLean, Nancy Foster, and Elva McLean worked alongside New Democrats like Beth Pater and Gary Wilson to produce a Yes victory. People like Ray DeSouza and Lauren André of the Queen's PC Club worked with Young New Democrats in common cause. Liberals showed up for the Committee Room opening then disappeared. At the central level, except for a handful of individuals, Liberals shared no information and did little joint planning to advance the cause. Jean Chrétien, by sins of omission or commission, contributed to the failure of both Meech and Charlottetown.

The decimating hit allowed the Bloc and Reform to build momentum in attracting candidates, constructing an organization, raising funds, and claiming a high ground, dismissing everyone who worked so hard for an agreement as pretenders to a reality in which Canadians had no interest. Of course, it was a breakthrough for the Liberals. That enough votes were gathered for the Yes side to elect a majority government nationally is comforting, but neither here nor there.

The Conservative Party has always put Confederation and its survival first and has always fought within itself and within the country to accommodate the Quebec reality. It may well be that the party's historic role in the process was to act as a buffer to take the flak and to protect the passenger compartment from greater damage.

I was comfortable with the efforts made on behalf of the cause. But I was saddened by the cheap and unsubstantiated criticism heaped on people like Harry Near and Bill Fox simply because the Earnscliffe Strategy Group, the company from which they took time to serve, had pre-referendum, long-term polling contracts with the government. Volunteering in an effort with questionable prospects, which essentially tied up two of Earnscliffe's principals, was probably neither well advised nor in the interest of their partners or shareholders. They did it for the country and the prime minister and stood to gain not one whit from the exercise. That the Yes votes were as high as they were in Ontario, Quebec, and the Maritimes was in large measure due to the massive effort and personal sacrifice that people like them made in support of the cause. But when people lose, the search for scapegoats is merciless and often unrelated to the facts.

The party did its best, despite its own misgivings around the cabinet table and in caucus and despite concerns among members of the Quebec caucus that there wasn't enough in the package for their province. But the party came together and worked with determination against immense odds to make the case for an agreement honourably reached and responsibly advanced.

The fundamental price paid was that the verdict made it difficult for Brian Mulroney to lead the party in a third campaign. A Mulroney campaign would have been difficult, but it would have been premised upon convictions on broad economic, social, and national-policy issues. It would have given Conservatives something to work for and believe in. Even if we did not succeed, we would have finished in a solid second place with our convictions intact. The referendum diminished that option for the election that had to come in 1993.

Another potentially deadly skirmish in the battle for Canada passed into the night with the nation preserved. The Quebec national assembly passed legislation after the Charlottetown meeting cancelling the sovereignty-only referendum, thereby taking the bullet out of the gun. But the toll the process took on the leader and the party was truly horrific. Less than four months later, Brian Mulroney announced his departure from the field.

10

FIVE DAYS IN APRIL

FROM THE BEGINNING OF MY ASSIGNMENT, my understanding with the prime minister was that my primary duty was to help see him, the party, and the country through the constitutional impasse, but if he chose to stay on in a position of command after the passage across the lip of the abyss, I would stay with him till the end, whatever that end might be. I had no illusions about the potential outcome of another campaign in the trenches against the Liberals and the new forces from Quebec and the west mutually bent on destroying the Canada I loved. But if he chose to lead the Tory family into one more electoral battle, I would be honoured to be in his service.

Privately, I longed to get back to the earning freedom of the private sector and revert to the local party volunteer status that twenty-hour days in the PMO make any sane family man crave. During my time in Ottawa, Donna, Jacqueline, and I moved house and home from Toronto to Kingston, a move we had discussed for several years before any notion of my serving Mulroney surfaced. In September 1990, I began a term as a Skelton Clarke Fellow at the department of political studies at Queen's University. When I had to disengage from that position to answer the call to Ottawa, the principal indicated that should I choose to reapply to finish the fellowship once my term of service was done, the application would be considered seriously.

Kingston is Donna's home town. She was a graduate of Queen's nursing program before getting her MBA from Western. Her grandfather had been superintendent of Kingston General Hospital for many years.

She had been a consultant in the institutional health-care field for Touche Ross before signing on with Ontario's ministry of health. When the ministry approached her about taking a position in Kingston, everything fell into place. We made an offer on a house a few months after I took up my position in Ottawa and we moved in September 1992, which allowed me to get home for dinner one or two nights a week.

How long I would stay in Ottawa was up to Brian Mulroney. Through the months after the referendum, he never shared his plans, assuming he had formulated them with any precision. Only about forty-eight hours before he met the press in late February 1993 to announce his retirement did he inform a few of his staff, the Privy Council Office, Donald Mazankowski, and Benoît Bouchard of his intentions. The next day, I discussed with him my desire to go back to private life, perhaps by the end of April. The morning of his announcement, a small band of brothers and sisters who had served the leader gathered at 24 Sussex for a bittersweet farewell with the Mulroneys. It was a subdued moment, a time to reflect on what had been accomplished over the previous nine years and on what the future held for the Conservative Party under a new leader. I was far more pessimistic than others about our chances as a party without him.

Many believe Brian Mulroney preordained the outcome of the leadership race. The prevailing media view was that he was enthralled with the idea of being replaced by an extremely bright minister from the baby-boom generation who happened to be a woman, Kim Campbell. Conceptually, the Conservative Party's election of that kind of leader would indeed signal a fresh point of departure, although only hindsight reveals the precise kind of departure from national politics her selection would entail.

In my view, Mulroney seemed more enamoured with the idea of a strong field—with Campbell, Barbara McDougall, Perrin Beatty, Mike Wilson, Jean Charest, Bernard Valcourt, and others all in—than a narrow field with Campbell dominant. In the three years before he announced his retirement, all kinds of senior ministers were shifted to give them a better vantage point from which to contest the leadership. McDougall was made foreign secretary, Wilson was moved to trade, Mazankowski was given finance and remained deputy prime minister, Bouchard went to health and welfare, Valcourt was given employment and immigration, Charest environment, Bill McKnight energy, and Beatty the urban and urbane communications portfolio.

In that context, Campbell's elevation to the ministry of defence was not as significant as many believed. But the excessive enthusiasm of a few supporters plus the support of deputy chief of staff Marjory LeBreton, a long-time and well-liked party worker, created the impression of a prime ministerial preference. The effect was quite significant, especially on key financial supporters in key parts of the country. The media preference for Kim Campbell, combined with the rush to her camp of such establishment figures as Guy Charbonneau, Gilles Loiselle, Marcel Masse, Libby Burnham, Doug Lewis, Paul Curley, Norm Atkins, and others, all for honourable and quite valid reasons, created a sense of *les jeux sont faites*. In fact, even an old and dear friend of mine, lawyer and collector Alan Schwartz, called me early on to indicate he was disposed to accept Kim's request that he become her chief fundraiser. I encouraged him to help any of the candidates he believed in. Campbell was lucky to get Alan.

This rush to hop on the Campbell bandwagon gave me a strong sense of foreboding. Early in March, in the post-Mulroney retirement haze, I had the chance to review the field over dinner with Jeff Simpson of *The Globe and Mail*. I was struck by the depth of his suspicion about Campbell's shallowness. There was no animus or hostility to his assessment. It was simply that, based on his observations over five years, he was convinced that a politically literate TV interviewer could, in an hour-long interview, demolish her. He believed that many senior people in the press gallery shared that view. With the media's influence over our public agenda, those kinds of beliefs can quickly become self-fulfilling prophecies.

Between the prime minister's announcement and the beginning of April, many people asked me about Campbell, whether I knew her well, and, if so, what I could tell them about her. I first met her at Whistler for a Young President's Organization convention in 1989 where we were both resource people. She struck me as an essentially cheery and quite bright proponent of a vigorous new right in the west. Her successful defence of free trade in the Vancouver area, along with MP Mary Collins, had been a welcome tonic in a difficult stretch of the 1988 election. As a volunteer in the campaign, I well remember the direct orders from the prime minister that we use extra radio weights in her riding and in Collins's riding to bolster their chances for election. The radio ads had both Mary and Kim passionately advocating the importance of free trade for British Columbia and Canada.

When I arrived in Ottawa, she was already attorney-general, the first woman to occupy that post in Canadian history. The last Conservative from British Columbia to hold the portfolio was Davie Fulton, a man Mulroney had worked for and supported for leader in 1967. Clearly, Campbell had been selected for great things. But the same could be said of Barbara McDougall, who had been given the tough job of minister of state for finance in the first Mulroney government, then employment and immigration before becoming foreign secretary. It's hard to look at their trajectories and conclude that either was disadvantaged when it came to options for the future.

There was, however, one fundamental difference between them. Barbara had spent more than twenty-five years in active Tory politics before being elected in St. Paul's riding in Toronto. She had no establishment help from PC headquarters in her quest for that nomination. She simply persevered and was not prepared to be put off by hints of some "star" candidate perpetually in the wings. She had run David Crombie's campaigns for Parliament and for the party leadership, and had been part of the Tories' urban political forces in Ontario for years. She had the scars to prove it. When she spoke in the corridors of power, she offered a seasoned voice, replete with a long Tory history, a broad national network, and the experience of someone who had won and lost her share. She brought soul, vision, and heart to the Tory crusade.

Kim had been a Social Credit MLA in B.C. and had run for that party's leadership at a time clearly predating her capacity to engender any meaningful support. She joined our party on the eve of the 1988 election and came very close to losing the seat Pat Carney had held for some time. She was intelligent, gregarious, and not without a tough sense of humour. She was a quick brief and passionate, but the causes she championed had little sense of rootedness. When she won cabinet battles, such as on KAON, the big science project in British Columbia, those opposed to her view were beaten up pretty badly.

My greatest initial anxieties about her centred on what I considered a serious gap in her approach. I never had the sense that she understood the dynamics of building or maintaining a team. She was a competent minister, as far as I could tell, and seemed to have loyal and determined staff. But after almost two years of watching her in cabinet, I gained no insight into Kim Campbell whatever. I had nothing of a negative nature to report to those who asked my opinion, except that I would have been hard pressed to enumerate any fundamental principles or beliefs to which she subscribed. I may have lacked the perceptual acuity necessary to divine them. There may have been answers that others understood, although to this day, I have not heard them or seen them.

Her support base consisted of those who believed in her and knew her well (largely limited to personal staff and B.C. friends), those who believed it was time for a bright leader from the west, those who believed a woman leader was long overdue and a genuine electoral asset, and those who saw her as the best way to advance their own agendas, whether they encompassed ministerial promotion, more decentralization, or more tolerance for an even broader strain of Quebec nationalism.

I encouraged McDougall, Valcourt, Beatty, and others to get into the fight. They reflected important philosophical segments of the party that should be represented in a leadership race. But the Campbell juggernaut crushed almost everyone in its path.

McDougall would have been an outstanding candidate, but she found not only that established financial supporters had gone quickly to Kim but much of her own riding's Jewish leadership committed to Kim before Barbara herself could make a decision. Beatty had served the party in Parliament loyally and with great dignity for two decades, yet believed he could not raise the funds for a creditable race. Financial support was no problem for Wilson, but the desertion of key Ontario ministers early on made victory an elusive proposition. At that point in his career, running simply to place would be a noble but futile gesture he had earned the right to avoid. Similar realities diminished the possibility of Valcourt or McKnight entering the lists.

Until Jean Charest entered, and for some time thereafter, the scent of a coronation was everywhere. For some, the odour was unbearable. To me, it had the smell of decay about it. Charest picked up some steam, but the sense of a process frozen in amber was extremely chilling. Especially troubled were a group of businesspeople from B.C. who knew Campbell and did not like what they saw, a group of about twenty caucus members from Manitoba, Ontario, Saskatchewan, and rural B.C. who were searching for another option, and a group of senior ministers: Wilson, McKnight, Valcourt, John McDermid, and Otto Jelinek.

The media slowly began to be somewhat less uncritical of Campbell, but the view that to be against her was to be against progress and decency itself was being given broad circulation by her more extreme supporters, with some articulating a neo-feminist imperative.

Their view was not that Campbell was an outstanding candidate whose sex was a genuine plus, which most thoughtful feminists, male and female, could accept, but rather that to apply normal critical standards to her candidacy was, in itself, to be anti-female. That kind of intellectual terrorism did both her and the party a great disservice.

The last weekend in March, I began to hear rumours that Wilson and McKnight were trying to find an alternative to add to the mix of candidates in the race. The first weekend in April, McKnight phoned me at home in Kingston on Saturday afternoon. The call was a surprise to me, a surprise in politics being anything with less than three days' notice. He said the field was devoid of anyone who could make the party feel comfortable with itself and with its fiscal, social, and economic mission. He offered no criticism of the candidates, other than expressing a genuine fear that Kim Campbell did not know the party and the party did not know her. He said he wanted to meet with me in Toronto the next day to discuss a Hugh Segal candidacy. I suspect he sensed the shock in my voice, but he persevered. He said I'd be hearing soon from Mike Wilson and Bernard Valcourt.

The Valcourt call came within an hour, and was, in the way that is so typical and decent of him, direct, frank, and hilarious. He argued that none of the candidates had been a *fils du parti* to the extent I had. He repeated the request that we gather the next day in Toronto. I told him I'd check with the prime minister.

Wilson's call from Dallas was the most intriguing. I had come to understand Michael better while watching him in cabinet and caucus, and had found him to be among the most determined and focused of ministers, often on fairly isolated ground. His case was simple and direct: the party would have a tough go in the coming election unless we had a leader who could confront Liberal hypocrisy and media biases and still keep the party a happy and humane vehicle for Canadians. He urged me to go to Toronto to meet with Valcourt and McKnight. He indicated caucus and financial support would not be a problem. This was all too much for me to assimilate.

Brian Mulroney was attending the opening of the Reagan library in the U.S. that Saturday. I phoned to tell him about the calls I had received and the discontent in the ranks over the field, a discontent and frustration that worried him too. The decisions of McDougall, Beatty, Wilson, and others not to enter the race had surprised him. I told him about what Wilson, McKnight, and Valcourt had in mind. I offered to shut down any exploratory process on their part, accepting his prerogative to have me disengage completely.

His advice could not have been more clear. "Hear what they have to say, keep your own counsel, and keep in touch."

I flew out the next morning, Palm Sunday, to Toronto's Pearson Airport and proceeded to the hotel there. Within the hour, McKnight and Valcourt arrived. Wilson and Jelinek joined in by phone. For the next three hours, the ministers forcefully advanced their proposal.

My protestations about never having held elected office held little water with this crew. They were outwardly enthusiastic about me but, more important, they seemed profoundly troubled by the shape of the race for the leadership and its implications for the country and the party. Their gist was that a coronation put the party at great risk. Campbell would be subjected to eviscerating criticism during the campaign and be found wanting. Jean Charest was decent, thoughtful, and likable, but lacked sufficient understanding of the party outside Quebec and of the media to lead the party just yet.

I did not buy all this. I was less critical of Charest's capacities and I doubted my skill set was quite as outstanding as they thought. The ministers were also clearly to the right of the spectrum in the cabinet, and their interest in a Reddish Tory on social issues was more than a little puzzling. I made it clear that my social-policy views were in the populist broaden-the-mainstream tradition. I had become far more fiscally conservative the closer I came to government, but reaching out to the poor and disadvantaged was a big part of my frame of reference, along with hard-line positions on foreign policy, defence, and capital punishment. They were adamant and determined.

"What's vital is your ability to communicate what our convictions as Conservatives really are," Wilson said.

"You're a son of the party," said Valcourt, "someone whom the country likes and the party knows and trusts. This is going to be a tough campaign."

"Look, Hughie," Jelinek said, "we've had our differences on policy, but you've always been there for the party and you're one of the few Conservatives the media and the public seem not to hate."

Bill McKnight added a prophetic and sombre note. "This is about you, not her. But Charest can't win the convention and she can't win the country. The party must have another option. With Mike and Barbara and Perrin out of the race, Ontario just isn't represented sufficiently to keep the coalition together. You have to give the party another option."

The meeting was emotionally destabilizing. Whatever the ultimate decision, I recognized those few hours as a defining moment. No one could be in party politics as a volunteer and staffer for three decades without the thought of leadership crossing the mind. But at that point, my thirty-year involvement with the party seemed less a precursor for a run at the leadership than a reason to move on. The latest Quebec crisis had passed with the country intact. The prospect of renewed leadership had pushed party numbers back into the competition zone. But the ministers' sincerity and intensity made it unavoidable that I think carefully on what it all meant. Not to do so would be to avoid facing some hard realities about where the party was and where I was.

Clearly, the basics of an Ontario–Metro Toronto–Prairie–New Brunswick coalition were in place, although the dimensions of delegatee support for any such coalition would be hard to measure. The ministers agreed to do quiet soundings. Wilson would canvass some business and political leadership, including a western premier or two, present or past. Valcourt would talk to one or two Quebec caucus and cabinet members not yet formally committed. McKnight would call his cabinet seatmate, Barbara McDougall, in Bangkok. I would take two days to speak to Donna and Jacqueline, and allow at least a week for assessment, reflection, and rational thought. The policy debates were to begin in ten days, and a decision could not be long delayed.

Before I flew home, I called Mulroney and reported the content of the meeting in considerable detail. I also made it clear that I was still prepared to call the whole matter off immediately without regret were that his wish. I was also prepared to resign so that even a few days of consideration wouldn't adversely affect his position of impartiality. I said that although the idea had come as quite a surprise, I felt I owed it to his cabinet colleagues to either pull out instantly or consider it with some seriousness.

He couldn't have been more gracious. "You should be flattered and you should reflect on it. I won't hear of your resigning. Take as many days as you need and don't worry about me. But before you do polls and check with financial backers or whatever, the most important thing you can do is have a long talk with Donna. If your family is on-side, if they understand what this could mean, then the other issues matter, but if Donna prefers not to, then, well, there's no relationship that matters more than that."

I never asked his views and he never offered them, which, under the circumstances, was quite proper, but my instinct was that his courtesy and generosity did not reflect any belief that someone other than Campbell or Charest could offer a meaningful option at that point. My sense was that he couldn't take my candidacy seriously because of the "upstairs-downstairs" phenomenon. The hired help—however trusted, liked, thoughtful, and bright—are the hired help. His ministers were the appropriate pool for new leadership.

As I sat on the flight home to Kingston that evening, I knew that assessing the viability of my candidacy would involve my family, some of my oldest and most trusted friends, and a larger network of friends, associates, and acquaintances, many of whom had long made little secret of their belief in the inevitability of my having to face this kind of decision someday. I also knew how many people would become hostages of a process of deliberation. Once I launched and made public the process, most in the media would declare open season on any relative, associate, former employer, or client. In the new journalism, the only dependable pathology is devoid of ethics or discretion. The operative principle is that of random violence.

I was even more troubled that after nine years of governing, the quality of participation in the leadership race from the cabinet and caucus ranks was such that seasoned ministers, some with more than a decade in the House of Commons, felt it appropriate to encourage the candidacy of a mere staffer who had arrived in Ottawa only a year and a half before.

As the plane began to descend to John A.'s old riding, I had a sense that the party was steamrolling towards a fundamental mistake, not so much in choosing the front runner but in what that choice said about how the party saw its most defining, central characteristics. An infatuation with Kim Campbell as a feminist and as a geopolitical and generational breakthrough would obscure and distort the normal countervailing forces that produce the crucible for a sound leadership choice. I felt that the new forces unleashed by Mulroney's decision to step down might have already become unmanageable.

When I got home, I was told that one or more of the ministers had phoned Harry Near and Bill Fox, two of my closest friends and two people whose judgement, integrity, loyalty, patriotism, and friendship have been a large part of my life for many years. That night, they began a cohesive and careful assessment of political reality.

The next morning, Monday, I again spoke with Bill and Harry, and with Bill Davis, Eddie Goodman, my executive assistant, Mark McQueen, Bill Liaskas, Rich Willis, Ed Stewart, and my brothers, Brian and Seymour. Each undertook to think about the initiative and about how we might assess the financial, party, electoral, policy, and media variables essential for a sensible decision.

Later that day, Donna, Jacqueline, and I drove to Toronto to attend Passover at my brother's home, an event none of us ever want to miss. It is always a sanctuary of sanity, good humour, family warmth, and Uncle Max's stories of his Italian World War II campaign with the Princess Louise Light Dragoon Infantry. As there were some non-family guests at the seder, the candidacy did not come up. What did transpire was a panic-stricken call from Marjory LeBreton, whom I had taken into my confidence throughout. We had a strong sense of loyalty to the prime minister and we had to manage any leadership process without diluting our primary responsibilities.

She had picked up a wire story out of Saskatoon attributing a draft-Segal movement to Valcourt and McKnight. I was not happy at the news; the reflection process would no longer be private. But I was more troubled by Marjory's reaction. Her angst was acute. She urged instant statements to shut the story down. This seemed both inappropriate and unnecessary. I had the prime minister's approval for a few days of reflection, if for no other reason than courtesy to the ministers involved.

The angst in her voice spoke to something far more important than whether I chose to enter the race. It spoke to a sense of lack of substance and organizational or thematic depth in the Campbell candidacy, a candidacy with which Marjory was clearly identified and strongly enamoured. Marjory had a sense of balance and reality unparalleled in the party. Yet because of the potential effect on Kim, she was put off balance by the mere mention of a run by someone who had been a friend of hers on the socially progressive side of the Tory ledger for years and a close ally through countless campaigns.

There was something fundamental at work if such a committed Campbell supporter and party loyalist could be upset by my candidacy being advanced by the seasoned and newer right-wing forces in the west and the Atlantic. She either saw my entry as a serious threat or had some unarticulated worry that there was less to Kim Campbell and the Campbell campaign than met the eye. Whatever the reason, it was the first of several straws in the wind in a very windy week.

When I returned to Kingston on Tuesday to complete the first two days of the holiday with my family, the phones rarely stopped ringing. Bill McKnight's enthusiasm had indeed led to a statement in Saskatoon on Monday saying that he was among a group urging me to run. The wire copy had moved to national TV, and what looked like a brushfire was gathering momentum. By Tuesday morning, Bernard had offered a similar comment in New Brunswick and Mike Wilson's staff had put out an announcement from Ottawa. This unleashed the unavoidable feeding frenzy of the media. The onslaught of calls, faxes, letters, and cards just about overwhelmed me and my family. So much for quiet reflection. That night, I called Alan Schwartz, who was by then Campbell's chief fundraiser. I assured him that I believed he was honour-bound to stick with Campbell even if I entered. His wife, Allison, indicated that she was going to support me whatever Alan did—a gesture I have never forgotten

That night, I called Barbara McDougall in Bangkok. Since she had dropped out of the race some weeks earlier, I felt I could count on her support. Much to my surprise, she said she would support Charest. My candidacy seemed to evoke some deep anger that overwhelmed our long friendship. All other ministers, including those who happened to be female, were committed. Her support for Charest meant that if there were to be a Segal candidacy, it would be subject to an attack as an anti-female effort.

Tuesday night, Bill Davis, Eddie Goodman, Rich Willis, and Bob Donaldson, an old friend and outstanding corporate lawyer with Heenan Blaikie in Toronto, reported financial pledges they considered solid of close to a million dollars, with pledges still coming in. Mark McQueen, who had contacted his network of younger business and political people across the country and party, reported that a steady stream of ministerial aides some two generations younger than me had called him to sign up. More than a thousand Conservatives of one kind or another—although not all were delegates—communicated support.

All declared leadership candidates, except Kim Campbell and Patrick Boyer, issued warm statements inviting me into the race. I took no offence at Campbell's inelegance on the issue, but worried about the defensiveness too much of that sort of thing might betray. That was one more straw in the wind.

Something about the prospect of a Segal candidacy had touched a nerve, with the Campbell people being the most hyperbolic and intense in their opposition. Two isolated acts of kindness from the Campbell camp were a call from David Camp, Campbell's key Vancouver strategist, and an offer of help from Ed Arundel, Benoît Bouchard's chief of staff, who was clearly in the sights of the Campbell people as a major Ontario recruit. But, by and large, that camp was unpleasant and unkind. Even Lowell Murray, a dear and old friend, not only made no contact but specifically and derisively condemned my getting into the race. I viewed the Murray episode much like the LeBreton panic. It was more a reaction to the weakness of Campbell than to the idea of my candidacy. He was also a dear friend of Libby Burnham—a New Brunswick-born lawyer in Toronto who was a key Campbell loyalist.

The media calls built to a point where the only sane thing to do was meet with the press and level with them about what was under way. So Wednesday morning, I got up early to drive from Kingston to Ottawa, both to get back to work and to answer questions. I drove with Donna on the back roads of God's country—Leeds, Frontenac, Grenville, and Carleton counties—allowing us an hour and a half to reflect on what all this would mean to us as a family and to Jacqueline. Typically, Donna's counsel was solid and utterly unaffected by hubris. The drive was a wonderful moment of peace away from the flurry of activity by my cohorts. Her concern was not losing—in fact a guarantee of losing would have increased her enthusiasm. What she was not sure we were ready for was winning.

Harry Near quickly assembled a national network, each node doing assessments. Rich Willis, an old friend dating back to the Wagner campaign in '76, with Bill McKnight, put together a Prairie and southwest Ontario group. Bill Fox, who was sharing his honest assessment of the motivations behind the candidacy with the media and offering me both tough-minded and caring counsel, gathered some welcome support in Quebec and Northern Ontario. Constructive and potentially helpful communications between leadership candidates came from Garth Turner and Jim Edwards. The Charest group, with whom Bill Fox was closest, was friendly but wary. Peter Lougheed was reported to have given neutral-to-positive signals to Mike Wilson, which, given my years of service with Bill Davis, was remarkable. Valcourt was pulling together a solid crew in the Atlantic region. Two Nova Scotia caucus members, along with one from Ontario and one from B.C., indicated they might shift after the debates if I performed well.

Bernard called several times during the week to make sure I didn't lose sight of the need to decide before the debates, which he felt would provide the chance to tear up the turf and pierce Campbell's lack of depth and identification with the party rank and file. He argued that the debates would clear any delegate uncertainty about my candidacy.

The interest from caucus during the week—especially of caucus members who had waited for Wilson, Beatty, or McDougall to get in and had found themselves with either Campbell or Charest by default—revealed a deeper problem. It became clear from several caucus conversations that, whether on abortion or gun control or Human Rights Act amendments, Campbell's caucus persuasiveness had limped through only because of prime ministerial support. Caucus support, even by those who were with her, was unsteady, unsure, and possibly fluid on the second ballot.

But a counter-movement had also begun, centred on the view that a right-wing, anti-female coalition was being established not to advance a cause or candidate but to stop a specific candidate. For many in the party, the thought that an alternative might enter the race was an attack on a woman's chance to be a leader, an anti-feminist outrage for people like Libby Burnham, Marjory LeBreton, and Jennifer Lynch, all of whom had been—and remain—outstanding party supporters, strategists, organizers, and leaders. For them, the move had to be combated at every turn. Only Charest, who had earned status as a minister from Quebec, was allowed to enter late without facing a vituperative attack.

Our initial canvass showed that for many in the party establishment who had committed early to Campbell, either because they believed in her or because they believed she was the shortest route to continuing in government and continuing their own role within it, the risks of moving were too high. This was not to be a convention where policy or conviction mattered much. This was about calculating the quickest route to keeping power, the kind of expedient thinking not uncommon in decade-old governments down in popularity and eager to reach safety.

As the anti-Segal machine got rolling, the anti-feminist cabal's tom-toms were beating pretty hard. While anti-feminism is about as far from my personal politics as is imaginable, the effect was real. Anti–Big Blue Machine stuff also began breaking the surface. One national TV correspondent, Craig Oliver from CTV, a close contact of Marjory's, made it clear on air that as I had failed to move Mulroney's numbers, it was pretty doubtful I'd be an acceptable candidate. Those numbers were at 9 percent when I joined in 1991 and 38 percent the day I left in 1993. I take credit for neither.

Moments before I met the press outside the Langevin Block around noon Wednesday to say I would be deciding shortly, a report from Los Angeles quoted the prime minister as saying that, to the best of his knowledge, I would be returning to the private sector. Quite properly, he expressed no view on the candidacy itself, although his statement seemed to signal his view that it was unlikely. I do not believe that to have been his intent, but that wide and unchallenged interpretation had a considerable influence. Some in our assessment process thought this was a conscious effort to dampen growing media and party interest. To this day, I have no explicit reason to believe that to be the case, although one network chief allowed afterwards that the network's senior Ottawa correspondent allegedly had been told by a senior confidant of the prime minister that the PM viewed my candidacy quite negatively and that it would not and should not happen.

The media conference was a gentle and balanced affair, for which I will be forever grateful. I levelled about what I knew about how the assessment process was going. I also indicated my intention to be quick about a decision. I didn't want to hurt candidates in the race and would certainly want to participate in the policy debates if I joined the race. It was at that press conference that I was asked—as Campbell, Charest, and Bill Clinton had been—whether I had ever smoked pot. I replied spontaneously that I hadn't, that I preferred corned beef, and, as was obvious, I had inhaled. Taking one's self too seriously was not my idea of serving in public life.

That night, we had a long and difficult conference call to assess exactly where things stood. The money, the broad support, the organizational stance, and the national network fell quickly into place. A clear, socially progressive, and fiscally conservative platform of conviction, which was our preference, was set. The financial side came to rest at about $1.25-million should I declare my candidacy. Mark McQueen had logged some twelve hundred messages of support from across the party and had also cobbled together a young brains-trust that seemed very much the party's future, from Don Mazankowski's chief of staff, Greg Ebel (one of the brightest and most capable among the chiefs), to Lara Zink from B.C., then on Mike Wilson's staff, and Jane Loblaw and Sarah Robertson, Benoît Bouchard's advisers who had guided the government towards more aid to breast cancer research. The party president, Gerry St. Germain, called to offer quiet support, and a Senate contingent of more than twenty from across Canada came forward. Seven other caucus members committed, with another ten waiting for the debates.

But the negatives in the positioning—the looseness of the delegate count, the strong anti-campaign from party feminists, the lack of senior female support from cabinet, McDougall's decision to support Charest, and the 98 percent of Quebec delegates who were already committed to either Campbell or Charest—all conspired to make my candidacy less than constructive. More worrisome were oblique messages to the effect that Charest might drop out if I entered the race because the competition for resources and people might become too intense. I was extremely troubled that a Segal candidacy would in any way weaken the presence from Quebec at the convention.

McQueen and Valcourt fought hard for me to enter. Bill Davis was more cautious. Harry Near and Bill Fox were cautious, but ready to roll if I wanted to. By the time the conference call ended, it was apparent that this idea had come too late in the campaign and too early in my family life. I was troubled that we would not shake the perception of being old guard and anti-female, and before the policy debates, any guess at delegate support would have been simply that. Only McQueen, Willis, and Valcourt were for declaring, on the assumption that the policy debates would alter party conditions. They may have been right, but others who had prepared for this race for at least three years had diminished the chance of any genuine dynamism. I was not convinced that conviction, experience, policy, or the capacities normally associated with a leadership choice would matter much. There was little room for a policy-based underdog campaign of the kind the party would benefit from and I would relish. In the search for the leader least like Mulroney, the issues of gender, generation, and geography would dominate. Others need not apply.

With the prospect of diminishing the running room for a Quebecker I admired and being cast as an anti-feminist force in the party, the issue became not so much the risk but my ability to make a constructive difference. Winning was not essential. Losing might have been more constructive in the right policy-driven cause. The issue was having the scope to make a contribution that helped the party choose a candidate with a firm policy framework and clear Tory convictions.

When I wandered into the press theatre beneath Parliament Hill on Thursday to announce I would not be a candidate, I was relieved to address the forces beyond my control that had made the decision unavoidable. Some of the best advice throughout the process had come from Donna, who said, "There is no problem should you run and lose. But I'd be more comfortable if you could assure me that you can't win. We really aren't prepared as a family to win." Jacqueline, who possibly would have paid the heaviest price, was all for my running, but I wasn't taken in by her motives. Despite her great support for her dad, she also believed that, on the off chance I was successful, we might get better seats at Montreal Canadiens games, which would be quite wonderful indeed. In all quarters of the Segal household, no other hockey team counts.

I felt great relief, plus gratitude to people from all parts of the country, the Young President's Organization, my old student friends, and even media people who offered to help, leave their jobs, sign notes, or produce cash were I to run.

On the afternoon of my announcement, I continued transition planning, preparing to hand over to a new chief of staff at the end of the month. David MacLaughlen, Valcourt's chief of staff and senior adviser to Joe Clark, was taking over while I resumed my Skelton Clarke Fellowship at Queen's. As I wrapped up my duties in the PMO, the sense of foreboding I felt some weeks earlier became steadily more intense.

The old Conservative Party, pre-Mulroney, was all conviction, conflict, and gang warfare, devoid of discipline or winning ways. Mulroney—through hard work, tireless campaigning, competence, conviction, and inspired caucus and cabinet leadership—had shaped a tough, focused, and efficient winning machine. That machine was fuelled by his personality and, above all, by the common faith and position on issues like the economy, free enterprise, free trade, less government, and all the rest. The party was about to lose the cohesive effect of his personality, and in the race to replace him there was no room for the politics of conviction or policy. The party establishment, without any sense of what Kim Campbell believed in, was trying to replace personality, the core of the party's belief structure, and its conviction with little more than form, a form contemporary in design but about whose makeup little if anything was known.

My potential candidacy was not significant in the broader sense. Much more significant were the forces arrayed to keep the field narrow and diminish the clash of ideas and competing visions. When a party allows itself limited choices, the population it is meant to serve clearly understands. That a high price would not be exacted as a result was the ultimate delusion.

With Campbell's win inevitable for many, I decided I would support Charest. His greater humanity and long-time association with the party made his candidacy more real and animated. Beyond his strong views on federalism, the environment, and economic opportunity for young people, he had deep and abiding conviction as a life-long Tory who had fought the endless losing battles of the Quebec organization in election after election. His politics were the politics of partisan conviction, and he spoke for a new Quebec generation tired of the old constitutional battles that had sapped so much economic potential from young Quebeckers.

The day after my leadership non-candidacy announcement, as I made myself a cup of coffee and sat in front of the fireplace on Friday night, I knew the party was heading off a cliff, facing a defeat of Hatfield proportions. I would argue for and defend the party till the end, but I sensed that end would be bitter indeed.

All political parties with any history or substance are held together and motivated by enduring mythologies. As a party more often out of power than in, Conservatives have often been glued together by the "outsiders" mythology that ennobles its losses, which had been, before Mulroney, continuous and repetitive. The myth speaks to the Tories being the party of the outstream—the old, the young, the farmer, the residents of the outports and smaller villages and towns. Positive elements of the mythology include populism, healthy distrust of the unduly liberal and urbane, and a concern for those not economically secure.

In a season of rising Conservative tides, this mythology can be broad enough to embrace outreach to the poor, feminism, and a Conservative world-view of foreign policy and defence. In a season of low tides, when constitutional quagmires and recession-weary consumers batter the party's ratings and reduce it to below core levels of support, a darker side of the mythology emerges. In English-speaking Canada, an anti-Quebec, anti-technocratic, anti-modern, anti–central Canada bias comes out, becoming an almost frenetic search for symbols of being anti-government generally.

The party was trying to gain re-election by selecting the candidate with the fewest roots in the party and in Canada's most populated areas. It sought a female, western counter-image to Mulroney's central Canada–Quebec roots and network. It sought to select the least partisan of its options in the hope that Canadians would somehow not notice the words "Progressive Conservative" under the candidates' names on the ballot. It sought to replace the positive reality of the Mulroney-Mazankowski-Wilson-McDougall-Crosbie-Valcourt-McKnight-Bouchard view of fiscal, trade, and economic policies with a candidacy not based on policies and in which "new" would be the compelling theme.

Many believed, especially in Quebec, that a patina of newness could best hide the enduring mythology while the party worked its way up from the low ebb produced by the GST, constitutional problems, high unemployment, and the net reduction in disposable income per household that since World War II has been enough to deny re-election to most incumbent Canadian (and American) administrations.

The new theology was that a British Columbian outsider female would countervail all our woes through a "new-old politics" choice that painted all but Kim Campbell in the "old" column. Coming from Quebec or Alberta was too traditional and memory-reinforcing. Being a male of any age and having served the party loyally were also too much of a memory-jogger to the allegedly amnesiac Canadian people.

In order to consolidate the steady increase in the party's standings since Campbell's victory had become apparent, it was essential to manage the upswing with nimble handling of the instruments of government, the mechanical and financial realities of the party, and a policy sure-footedness based on conviction and experience for choices that would have to be quickly canvassed, then quickly made. The leadership could be won on form, but the election would be won or lost on substance.

It is remarkable how history repeated itself. At the end of a sixteen-year Trudeau regime replete with allegations of corruption, alienation spawned by intellectual arrogance, insensitivity to the regions, constitutional obsession, policy biased towards central Canada, excessive regulation, the NEP, and so on, Liberals turned to form instead of substance by choosing the attractive John Turner over Jean Chrétien. Turner's alleged winnability traits of being the opposite of Trudeau produced a cabinet without focus and a government without conviction. In the post-convention sizzle, Turner eclipsed Mulroney by 14 percent in the polls, revivifying Liberal campaign hopes. Mulroney, like Chrétien in 1992–93, was dismissed by many in the press as too glib, too superficial, too Quebec, etc., etc.

The Tory victory in 1984 was larger than the Liberal victory of 1993 by many measures: voter turnout, popular vote, width and breadth of coalition, seat count. Although the Liberal collapse in 1984 was back-stopped by ethnic and traditional core seats Tories never held and the absence of two parties spawned by the recession and constitution, the Bloc and Reform, the dimensions and trajectory are roughly parallel.

Yet, having been great beneficiaries of the Liberal grasp at the straw of form over substance, Conservatives seemed determined to head down the same road. To question it was to be at once anti-feminist, anti-B.C., anti-new, and anti-change. Although their motives could not have been more noble, even great totems like Flora MacDonald, Bob Stanfield, David MacDonald, David Camp, Dalton Camp, Norm Atkins, Tom Hockin, and Perrin Beatty got swept up by the momentum.

The courage Charest showed as an alternative—of a young, solid, truly bilingual son of the party stepping up to the plate, quite comfortable with the past and able to pick the best from it without being its hostage—was too predictable for those in the salons of Toronto and Vancouver and Montreal who wanted the easy route to staying in power.

My anxiety was lightened only by a hope that when my last day came—April 29, 1993—there would be ample time for Campbell to reverse some of the trends her tacticians had set spinning against her. She would be able to build an organization that truly understood whatever she stood for and make the best of it. I also hoped, in the compulsively optimistic way Tories have had for decades, that old hands like Valcourt, Hockin, Beatty, Edwards, Ross Reid, the MP from St. John's East, and Loiselle would coalesce around a policy agenda and that Charest would exert partisan reality upon the inevitable Campbell government.

I knew that the sin of even reflecting for ninety-six hours on the possibility of entering the race would, among her mow-'em-down tacticians, consign me to an outside observer's role as I began my fellowship at Queen's. As a Tory with specific policy views and a belief in the policies of nation, decentralization, and economic freedom, and as someone honoured to have served Stanfield, Davis, and Mulroney, my history was too linked to the past to be of any value to the forces of "new at any price."

In other times and places, this would have been troubling. On this particular night, as the first taste of spring made progress on a Kingston evening, the feeling was rather one of liberation from a circumstance that could not be helped. It was liberation from the tyranny of newness *über alles* that seemed about as un-Conservative as this Tory could imagine.

At the end of April, the prime minister and I had a warm and friendly lunch to reflect on our twenty months together and trade stories as partisans are inclined to do. I declined a generous offer he made to ensure a continuing role for me in public life. The call to private life and to the warmth of my family was stronger than any other force on the planet. Besides, there were many volunteers in battles past who had never had the opportunity to serve, as I had, in a capacity that actually paid. They were far more worthy of any appointment.

I watched the leadership race play out to its inevitable conclusion from afar, still haunted by the memory of the ministers who met with me at the beginning of April and who spoke from their visceral, intuitive fear that we would shuck our heritage and policies in favour of a pervasive newness that hoped Canadians would somehow think that Conservatives either didn't believe in what they did between 1984 and 1993 or, worse, might conclude that Conservatives did not mean it.

The five days in April were about not breaking with a policy past that was creative, courageous, and clearly Conservative. They were a wake-up call to many who seemed to forget that genuine social progress and justice could be advanced only through fiscally responsible policies. Only through linking the principles of the past to a creative redesign of Canadian capitalism could the Conservative mission remain compelling.

It was not to be. The narcotic effect of government had done its job. The party chose Kim Campbell to replace conviction with personality and substance with form. She was what her campaign promised. It is not fair to blame her. She could not know what it was she did not know.

When I headed home from the leadership convention, I felt the party had made a profoundly self-indulgent and horribly wrong choice. As I drove home, eastern Ontario's rocky Shield seemed especially hospitable and comforting. Here was a bedrock area of our party and our country, where individualism, loyalty to the Crown, and traditions that mattered—community spirit and concern—had always blended with the pragmatic Tory values of nation-building and economic freedom. As I drove down the causeway linking the King's Highway 2 to the city of John A., I knew that however the federal party, trance-like, might be setting aside the politics of Conservative conviction, those politics would be alive in cities like Kingston and towns larger and smaller for many years to come. The party could try to manoeuvre without those politics. It would founder badly. But the convictions would still be there awaiting a Conservative Party of purpose and principle.

11

CRUSHING DEFEAT

I N A PLURALIST DEMOCRACY, there should be no easy route to staying in power. By 1993, conservatives of varying stripes like Bush
and Thatcher were already gone because of party revolts or splintered
coalitions. The governments of France, Japan, the U.S.,
Saskatchewan, Nova Scotia, and British Columbia had all changed
during the harsh recession. For Canada's Progressive Conservatives,
the likelihood of an easy election was zero, yet people still searched
for the easy way. Sadly, to a majority of Tory delegates Kim Campbell
seemed the only possible route to circumvent reality.

After two tumultuous terms when more jarring and often unpopular changes had been brought in than at any other time in the party's
post-war history, we needed a leader with deep roots who would have
known intuitively how to fight hard on our record and on a clear and
distinct vision for the future. Barbara McDougall, Flora MacDonald,
Bette Stephenson, and Mary Collins were just a few of the women in
the party who could have done it and done it well. Kim Campbell
might have been able to do it five years down the road. But this election was about perceptions of competence, not male versus female. A
mix of genuine supporters and party power brokers thrust Campbell
into a position she could not possibly sustain. The press knew it, the
opposition knew it, and, on occasion, TV caught Campbell in a way
that implied that at some level she knew it too.

She had every right to seek the leadership, tip off the party with
an opening statement devoid of historical reference, and campaign her

heart out. She also had the right to win. What she did not need and was utterly and permanently hurt by was the phalanx of protective tactics, perhaps launched without her knowledge, that sought to mow down all challengers before they reached the starting gate. The effort that saw the drying up of financial resources for McDougall and Perrin Beatty, the sealing up of a top-down Quebec camp almost forcing Jean Charest from the race, and the reduction of delegate races to gender and "new–old" fights devoid of policy, and which divided the very troops she would so desperately need for the election campaign also sent a message to the bureaucracy. A Campbell government would be devoid of pre-election policy.

She had perhaps the best chance ever for a Tory leader to shape a fresh media presence and, to her credit, did so skilfully. A month after the leadership convention, she was the most popular Canadian prime minister in thirty years. But in the end, no one can hide behind the glib and inconsequential in the face of the probing media presence during a campaign. Many in the press gallery began Campaign '93 with a real worry that with Kim Campbell, there was no "there" there. That view was perhaps a touch unfair, but the campaign and her performance lent daily credence to it.

Campbell's people barred her campaign committee from working with me, and me with them. I could only watch the campaign from Queen's University and my home riding of Kingston and the Islands. What I saw was a party that offered nothing on either the nation-building or economic fronts. When conservatives effectively bring together the notions of nation-building and enterprise, we're a great success. If we don't provide the balance defined by nation and enterprise, more marginal and fragmented groups will offer their own distorted balance. The Bloc answered to the issue of nation for Quebeckers. Reform responded to both anxiety over enterprise and anger over the direction of the nation, doing what it was supposed to do and doing it relatively well. Reform had an open field, because when Conservatives desert the field of nation and enterprise, Conservatives are not necessary. These days, if you're not necessary, people don't keep you around for nostalgic reasons.

What I saw was a party offering nothing but newness. That newness would mean little to those who had left the Conservatives for Reform not because they were anti-Quebec, anti-immigrant, or against social justice but because the rate of change in the world—in our economy, global patterns of trade, our population mix, and our social practices—caused them to crave what conservatives often crave: a measure of order and stability.

That newness could offer little to those on the left of the Tory coalition who believed that genuine economic hope could be found only in a rational and conviction-based plan for economic and social priorities.

That newness would pre-empt a bold confrontation with the Bloc and the PQ on the contradiction between what they said in the 1992 referendum and what they were saying in 1993.

That newness could not possibly embrace new ideas or a new program because that would require addressing the link with policies like privatization, trade liberalization, the deficit, and tax reform, and that would involve debate over that past and a defence of it. Defending one's past after ten years in office is never easy, especially in elections fought amidst the anger and pain of a post-recession recovery. But failing to defend it is a sure formula for collapse.

Two mistakes made the difference between a respectable finish of fifty to ninety seats and total collapse. The first was the prime minister's ad-libbing, on the day she called the election, about future unemployment levels. By trying to be honest about economic forecasts and not create false expectations (a candour people applauded Paul Martin for a few months later), she inadvertently removed all hope from the Tory campaign. That had just begun to gell when, in Quebec on September 13, Campbell suggested that detailed social-policy matters were too important to discuss in an election. She was clearly trying to make the case that an election campaign was not the best time to get into the intricacies of block funding, equalization formulas, or federal-provincial fiscal arrangements, yet her comments were construed as suggesting that the people could not be trusted with social policy. From that moment, the party collapse was inevitable.

I heard nothing about the famed Jean Chrétien ad before it appeared. When I first saw it on the air, it struck me as the same kind of negative ad Liberals had used against Stanfield and Clark a hundred times before. Far more unflattering pictures of Chrétien had appeared in *Maclean's* magazine and other places. There was an even more unflattering image of him on the outdoor posters in Quebec during the campaign, prepared by the Liberals' own agency. The posters had the slogan "Strange-looking forehead. But reflect on what's inside."

Without knowing what other options the campaign team had, I can't judge whether the ad was the most appropriate vehicle. But it did spark discussion about Chrétien's competence and depth. Tory numbers started to trend upward when the ad hit; clearly, it was working. So it was imperative for the Grits to get it off the air. I was told it was Roméo LeBlanc, then a senator and now governor-general, who ran the Liberal war room that organized a phone blitz, for which the Liberals deserve great credit. By calling Tory campaign rooms, newspapers, and radio and TV stations across the country, they rolled both the party and the media. They counted on a weak Tory leader to cave in. They counted right.

I was angry about the decision to pull the ad. It was the kind of ad a campaign crew uses if it both tests well in research and there is no other choice, and it should have run its course of a few days. From the outside, the sight of Prime Minister Campbell caving in without even a fulsome apology was almost too painful to bear. Even if the ad was a mistake, which can be argued by many reasonable people, pulling it that way was a bigger mistake. She should have either stood her ground or apologized fully. In the end, she did neither. That probably cost us the last fifteen seats.

The morning of the election, I voted for the PC candidate in my riding, Barry Gordon, who, along with his much-admired wife, Alicia, had done a magnificent job campaigning in the seat. Barry was the reeve of Pittsburgh, one of the most progressive townships in Ontario, and one that had achieved a remarkable restructuring of its services and administration to adjust to the recession and save taxpayers money.

The sadness I felt as I left the poll came from the knowledge that Barry, through no fault of his own, did not have much of a chance. My canvassing for him in traditionally Tory parts of the riding turned up lifelong Tories who could not have been more direct or frank. The gist was, "This is not about Barry, who's a great guy. It's not about Brian Mulroney. He's not a candidate. It's about how with Kim Campbell's collapse, the only way we have to make sure Bouchard or Manning don't have too much influence is to give Chrétien a strong government."

I got the message at door after door. It was the same message being heard at doorsteps across Ontario. For Progressive Conservatives who wanted a strong national government, the Campbell collapse afforded no other choice.

When I left Ottawa, the conservative perspective on the *Canada A.M.* panel had been handled quite well by Bill Fox for the better part of a couple of years, so I did not go back to CTV. But I was asked to appear on the CBC *Prime Time* election-night panel with Stephen Lewis and Heather Reisman. As I left my hotel in Toronto for the CBC studios, I was prepared for a defeat of meaningful proportions. My sense was that we would get one or two seats in Quebec, maybe three in the Maritimes, about ten in Ontario, and perhaps another five elsewhere. I saw our maximum as a corporal's guard of about twenty seats. I tried not to think about what would happen if Reform further split the right-of-centre vote.

As the results rolled in from the Maritimes, it became obvious that we were not only toast, we were headed for breadcrumb status. As the results came in from Quebec and Ontario, it was quickly apparent that this was not one of your everyday setbacks, although I called it a mere setback all night just to unnerve Lewis and Reisman. In the end, we were reduced to two seats, with even the NDP pulling ahead of us.

One of the joys of serving as a panellist on election night is that one's reaction to calamity is utterly public. Private contemplation or rationalization simply do not exist. What happened that night in October shocked me and many other Conservatives. I felt I was watching a bus with many friends and close acquaintances aboard driving off a cliff.

I did not say, that night, all that came to mind. The wounds out there were so deep. I felt the needs of triage suggested something less than total candour. Viewing the wreckage of a bus and the body parts scattered hither and yon, I didn't want to offend the grieving relatives by being too candid. I said to myself, "This is not a moment to be morose or sad. It's a night to be cheery and give heart to all those people out there who have been Conservatives for all the right reasons, who have worked hard for their candidates, and who are going to be feeling pretty low." (For much the same reason, on the Thursday before the vote, I had predicted on national TV that the Tories would win ninety seats.)

My responsibility was to be as upbeat as possible, to try to bring a smile to the faces of the many Tories watching. I didn't want to diminish the seriousness of what had happened. But, with a nervous laugh, I wanted to let them know that the sun would rise tomorrow and we could rebuild. The party, its history of service, and its courage could be removed from government and its MPs sent packing. A government could be destroyed by the voters if that was their wish. We had fought wars to preserve that very principle. But the Progressive Conservative Party would rise again. The near death of the parliamentary wing did not kill the ridings or the campus clubs or the provincial parties or the rank and file.

So when asked for my response to the crushing defeat, I said only, "The people are always right. But in a democracy, on occasion, they can be a bit excessive."

As I drove back to the hotel, I thought of the people I would call in the morning. Dear and close friends like John Tory and Harry Near, whom I had begged to step aside after the leadership convention, had soldiered on as volunteers despite the hopelessness of the task. Both could simply have said between the convention and the election that they had been on the Mulroney campaign team and would let Campbell appoint her own people. When I made that case, both argued that standing down would unfairly leave both Campbell and the party in the lurch. Both had volunteered and persevered for the best patriotic and partisan reasons of loyalty. Election night would be painful in the extreme for them, as it would for the candidates who were wiped from the slate, for the incumbent members who had lost their deposits, for those who would be in great personal debt because they had signed for campaign loans that would now be hard to repay. There were so many victims.

Then I thought of the interview Jean Charest had given that night from Sherbrooke. I thought of how poised, relaxed, and comforting he had sounded, and how loyal he had been to Kim Campbell despite the magnitude of her collapse and of the campaign under her. Then it occurred to me that Canadians had not only chosen a new government. They had also chosen a new leader for the Conservative Party.

That was the one bright spot to contemplate after a collapse that need not have happened. There are many reasons it did, all of which have to be understood and analyzed. It is important to separate facts from mythology and reality from wishful thinking. Mythology and wishful thinking can be warming, comforting, sometimes even inspiring, but rarely terribly helpful.

I don't blame Kim Campbell. She was more victim than predator. She was victimized by circumstances beyond her capacity to understand or control. With little knowledge of federal politics or the country and almost no deep roots in the party, she was swept up by the forces of expediency that crushed competition, put regaining power ahead of conviction, and ultimately crushed her and the party. Expediency in its most raw and virulent form has a way of doing that, time and time again.

Facile pundits and Mulroney-haters (often one and the same) argue that Mulroney's date of departure left no route but the road to a rout. Could he have left before the GST passed the Senate? During the Gulf War? Before Charlottetown? He left less than four months after the referendum results. He could not go sooner. He left the party in substantially better shape than had John Diefenbaker, the last Tory prime minister of any length, and certainly in far better shape than the Liberals were left by either Trudeau or Turner. The party had assets: a well-planned campaign, a treasury in responsible shape, a wide range of policy choices carefully worked out to strengthen the decisions a new prime minister should make. But these assets meant nothing if they ended up in the hands of a leader who had no idea how to use them constructively.

The organization put in place by Brian Mulroney was ably led by John Tory and Pierre Blais, but it could not but founder if it served a leader it did not know and who could not possibly know it. If John Tory was not so loyal to the party, he would have resigned so Campbell could appoint someone who understood this and could craft a campaign accordingly. John was used to campaigns where the leader had a commitment that sustained a platform and direction. In this campaign, he and his organization of volunteers never had a chance.

Neo-conservatives believe as a matter of principle, as do many Reformers and others disdainful of partisan politics, that the party met its fate because it was too much of the centre, too much of the progressive and not enough of the conservative. Many urban and small-town conservatives believe that the harshness of measures conservatives imposed when in government—the GST, the relentlessly tough monetary policy that kept interest rates high and stymied employment growth—all contributed to a dislocation of Progressive Conservatives from their natural middle-class constituency, giving an opening to Reform on the right and Liberals on the left.

Those in English Canada who have no time for Quebec and its legitimate aspirations within Confederation united with those in Quebec who have little time for Canada to argue that our undue focus on—or, latterly, our so-called failure on—the constitution opened the floodgates for a Reform and Bloc protest vote throughout Canada.

Early Campbell proponents are often heard expressing the view that Mulroney's unpopularity was so massive and intense that any patch of bad luck, which is unavoidable in all campaigns, would have had disastrous results. Some who had been part of the 1984 and 1988 campaigns, and had an abiding respect for Mulroney's campaigning talent and his focus on loyalty and unity, believe Campbell is to blame because she had it within her power to win without difficulty.

This is all wishful thinking. Our fundamental problem was government itself, which is the ultimate exile for Conservatives of conviction. It is one thing when in perpetual opposition, as we were before Mulroney came along, to want desperately to have the chance to put principles into effect by winning the privilege of governing. But to become part of Ottawa, its processes, insensitivities, excesses, and disengagement from economic reality, is, for a Conservative, the equivalent of original sin. It is the primordial miscalculation and the ultimate indulgence. Its effect has always been explosive.

Conservative initiatives opposed to the conventional Ottawa wisdom were in fact the high points in nearly a decade of service. Each attracted the opposition of many and sometimes the virulent opposition of the press, but they were positions of conviction taken on the basis of strongly held views out of sync with the don't-rock-the-boat approach of Ottawa's senior public service. The government won an election on free trade. It won an election after it tried to support the defence department and its material requirements. It won an election after controversial privatizations. It won election on solid Progressive Conservative Party principles.

The party's collapse became inexorable and overwhelming only when expediency led the party towards the politics of making choices aimed only at keeping a government in power. That was the core flaw in the Campbell candidacy. The roots of that candidacy and the party establishment's unthinking embrace of it run back to the difficult days of perpetual opposition. Many chose Kim Campbell because they believed in her, her politics, and her capacity to lead. They did so honourably and in good faith. As many chose her because they believed that the very difference of her image, geography, sex, and generation would allow people to forget those things that had made the party unpopular. They believed Tories could win a mandate for the future by repapering the past. At the very least, they believed Tories could win a mandate for the future by changing the subject.

It did not work, nor should it have worked. It would have been better to have run a campaign on policy and conviction and lost than to have won by squeezing by on personality, newness, and changing the subject. Having tried to take the easier route, we ended up deserting both our Progressive and our Conservative base. The Progressive voters largely voted Liberal, particularly in the Maritimes, Ontario, Manitoba, and Saskatchewan. Much of the Conservative base moved either to the Bloc in Quebec or Reform in rural Ontario and our ridings in the west. It's too soon to tell whether our policy abdication spawned a one-parliament aberration or a permanent multi-party system more in line with most of the world's older democracies.

Whatever reasons the Campbell cabinet may have had for not imposing a focused policy agenda—an agenda presented to the cabinet by the public service, after months of work and preparation, for a policy-based pre-election Throne Speech—the effect of the decision was to leave the leader and the party without any capacity to sustain or build a coalition on new priorities and historic principles.

Having left the government months before those decisions were taken, I can only wonder at what the motivation might have been. My suspicion is that choosing the path of least resistance was just too attractive. The new prime minister was up in the polls and experiencing many weeks when she was the most popular prime minister in three decades. When faced with the potential divisiveness of any serious policy debate on such fundamental questions as income security, labour training, middle-class tax relief, and government restructuring, the path of least resistance must have seemed more attractive.

Perhaps the absence of senior ministers who had retired after long service—Don Mazankowski, Bill McKnight, John Crosbie, Barbara McDougall, Mike Wilson—meant that discussion around the cabinet table was uncoupled from the discussions that had motivated the cabinet, the caucus, and the party to make tough decisions and take the courageous stands they had in the previous nine years. But it's fair to reflect upon why any minister sitting around the table, including the prime minister, would be more focused on finding a way to stay in government than in fighting for the things they knew to be essential in the Conservative mission for government. That they became averse to policy risk cannot be laid solely at the doorstep of any group of ministers nor of a prime minister with barely five years' experience in federal politics and the party.

The problem is government itself.

There comes a moment in every prime minister's first few months when a decision is reached that may not seem significant at the time but that has far-reaching implications. After winning the 1984 election, Mulroney made modest changes to the public service of Canada, involving no more than half a dozen senior officials. Those few changes prompted a huge outcry from the media and others about the politicization of the public service, but the core system was essentially unchanged. The chief-of-staff system, set up in hopes of counter-balancing the influence of the bureaucracy, was also attacked by the denizens of the permanent public service and their friends in the media as a serious misuse of public funds.

Those early Mulroney changes were not enough. Senior public servants sent the message to the prime minister that they were relieved at the departure of the previous Liberal government, which had become tired, inept, corrupt, and unfocused, and were just so gosh-and-golly pleased to see a new government with fresh ideas, fresh focus, and fresh determination. Boy, were they eager to serve and be helpful. This was the same message I'm sure they sent Jean Chrétien in 1993.

Mulroney's decision not to fundamentally restructure the senior ranks of the public service and repeople those ranks with individuals of standing and ability from the private sector, academe, labour, and other governments who believed in the need for fundamental change was a mistake that sowed the seeds of many of the difficulties that overwhelmed the brief Campbell administration.

When the lines of authority to senior public servants remain unchanged and the public servants' own patronage system—which is far more extensive, excessive, and unaccountable than anything politicians could ever dream up—remains unchallenged, the government is always on the verge of becoming hostage to the forces of inertia and systemic self-preservation.

It is not hard to understand why Mulroney decided to work with what he found. He always prided himself, justifiably, on winning the leadership without being an extension of the Big Blue Machine, the

Lougheed organization, or their respective affiliates. There were all kinds of competent people in Crown corporations and senior deputy positions in Ontario, New Brunswick, Nova Scotia, Newfoundland, and Alberta who could have been helpful. But reaching out to any of them might have been seen as tilting towards one element of the party. Mulroney won the election because all factions felt comfortable with him, so choosing bureaucratic talent from among the factions was not an option. As for recruiting successful executives from the private sector, the salaries, obtuse accountabilities, and unwieldy bureaucracies that accompany a posting in Ottawa are neither rewarding nor attractive. It is easy to see how a new government that had been out of office for a quarter of a century might not feel any great sense of riches about competent replacements for those in charge of the bureaucracy they inherited.

There was also the common and naive belief—in this case, a prime-ministerial excess of trust—that with civility, decency, treating people as professionals, and respecting their contribution and abilities, a prime minister can expect a bureaucracy that had served others with loyalty and determination to serve a new government. If the prime minister could win the hearts and minds of millions of voters, surely he could campaign successfully to win the hearts and minds of a small cadre of senior public servants.

The problem was not in that spirit or purpose but in the futility of trying to get those who have systemic power to share it with those whose goal is to dilute the importance of government and diminish its capacity to spend and tax. It is hard to know which was the more prevailing: the innocence of the early Mulroney administration or a measure of self-assuredness in managing the public service. The resulting dysfunction, though ultimately unavoidable, was through sheer strength of will delayable.

The negative effect of accepting the structural and individual status quo in the public service was delayed only by the sheer weight of the massive policy agenda Conservatives embarked upon between 1984 and 1988. This agenda created a momentum for change that, along with buoyant economic times, allowed the Conservative coalition to develop enough to sustain a second majority government. That the prime minister had to work double time to move a public service that opposed free trade, tax reform, joining the Organization of American States, privatizations, supporting

Israel, and the decentralization implicit in Meech all reduced the time available for the government to listen to the public, explain policies, and reshape public understanding.

Much of the policy momentum ended with the 1988 election. The constitutional formula agreed to by Trudeau in 1982 forced Mulroney into a fresh constitutional mode that made the government dependent upon a public service that, as the price for support of the constitution, sternly opposed any devolution of federal power. There could be no burden more profound and no process more likely to liberate the forces of western frustration about Quebec, nor Quebec nationalist frustration about English Canada's inability to get itself sorted out, than the one the post-1988 period imposed on the Tory party.

This is not to suggest that the public service is wilfully disloyal. It is to suggest that outside narrow military applications, a large bureaucratic system organized along lines of vertical and statutory responsibility is, by its very nature, dysfunctional. Vertical organizations in the public service tend to draw people away from problems, not towards them. They tend to impose centrifugal pressures upon the public policy process that often make pragmatism and common sense the last available options.

The problem is government itself, but conservatives have a fundamental problem. They care about institutions and their validity because institutions are instruments of order. If legitimate, effective institutions are not in place, society tends to get a little ragged around the edges. Reforming institutions that are ineffective or whose legitimacy is questioned should be high on any Tory priority list. Yet conservatives are also bound by some traditional ideas and ritualistic constraints that make them feel comfortable. Institutions that have operated in a similar fashion for a long time acquire, for conservatives, a kind of validity tied to the mere fact of their history. So what to do with national institutions that have for the most part served us well for more than a century is a question conservatives approach cautiously. But it is a question that must be approached directly because Canadian society has changed so fundamentally that common points of heritage—like parliamentary government itself—have become distanced from people's everyday perspectives and what they want from the state.

Canadian values are tied to the notions of peace, order, and good government. Yet our institutions do not imply anything terribly peaceful. They imply dysfunction not only by the way they operate but by their very existence. Our institutions do not imply order. They imply disorder, narrow agendas, and intense factionalism. And good government is one of the great oxymorons of our time. Canadians know that no matter how good someone is when he or she gets elected and no matter how he or she may reflect legitimate public aspirations, the very structure of our government institutions will inevitably diminish that person's effectiveness.

What feeds the sense of dysfunction is the remoteness of Ottawa, a remoteness that isolates the federal public service and almost ensures the lack of any relationship between that public service and the country. Ottawa has a transient senior government village of about ten thousand people. There is a real community there on the river that has nothing to do with government, but the transient village exists for the purpose of serving government. The people of that village are not rooted by any other way of making a living, which puts them at some disadvantage in understanding the concerns of the rest of us.

When I served in Ottawa in the early 1970s, the Liberal government came in for some pointed criticism for not recognizing, or at least not admitting, that we were sliding into a recession. But at the time, it was hard to find in Ottawa any symptom of a recession. People in the village were moving along pretty well. Before a budget freeze on salaries, public servants were preparing to settle on a 6 percent annual pay raise and getting set to exercise a moderate level of self-denial. Employment was stable and condominium prices were holding firm.

This was not the case with people serving provincial governments, who lived and worked in the communities they served. In provincial capitals, both legislative members and civil servants would have had regular contact with neighbours walking away from mortgages, stores failing, and businesses being unable to make the payroll. They would see it and hear about it every single day, which makes for better government.

Ottawa is so cut off from the rest of the country that it is difficult, maybe impossible, for any party to govern effectively. The advice politicians get from the best minds in the capital is isolated advice, directed towards the continuity of the system rather than genuinely responding to problems. The remoteness spawns problems of legitimacy in myriad ways.

Any government that comes to Ottawa tries to search the country and find good people to come and serve temporarily in policy positions. Many good people, however, cannot come. The conflict-of-interest rules and the rules about what job holders can legally do after a temporary period of service are so onerous that only the independently wealthy or the independently poor are really eligible, which takes a lot of good people out of consideration. That leaves the country with a permanent civil service and its permanent capacity to generate talent based on an internal patronage system that operates on the basis of who has made the right contacts, who went to the same language school with particular senior officials, or for whom a deputy minister may have been a mentor. It's an interesting system, no different from any other large bureaucracy, and it has nothing to do with political parties. It is a system that is utterly unaccountable to either politicians or the electorate.

It is a system that feeds on itself, advancing its own names for its own purposes. The Mulroney administration appointed many people to positions in federal–provincial relations, for example, who were prominent proponents of the Trudeau-Pitfield centralist approach to government. Such people should have been anathema to any Tory, but those names were likely the best names the system produced. With Ottawa being so remote, political leaders and their advisers have no opportunity to circulate in academic, business, or government circles outside the capital and so cannot come up with any better names. The result is an internalized, self-centred public service that constrains the range of advice and the range of options it provides.

There are people wandering around Ottawa who have never done anything except work in government. There is nothing wrong with having a career in that setting, but people who are without a grounding in practical experience shape policy that emerges as shoeless and toeless. Nowhere else in society could someone get ahead—whether in a corporation, small business, or on a farm—without demonstrating some understanding of the issues involved and the way things work. It is inconceivable that anyone could become head of a tool-and-die company unless he or she had sold the product, been an engineer, or had been in some other position where practical understanding was required. Yet there are people working in the federal Department of Health who do not know how a hospital works. They've never been in one, perhaps, except as patients. Why would working in a policy role not require some background in how the healthcare system operates?

Senior civil servants like to promote people who have had some line responsibility in government policy roles, but there is no such rule when it comes to having been a service deliverer in an organization that relates to government policy. It should be the norm, with no one allowed to progress through the ranks to senior positions unless they have spent time in the volunteer or community sector, the private sector, or at least somewhere on the front lines.

The entire system is premised upon government as the source of all solutions because that notion is what serves the public servants' interests. Even the best public servants—who are there trying to do good, rather than do well—know that their advancement is tied to their ability to expand what they do and manage the expansion effectively. Historically, opportunities to advance and have influence have not been tied to their ability to reduce what they do because it can be done elsewhere more effectively.

All the accountabilities in the public service relate to matters of process and form, not to results. Public servants are accountable for how many people of different language groups they hire, how many handicapped folks they hire, how their programs are evaluated, their adherence to civil service commission hiring rules, and their careful pursuit of life under Treasury Board guidelines. There are often conflicting accountabilities in the career of a public servant that leave not much room for any accountability for results. In our parliamentary tradition, the responsibility for results—good, bad, or indifferent—is that of the elected ministers. The only way a minister can avoid being held hostage by the bureaucracy is either through a massive act of will—which will be viewed in Ottawa as imposing one's political biases upon the due process of the system—or by simply refusing to meet with them, which is both illogical and unconstructive.

When the Mulroney government announced higher immigration levels, one of the criticisms levelled within the civil service was, "Wonderful, but where is the infrastructure to assimilate all these people?" This question is based on the social-work model, which assumes that if we do not have a special capacity for housing grants, instruction in English as a second language, and social workers to help immigrants settle, they simply will not integrate. This is a classic example of the policy-making notion of "If all we have is a hammer, then every problem is a nail." If what the civil service does is dispense certain services, obviously immigration policy cannot be addressed unless more of those services can be delivered.

That is the sealed mindset public servants often get themselves into, and for all the right reasons. They are well-meaning people who genuinely care and want to be helpful. But in looking at any of the waves of immigration we have had in this country—from the Irish, Scottish, and English in the 1800s through the Ukrainians, Italians, Hungarians, Czechoslovaks, West Indians, East Asians, Chinese, and many others—there is not one shred of evidence that the newcomers' integration into our society was determined by their ability to get counselling when they arrived.

They came because they had prospects for work, they had family members prepared to sponsor them, they were fleeing war or oppression, or they had independent means. Whatever their category, there was some expectation that they were going to make their own way and enrich the country substantially, which is, in fact, what they did. Government services were somewhat supportive and helpful at the outset, but the notion that migration and population policies should be tied to the bureaucracy's ability to hire social workers is insane.

Ottawa is premised on the notion of a universe so contrary to the way things work that dysfunction is systemic. It is essentially a nineteenth-century organization resting upon the questionable hypothesis that the issues in a modern industrialized state can be approached in narrow vertical ways through discreet allocations of resources and statutory mandates. It is like suggesting that a father and mother in a household could precisely separate their responsibilities.

Yet the structure of government means that ministers can do nothing about this state of affairs. They're so caught up in internal cabinet structures and processes that they are managed by the system rather than managing the system themselves. A politician who enjoys the cerebral assessment of how many angels can dance on a pin, as Pierre Trudeau generally did, can thrive in such a system. But anyone who does not feel comfortable with that approach is soon worn down by the process.

The civil service often produces a Goldilocks approach to public policy. In presenting a range of options, civil servants essentially say, "This proposal's too hot, this proposal's too cold, but this proposal, Minister, your advisers having met, we think is just right." Unless the minister has the presence of mind or the time-management skills to reach out for eight or nine other proposals from the real world, his or her freedom to act in the public interest is seriously constrained. Some do make the effort, but ministers who put new ideas into the public service often find it's like serving a tennis ball into the Atlantic Ocean.

New ideas are risky, and the generic attitude of the civil service is, "This minister is temporary, this government is temporary, and so, considering my twenty-year career plan, I'm not about to take any risks." The system does not reward public servants who take risks and support new policies. Any official who becomes too closely associated with the policy initiatives of an administration finds that the system takes quite a negative approach to his or her future prospects.

In the end, we're saddled with a system that diminishes creativity and dilutes courage, that produces a monotonous, self-perpetuating leviathan that serves no interests but its own. It is only human nature for the interests of personal advancement and interministerial relationships to be at least equal to the public interest on any given issue. It is not surprising that, until very recently, when a federal government sought to make major cuts in expenditures, all the cuts recommended by the mandarins happened to be in places where mandarins do not live. The process is not wilful, nor is it conspiratorial. It's just the nature of the beast.

The only way to deal with the bureaucratic colossus that is Ottawa is to gut it, radically and quickly, when a new government takes office. The risk of a totally new senior mandarinate brought in by a new government is that of six to seven months of modest administrative chaos. This is not a particularly high price to pay compared to the very high price our society pays when governments elected to bring about change seem unable to do so. For the system to keep ministers in hand while change is diluted or destroyed, the comforts of the department—ministerial expense account, driver and car, conferences here, there, and everywhere—are eagerly imposed upon ministerial schedules. Human nature being what it is, these comforts are often equally embraced.

Mulroney could not move quickly enough. He essentially paid the price for his commitment in his acceptance speech on the floor of the leadership convention that he would reappoint Erik Nielsen as deputy party leader and House leader. Nielsen had been interim leader when Joe Clark stepped aside. He had been identified with the

Diefenbaker rump, the centre right, the west, and, to an extent, elements of the Clark loyalists. He was seen as one of those who had hung in there year after year, causing the Grits great grief, pain, and suffering, so he was generally well liked and respected in the party. Mulroney made the commitment to cut factionalism off at the pass. That did help focus party energies long enough to get through the election, but at the cost of associating Nielsen's prominence with a fundamental redesign of how government worked.

The task force put in place to make real the commitment to a more efficient and effective government, one disengaged from many activities government could neither afford to do nor do well, unhappily became a focused target for the civil service and all the interest groups who depended upon civil service support and funding and vice versa. Combined with the somewhat hardline views often associated with Erik Nielsen, the government unwittingly surrendered one of its most important instruments for fundamental change by putting it in the hands of the wrong person.

Early setbacks didn't diminish the government's capacity to move forward on critical priorities. But one price of maintaining that momentum was setting aside what would have been an internally disruptive and destabilizing process had the substance of the Nielsen task force been put into effect in any significant way. The choice facing Mulroney was either to dissipate scarce political capital to support internal operational changes or to deal with the larger issues of the Conservative agenda. Trudeau moved the country so far to the left on foreign, defence, and economic policy that there was a massive need to drive through the centre towards the right to bring back some balance. The political capital necessary to make that happen was also massive. Dissipating that capital on internal rejigging of the government's activities would be akin to renovating the house while the barn and equipment shed burnt to the ground.

It is hard to fault the choices Mulroney made. Serious changes in foreign, trade, and economic policy were far more fundamental than cleaning house. He was a prime minister with an agenda he was determined would not be deterred. He brought to Canada the most conservative administration since the country's birth. Official Ottawa never forgave him.

Because the media concentrated in Ottawa are the primary source of information about Ottawa and are captives of the same forces, the same limitations constrain their ability to assess a minister's performance or a government's effectiveness. This is truly the blind reporting on the visually impaired. The prime ministerial will necessary for Mulroney to break this mindset, as he did on free trade and other issues, took all his thirty years of experience in the party, the law, and business to execute as effectively as he did.

The system creates a gulf between reality and what some believe to be reality. In the end, judgement is seriously impaired. So it is not hard to understand how a new Campbell government, eager to hold on to office and getting great reviews that produced even more encouraging polls, would choose the path of least resistance in seeking re-election. It is equally unsurprising that when the core information about the prime minister changed dramatically—as it did when she explained why social policy couldn't be discussed in detail during a campaign—public opinion also changed dramatically. In the end, the party's obsession with finding a way to stay in government became the primary reason it was booted out of government and almost out of Parliament itself.

On the great and pervasive media issue of who is to blame, the answer is simple: all Conservatives who became enamoured with serving a nation from within government, all who believed we were so right and others so wrong, and all who were convinced that the party could change reality by changing the subject. I certainly accept my own share of the blame.

The long years in opposition under Diefenbaker, Stanfield, and Clark, the tantalizing taste of government ripped away by our own incompetence under Clark, and the final winning of government under Mulroney set up an almost narcotic appeal for those who had been perpetual outsiders. In that narcotic haze, all who were smitten forgot that we are best when we are outsiders. We are most effective when we are not infected by the virus of self-importance so often associated with being in power.

The true meaning of our mission and the moments when our contribution to the future is most meaningful come when we're campaigning to change what's wrong, to represent those outside the mainstream, to broaden the mainstream, and to work against the established forces opposed to real change and progress. We are best when we are about liberation of economic forces and protection of the vulnerable, not the preservation of elite economic power and denial of the disadvantaged.

Government can be a positive force for good only when it is not the only force for good in a society. If the burden of fighting for change as Conservatives sometimes means we risk forming a government, we should face that prospect with good cheer. But we should always remain outside the circle of those who see government as an extension of their career plans. This may mean that Tories do not have fifteen- or twenty-year periods in government, as is the case for many in the Liberal Party, for whom government is the family business. What it does mean is that when we make a case and have the cohesive party and focused policy to justify their trust, Canadians will turn to us with a specific task that we can discharge with them and for Canada. The length of the engagement matters not. It matters only that we were asked, we had the ability to deliver, and we discharged our mission with honour.

12

TO RISE TO FIGHT AGAIN

THE PRESENT STATE OF THE FEDERAL Conservative Party is, except for a matter of degree, consistent with the state it has been in since the demise of John A. Macdonald. This country prefers the sophistry of Liberal governments. There is a view that the large issues that have undone the coalitions Conservative governments have built have always been efforts for reform or reconstruction, massive tax changes, substantive disputes with our neighbour to the south over defence or economic policies, or points of principle defended sometimes at the expense of electoral support. In this view, the party is kept from power not because Conservatives fail but because they show too much courage.

Not even a partisan like me could sustain so brazen an analysis. The party is often kept from power because, with Conservatives historically being outside the government mainstream and so uncomfortable with the levers of central power, the party has often proceeded in the sweep of governmental activity in fashions so blunt, naive, and insensitive as to produce more negative response and alienation than the substance of our policies would justify. This was true of Diefenbaker, of Clark, of the anxiety over Stanfield's ninety-day wage-and-price freeze, and of the antipathies that arose during Mulroney's relentless and radical reforms. The public hostility during the few times Conservatives have formed a national government in this century produced pressures on caucus unity and party cohesiveness that have often dictated a posture upon the leader that makes him or her seem insensitive to public angst and outwardly complacent about public opinion.

To understand the inside of the Conservative Party, it is essential to understand the reality of being an "outsider" surrounded by hostile forces. Without that understanding, there is little chance of coming to terms with Conservative partisanship and leadership from Diefenbaker through Charest. It is the core concept and self-image that unites all Conservatives, whatever else may unite or divide them geographically or in policy.

Any effort to bring the Conservative Party out of exile must be tied explicitly to offering choices that will preserve and advance the country. To be relevant in the politics of the federation, Conservatives have a responsibility to embody a conservatism of ideas, a civil Toryism of principle, and a community-based approach to self government. Anything less will certainly mean the permanent marginalization of the Progressive Conservative Party as a national force.

The challenge is to reach out to a new coalition and build from the heart in a way that reflects the best of who we are and what we believe. A future for Canada—which is far more important than the future of any party—depends on the intensity, clarity, and precision with which Canadians can make the choices necessary to preserve their future.

Liberalism's core problem, in its self-indulgent belief in the endless ability of the state to improve and expand the individual's opportunity, is as perverse as the neo-conservative view that the state is always wrong or out of place. Government and bureaucracy unchecked or bureaucracies without accountability are as dangerous as complete licence for the invisible hand of the free market, a hand that often ends up subsidizing a tax-financed socialism for the wealthy while permitting a cruelly inhumane free enterprise for the poor. The middle class finances the former and tries to sort out the cost of the latter, in the process being deprived of its own economic opportunity.

Our socialist opponents, while not giving up on society, seem to have lost their internal will to advance genuinely socialist options to existing public-policy processes, or they have found it difficult to reconcile economic realities with the rather puerile and naive collectivist idolatry at the soul of their philosophy. When any of their leaders attempts to address that reconciliation, the schism is wide and the sense of internal jihad launched by the purists (usually in the taxpayer-financed public-sector unions) is intense and corrosive. Bob Rae experienced this firsthand.

In Canada, the recently contrived Social Credit/Republican/Pat Buchanan/reborn/ersatz coalition calling itself Reform exudes a conservatism without root or history in this country. Preston Manning has simply benefited more from the pervasive U.S. media shower than any Canadian politician since Mike Pearson. Not since John Kennedy and the American media empires poured anti-Diefenbaker material into Canada to help Pearson has a Canadian politician been so profoundly aided in his political pursuits. Unlike in 1963, there is no specific desire to help Manning. He profited from the huge buildup of a peculiarly American neo-conservative framework tied to atmospherics like the "right to bear arms," the "sinister nature" of all state activities, the focus on freedom over responsibility, which he has translated into notions like equality of the provinces, the preference for individuality over community, and the denial of the historic role of English and French settlers in shaping our political framework, all of which reek of the *E pluribus unum* version of the conservative cause.

For those who hunger for simple solutions, clear lines of demarcation, and the clarity often associated with the certainty of youth, neo-conservatism is a genuine and attractive option. For those unable to distinguish between the excesses of the welfare state and the need for some welfare, or between the wastefulness of large bureaucracies and the limited but real capacity of government to be a force for good, neo-conservatism is awash with politically attractive pleasure. For those who wish to establish their own piece of iconoclastic turf in the interests of their career plans or political aspirations, the neo-conservative allure cannot be discounted.

The simplicity of the neo-conservative ethic and the incompetence of American liberal-Democratic coalitions have produced a consistent reassertion of neo-conservative values. Because of the cultural sea in which we swim, it is inconceivable that we could live where we do and not be affected by that view. But the neo-conservative bias of our American friends has little to do with the conservative tradition in Canada.

Successful conservatism in this country, federally and provincially, has been tied to a belief in our responsibility to make society more open and fair, and to afford people a chance both to have responsibility for each other and to pursue their own aspirations. That belief has been coupled with the tidy bedrock "you shouldn't spend much more than you make" approach to life that underlies an understanding of government's place in society and an aversion to expanding it excessively.

The Canadian Progressive Conservative tradition is rooted in the essentially Tory view that there has to be a balance between collective rights, opportunities, and benefits on the one hand and the imperative of freedom on the other. The Tory view is that collective wealth and collective opportunity can result only from personal wealth and opportunity. A fundamental role of government is to maintain the balance. A fundamental role of a political party is to put forward ideas as to how that balance can be maintained under contemporary pressures.

The genius of the Tory proposition as opposed to the neo-conservative abdication is that it looks for mixed instruments to maintain the critical balance and achieve social and economic goals. The Tory proposition says there are some things only business can do, some things labour can do, some things only government can do, and some things all should do together. Government should be prepared to be involved in areas of the economy only when necessary, as was the case when Tory governments created CN, the CBC, Air Canada, Ontario Hydro, educational TV networks in Alberta and Ontario, and other Crown corporations, federal and provincial. But needs change, such state institutions are not eternal, and there are some areas where government clearly might not do as well as the private sector.

A Progressive Conservative government in the Canadian context encompasses fiscal conservatives and social progressives who cobble together a balanced path between fiscal prudence, deficit reduction, and necessary social reform. That balanced path has never been more essential. Society will ultimately reject economic frameworks that are too narrow and limiting. Traditional conservatism has always been the best possible steward of a genuinely dynamic and humane capitalism that broadens horizons and promotes opportunity. Toryism is the natural bridge that builds on the best of our traditions and sets aside more extreme elements. Neo-conservatives traffic in artificial polarities. Tories seek social cohesion.

Canadians know that the notion of the unleashed invisible hand is a euphemism for someone getting greedy on us while our interests are left unprotected. That philosophy is simply irrelevant to the realities of keeping a country like ours together. We are a disparate band of citizens spread over a huge landmass, which means we have some needs that require a constructive, if limited, view of government.

To campaign for the opportunity to do things for people through government by changing society, all the while stating that you have no belief whatever in government or its capacity to make things right, is a philosophical flaw. It is the core of the neo-conservative position and has no durability. Philosophically, it is hollow. It also contributes to the sense of ineffectiveness among voters, because if government itself is worthless, of how much value is the process by which we elect people to govern? That philosophy has been unsuccessful in defining a distinct purpose for the Progressive Conservative Party.

Progressive Conservatism will not remain a dynamic political force if Tories are ashamed of those things they do that seem more progressive than conservative. Yet some Conservatives tend to be afraid of that part of their heritage. If they are not prepared to embrace it and tout it, they cannot expect anyone else to do so. Their political opponents won't, and it's not the media's job. But if Conservatism is to survive as a national political force, Progressive Conservatives must state clearly that there is a brand of conservatism that is determined never to be hostage to limited business interests or the quarterly earnings statements that some would have replace all social assets and spiritual and community values, but to be an advocate of society's broader interests.

The Conservative Party is a voluntary association of individuals in about three hundred riding associations across Canada who have come together for differing reasons of policy or regional priority, supporting individual candidates, leaders, and programs. There will be no lack of recruits within some PC ranks to the neo-conservative call to prayer, especially when fundamentalism is rising in North America, Europe, the Middle East, and Asia during these complex times.

To be fair, there is a strain of the neo-conservative option that, in its candour and fiscal frankness, can be quite constructive, providing clarity and strengthening political resolve. That strain looks at fiscal and economic outcomes and argues that they are the ultimate reality. That strain argues that we are headed for substantial trouble indeed when matters like debt and deficits are not addressed, when government borrowing is profligate and wasteful, or when bureaucracies and politicians of the centre and left try to engineer a society rather than tend to the plumbing. By doing so, they prevent individuals from making their own choices and decisions—and that is the best contribution of the recent neo-conservative tradition.

But one tune does not a symphony make, and this tune does not constitute a battle hymn for the Tory tradition. Progressive Conservatives cannot embrace the nihilistic defeatism that masquerades as a neo-conservative polemic in support of individual freedom and disengagement. It is not a recipe for political relevance or certainty. It offers neither the politics of genuine insurgence nor real reform. It's American fast-food conservatism served up from its fresh-frozen state and not high quality at that. To confuse it with genuine nutrition, especially when pursued as a steady diet, would mean the Conservative Party faces a long political famine.

A Tory rebirth must be based upon a politics of insurgence that speaks to larger realities unfathomable within the neo-conservative mindset. Surely, turning one's back on the poor simply because there are no easy solutions or because previous state efforts have had paltry results is choosing defeatism and selfishness when neither is acceptable.

Tories do not yield in the face of poverty or economic dislocation or bureaucratic excess by advocating a withdrawal of the state from society. They don't advise as expatriates from Great Britain or the U.S. about what Canada should become in their absence. They stay and they fight if they truly believe and if the politics of real change are more than a passing fancy. Tories are prepared to work within a society where their views do not prevail, where tolerance for the views of others is a mark of civility, and where pluralism and political diversity are strengths and instruments for social consensus, not ills to be spurned.

Politics is not about individual gratification. Politics is about serving the broader public interest and the national interest. It is about peace and war, poverty and opportunity, freedom and oppression, excellence versus mediocrity, competitiveness, productivity, and economic prosperity.

Conservatives are about preserving the best of our past by weeding out that which requires change. At our best, we have the courage to disengage from the Liberal myth of entitlement, the socialist institutionalization of envy, and the neo-conservative embrace of greed. We embrace the more practical, rooted, and

Canadian expression of conservatism that speaks to community, responsibility, nationhood, and the true freedom of citizens in a nation that pays its way, defends its interests at home and abroad, and has the national resolve to prevail.

Neo-conservatives have every right to take the narrower view that sees society as little more than an intrusion upon an individual's right to advance his or her own cause at all costs. But in the end, neo-conservatism is a politics of premature withdrawal that does not have relevance in society as a whole. It is the politics of no politics at all. It is not the stuff for a Progressive Conservative rebirth, nor the stuff to reignite the Tory mission through a broad insurgency from coast to coast.

The challenge facing Conservatives is how to articulate a national vision when the role of government is not only changing rapidly but being replaced by a series of competing sovereignties that should cause all political parties to reflect on their raison d'être, their organization, and their strategy. Conservatives have no right to be part of Canada's future simply because we played a major role in its past. We will be a part of the future only if we earn it. The only way to do that is to understand and explain what we believe in and why we are necessary.

If we can't do that with authority, good cheer, and an ability to reach out that is compelling and humane, we will face a serious battle for relevance. But if we remember who we are and what our purpose is, we'll rekindle a larger Tory flame and ignite a popular Tory insurrection that hungers for the community Canadians build and the immense benefits each Canadian can earn from that kind of confident and self-assured national community.

The opportunity for a meaningful Conservative revival will never be better than it is now. Renewal has always begun in the provinces and it has begun in the provinces again. The challenge as Tories is to see it through not to some Gingrichian dialectic between good and evil but to a Canadian resolution that is a balance of pragmatism, common sense, and a lot of heart.

Conservative parties in Canada are more comfortable at the provincial level, and voters have traditionally been more comfortable electing them at that level. In the post-war period, Shaw in P.E.I., Flemming and Hatfield in New Brunswick, Stanfield and Buchanan in Nova Scotia, Moores and Peckford in Newfoundland, Duplessis and Daniel Johnson Sr. in Quebec, Drew, Frost, Robarts, and Davis in Ontario, Roblin, Lyon, and Filmon in Manitoba, and Lougheed in Alberta all came to represent the pragmatic Tory provincial tradition.

Ralph Klein in Alberta and Mike Harris in Ontario should be seen in that perspective. Both were given long odds. Both campaigned on a down-to-earth "we can't spend what we don't have" fiscal message, calling for a better targeting of scarce resources and a move to preserve what really matters in health care, education, crime prevention, and the safety net by paring back what matters less. This is simply a reassertion of the party's pragmatic roots that help define it, locally and nationally, at its best. The continuity between Bob Stanfield running a frugal Nova Scotia government and the economies brought in by Klein and Harris is unbroken. The more moderate and frugal approach employed by Gary Filmon in Manitoba is in keeping with this tradition. Conservative pragmatism and frugality are alive and well and being practiced.

Nationally, there will be triumphs to incorporate and mistakes to learn from. The challenge in 1997–98 will be to find the way to sustain the progressive social framework around health care, the poor, and education while liberating the forces that generate profit, diminish deficits, and advance economic growth. The Conservative tradition is at work in the provinces to find the best way, with clear mandates to do so. (In this vital national process, Reform is neither relevant nor a player. It will enter the next election without roots or wings, and can only hope to propel its interests through stirring up interregional or linguistic rivalries that play to the worst side of the Canadian psyche, an approach the party took throughout Charlottetown and the most recent Quebec referendum.)

Progressive Conservatives now have the opportunity to devise a new agenda for Canadians. In that process, government's role is a point of fundamental consideration. While the perception among neo-conservatives is that being in government is somewhat like being in a common bawdy house—if you are involved, you don't want anyone to know—Tories can still see government and the governmental process as involving the positive pursuit of innovative, collective responses to issues that are a mix between competing interests. Tories believe that government can be a legitimate instrument to deal with fundamental issues and that a government, accountable to a parliament, that attacks a specific problem with common sense can be effective.

This is not an argument for more government. Government that is bloated tends to become too pervasive, overbearing, and oppressive, its legitimacy becomes questioned, and its capacity to provide leadership is weakened. Bloated government often makes a common mistake in the public-policy process, which is to assume that to govern means always to act, always to intervene, always to try to artificially redirect where society is headed. Sometimes governing is just being there when the phone rings. Sometimes governing is being able to respond to a problem that is too large for any number of citizens to deal with on their own. Sometimes it is just competent case work, pointing the way to existing programs. Governing does not always have to involve the reconstruction and realignment of policy priorities. There is such a thing as doing too much, as being too ambitious and insensitive to the constraints on what government is. That said, there are times when government does have to intervene and say, "There is a higher public interest here and this is what we must do."

Those basic tasks that all governments must carry out have not been re-examined in years. We have not asked, what it is that we are doing in government? How are we doing it? Why are we doing it? Does this or that government activity relate to our core values? If not, why are those activities being performed? What does government do that it perhaps need not do? What does government now not do that it perhaps should? Given some answers, the nation's resources can be applied appropriately.

The fundamental question is: what is the mission of government? Without understanding why government is there, all the countervailing arguments over policy choices will produce nothing but the normal government stance, which is inertia.

Of all government's missions, none is more important than ensuring equality of opportunity. Government is not for helping the wealthy, the powerful, and those with vested interests. Last anyone checked, they were doing okay. Government is for the people who don't have a large union to protect them on their job sites. It is for low-income people who despite all their efforts cannot break out of the cycle of poverty. It is for coming to the rescue when the odds are so stacked against the "little guy" that only government *can* come to the rescue. If government isn't about reaching out to people whose circumstances are difficult, what is it for?

Government has a duty to guarantee all Canadians a measure of fairness and a measure of equal access to education, health care, a clean environment, and a reasonable place to live. There is a fundamental imbalance when entire groups of Canadians are outside the mainstream of economic and social participation. Conservatism especially has to grapple with the issue of reaching out to those who are permanently disenfranchised. The alternative is to accept a permanent waste of human resources, a permanent locking out of individuals who have as much right to participate in society as anyone else. Ultimately, the alternative is to accept a permanent class structure, which is inimical to what conservatism should be about. Income security and a taxation system that facilitates freedom of choice for people who are trying to improve their circumstances should be addressed as a matter of priority.

Equality of opportunity should be first and foremost, and every policy put forward in every government department should be put to the test. Does the policy contribute to equality of opportunity, is it silent on the issue, or does it effectively thwart such equality? If we looked at our policies on health care, education, skills retraining, family support, child poverty, and a host of others in light of equality of opportunity, we would change them radically. We would have fewer dollars going into programs everyone knows contribute to equality of opportunity not one whit and would then have the fiscal flexibility to direct financial resources into programs that do.

Insensitivity to issues of social justice will spawn challenges to the legitimacy of democratic and capitalist values. Some business theorists may pooh-pooh the relevance of any such challenge and point to weakening trade unions as proof of their lesser concern. But we should not assume that our infrastructure is so strong as to resist riots by the unemployed, immigration backlashes, housing crises, or insolvency of the healthcare system. All are more real threats than we would like to admit.

Social justice can be sustained through a creative commitment to a capitalism premised on values intrinsic to human well-being. Government, as an arbiter of fairness and the only instrument ultimately accountable to public will, is not an evil to be avoided in this process. It is a limited instrument that can be immensely constructive in shaping society and articulating the values we share and hope to maintain. In the end, social justice—the right to security of person, the right to work and to equality of opportunity, with all that that implies—is the ultimate fruit of capitalism and freedom living together in a democracy.

Government would do well to remember that nationalism is not just an extension of ethnicity and geography. It is an extension of a shared commitment to a quality of life and to the values of a way of life that people feel at home with and warm towards and are very much a part of. A nation cannot just be some sort of hotel where people live for a time, order up room service, and leave. There has to be more to a country than that, and government has to be the provider of the atmosphere in which the "more to it" can be defined.

Certain values, one hopes, may be perpetual, but the ways those values are expressed change over time. It is a primary duty of government to give contemporary expression to those values, not only to help give shape to the foundations of social cohesion but also to help citizens see some legitimacy in government and the political process. The legitimacy of government depends on a relationship with the people whereby individual citizens can look at their government and see a reflection of themselves. The reflection may not always be pretty, pleasant, or terribly noble. But a government's capacity to reflect the country and articulate national values is critical to the survival of the nation.

Leadership in a social or corporate organization is tied to team-building and making sure that every representative of the organization understands the same issues and has the same positive attitudes about serving the organization's clientele. In a similar way, government as a collective but indivisible entity has to exercise leadership in a society by what it says and the positions it takes on issues of concern.

Politicians of all political affiliations have too often and for too long believed that the way to exercise leadership is to use one of the regulatory, legislative, fiscal, or economic instruments available to show that "we mean what we say and we say what we mean." The desire to do that has increased as cynicism about the political process has increased. What the politicians are really doing is playing to the media bias towards "solutionism."

The media have a rather liberal view of society and believe that every problem has a rational solution. The effectiveness of any leadership is often judged by the people, through the media, in terms of who finds the best solution and who finds it first. But the fact is that there is a host of problems that do not have rational solutions and will be with us in some measure for a long time to come. The leadership that can be shown on those issue is one of demonstrated sensitivity and interest. Leadership is shown by what the government's values are, how well those values are articulated, and how coherent government is in finding concrete expressions of them.

The same kind of leadership can be shown by a political party, which is, after all, a public instrument, not a private gathering of aficionados. One of a party's most fundamental roles in a democracy is to afford some leverage to voters who have more important things to do with their lives than immerse themselves in the trivia of day-to-day politics. The critical issue for Conservatives must be how to fashion a public instrument that is of as much use to people between elections as it is during them.

Conservatives have a duty to think about the context within which we must operate as a party and how that context can be made clearer, more precise, open, and democratic and less prone to the isolation and incestuousness that political parties often breed and the system can unwittingly promote. We must have some fundamental views about how parliamentary democracy operates, what must be preserved of what is best about the past and what can and what must be changed. Fortunately for Conservatives, what is best about the past constitutes about as firm a premise for making changes as could be hoped for.

There is nothing more isolating and divisive between a party as public instrument and the taxpayers who wish to make use of it than the notion of the fulltime elected career politician. In the past, Canadians elected to public office left their businesses, stores, farms, schoolrooms, law offices, surgeries, and factories to go to their provincial capital or Ottawa for short periods. They spent most of their days in their constituencies earning a living like the taxpayers who elected them, remaining in daily contact with the people on the street who determined the priority of issues.

The growth of the bureaucracy under successive Liberal administrations caused thoughtful people to propose longer parliamentary sessions in Ottawa and many of the provinces so that parliamentarians could "be in charge" and be held accountable to the people for programs that required fulltime oversight. This produced a call to professionalize the MP's role, broaden his or her staff, and provide larger salaries, greater benefits, more travel costs, local constituency offices, and all the rest so that MPs could discharge their gruelling duties in Ottawa while still addressing local constituency problems.

The professionalized politician produced advisers, staff, secretaries, drivers, bureaucratic aides, and outside consultants.

The media almost involuntarily responded to the professionalization by concluding that politics was the most important news to cover and broadcast, mainly because it is also the cheapest to cover and broadcast.

The cycle of politicians in all parties and media conspiring, often unwittingly, to create the notion that all community problems have political and governmental solutions produced a cult of "solutionism" that created expectations no reasonable person could otherwise think appropriate. All political parties have been part of this process. All have profited from it. All have been ambushed by it. The travails of political parties themselves pale into insignificance when compared to the damage this professionalist cycle has done to the country and to democracy.

The populism that demands referendums on almost everything— which the Reform Party would use to advance its case against the elites in Ottawa—stems not so much from right or left, but from the hard fact that government's agenda has grown so massive and beyond its capacity to sustain, intellectually and fiscally, that the only possible response for those who finance it from afar is to get some of the decision-making power back into their own hands and rein in those who have drifted so far from the realities of life.

There is no need to throw one's hands up in despair and dismiss all this as the way of the world. Conservatives can advance the cause of less and less intrusive government and a less unworkable and unaffordable agenda by insisting that no parliament or legislature should be meeting more than every second month and never for more than two weeks in any one month.

Conservatives can advance an approach to electoral politics that encourages people to run for office who intend to keep their jobs, remain in their communities, and visit Ottawa only when necessary. If bureaucracies are too large to be managed in this fashion, then bureaucracies should be slashed, with fewer responsibilities and jurisdictions and fewer programs and expenditures.

The premise of democracy is that people choose representatives from their own community to go forward and make the right decisions on public policies that must be decided on a level broader than just their community. If those representatives become separated from the community, that premise is weakened at its foundation. The premise of government by one's neighbour is a Conservative and democratic one we should embrace with renewed vigour. The systemic exigencies of large governments are all self-justifying, imposing constraints upon the democratic part of the system necessary to respond to those exigencies. That's not what democracy is about.

This is not to suggest that for important national matters like monetary or defence policy, or areas where technical expertise and continuity are required, a permanent bureaucracy of modest size and standing is inappropriate. It is to suggest that the massive size of the federal bureaucracy, the massive agenda that the federal government has appropriated unto itself since Confederation, has gone too far, costs too much, and dilutes the influence of average citizens upon decisions that are most important to them, their families, and their communities.

Conservatives would do well to get back to basic principles, to the greater role of provinces, to diminished national jurisdictions, to less forced and contrived parliamentary activity in, and less public spending from, Ottawa, and to the return of more authority, spending control, and decision-making responsibility to levels of government closer to where we all live and build our lives.

Our national vision as Tories must also extend beyond the repair of the system and the democratization of a parliament to a view of how we maximize the balance between freedom and responsibility in a way that generates opportunities for economic and social progress. We must have a view of what instruments beyond, as well as within, government are most appropriate to use in that cause.

The role of government beyond maintaining order, sustaining the cohesiveness of the nation, contributing to equality of opportunity, and ensuring coherent trade, monetary, defence, and foreign policy should be limited. Returning taxpayers' dollars to taxpayers, or at least to provincial and municipal jurisdictions closer to the taxpayer, should be an abiding priority.

As we reduce counterproductive areas of expenditure, we also have to ensure that in those areas where the national government does have fundamental responsibility, the government does have at its disposal the tools and cash to do the job. We have lived for too long in a world where federal governments did not have the money necessary to discharge their primary responsibility for national defence while federal politicians competed with provincial and municipal politicians to hand out grants for community centres well beyond the purview of the federal government as envisaged in the constitution.

The government that does substantially less but does it well would sustain national legitimacy and consensus far more effectively than a government whose agenda is too large, whose budget is too stretched, whose taxation is too excessive, and whose intervention in the economy and society is far too pervasive and unhelpful.

A Tory who believes that government can be a constructive force for good understands that cooperation between volunteer and private forces, and the efficient movement of capital to support investment, will be enhanced by a national government that doesn't set the agenda but tries to be constructive to the agenda set by the economic, social, and human forces in society as a whole.

This is not about *laissez-faire* government. It is about government consistent with the new realities of international agreements, international capital flows, and international mobility of labour, technology, goods, and services, all of which are well beyond the purview of any national administration in any free country to control. A government that doesn't understand that, as many Liberal governments have failed to do, is a government destined to be a disruptive and destructive force, however unwittingly, in the growth of society. This is about liberation, not abdication. This is about reality, not withdrawal. This is about engagement, not surrender. This is about making the case for a conservatism rooted in the communities and values of generations of Canadians, a conservatism that is activist and crusading, progressive and humane. It is about the kind of insurgency Conservatives must be prepared to mount in the marketplace of ideas if we are to repel not only the forces of "expediency at any cost" but the equally dangerous neo-conservatives who use populism to mask the destruction of much that is good about our way of life.

If Conservatives have learned anything in the period from Diefenbaker to Charest, it is that when we know our way, understand the larger forces we are trying to address, reflect and respect the will of the people, and hold fast to our conviction about a society dominated by no single power base—especially bureaucratic and governmental—then we have made our most significant contributions, experienced our most substantive successes, and moved the country most dramatically ahead despite the difficulty of the issues.

The Conservative Party now has more options and opportunities than a superficial assessment of its prospects might suggest. Every insurgency must have its core of supporters who are with the party for the right reasons, in good times and bad. October 25, 1993, saw more than two million Canadians stand fast with a party that in the election campaign offered neither leadership nor compelling ideas.

Since the 1993 collapse, I've spoken at countless federal and provincial party riding meetings, fundraisers, and PC Youth Federation events across the country. What I have found is encouraging. The electoral setback, despite its monstrous proportions, has had a liberating effect. There is a new vibrancy about both party democracy and policy development. There seems to be no discouragement. Membership numbers remain strong. Two years of small-minded and ineffective Reform activity in the House of Commons has been an added tonic. There is nothing so refreshing as seeing the party that split your vote and helped the Liberals into power come a cropper over its own hypocrisy and diminished perspective.

We're extremely well served by a young, dynamic, competent leader whose intensity, humour, and personality strengthens our capacity to rebuild a bridge with each and every Canadian. Jean Charest is the right person for these difficult times, and Conservatives are fortunate to benefit from his leadership. With the relaxed demeanour and comfortable conversational fluidity of a cross between Peter Gzowski and Tom Snyder, Charest has an outstanding media opportunity. The schoolmarmish hectoring of Preston Manning and the tortured, timeless, unimproved syntax of Jean Chrétien all plant the seeds for a warm and engaging Charest with something important to say making great gains.

As leader, he has begun rebuilding in an exemplary fashion, tending to the rank and file, flattening the party hierarchy, and making the party democratic in a way that creates direct accountability to a new National Council made up of all riding presidents. As local associations renew or elect new executives, the nature of the National Council will change, producing the kind of dynamic that will secure the party to its own grass roots in a way never seen before. Making the party more democratic also gave Charest good reason to visit many parts of the country and offer support and encouragement to the membership. The affection for Charest and the loyalty to him in the party are palpable. Some neo-conservatives have been critical of

his lack of focus on policy, but any failure to address the sense of dis-
enfranchisement party members had the right to feel after the Campbell campaign deserted both the left and right of the Tory spectrum
would have been a serious miscalculation.

As the runup to a 1997 election begins, the challenge will be not
only policy process but also policy substance. The simplistic neo-con
"self-evident" and exclusionary truths of the Buchanan-Gramm version of barbed-wire conservatism will not suffice, nor will the make-
it-up-as-you-go-along policy-by-pollster tradition. A process by
which rank-and-file Conservatives can shape policy and develop the
party's manifesto for 1997 is vital.

But Charest also has the opportunity and the duty to put his own
stamp on policy debate and development. Who he is and what kind
of party democracy he believes in are what the party and the broader
conservative population beyond the party now have the right to know.
Leadership is about civility, integrity, and links to the real world, as it
was with Bill Davis. It is about process, as it was with Joe Clark. It is
about populism, as it was in the early days of John Diefenbaker. It is
about courage, as it was with Brian Mulroney. It is about moderation
and balance, as it was with Robert Stanfield. It must also be about
conviction. Jean Charest's capacity to embody and amplify that conviction will be vital to his success and to the revitalization of the
Conservative Party.

We are best when we are outsiders, and the insiders now are the
Liberals, Reformers, and Bouchardists. It is they who are responsible
for the lack of fiscal progress, failures in foreign policy and constitutional issues, the destruction of our armed forces, excessive centralization, and the disregard for locally driven social justice and decency
that Ottawa so clearly reflects. And in the eyes and hearts of the men
and women, young and old, whom I speak to at meetings across the
country, I find no lack of will, no lack of optimism, and no lack of
fire in the belly for the fight to build a broad, conviction-based coalition that will attract moderate Reformers, disenchanted Bouchardists,
and uncomfortable business-oriented Liberals back to a Tory banner.

We have a chance to shape a cohesive national vision within a
Tory framework of order, stability, and responsibility. We have a
chance to expand on the freedoms and opportunities of our people by
making our party into an instrument as active at the local level on
community concerns, with or without seeking local office, as it might

be at the national level in support of national goals. We have the ability to articulate a role in Canada and international affairs that is neither satellite nor non-combatant but reflects our democratic institutions, our national values, our history, and our genuine interests with the might and will to defend them at home and abroad, diplomatically, economically, and militarily when necessary.

We have the capacity to propose a massive redesign of our bureaucratic systems to liberate creative and communitarian forces now stymied by systemic exigencies that have little to do with democracy or the human condition. We have the ability to build from the grass roots with a civil Conservatism of hope, a Toryism of principle, and a self-knowledge that reflects the premises we bring to public life in this country.

This is not a time of setback or dislocation. It is a time when the foundations of our approach to public life, public affairs, community development, and economic opportunity can be put in place. Being honest with ourselves about the strengths and weaknesses of those from Diefenbaker to Campbell who have led our coalition neither diminishes our prospects nor dilutes the Conservative family we share with millions of Canadians who understand fundamentally that when we get it right, we are right for them, for their aspirations, and for the country. This is a time of opportunity the likes of which we shall not see for many decades to come. We must not let it pass.

Our established roots should not prevent us from reaching out to less-established communities. Our experience in government should not constrain us from relishing the role of reducing and restructuring it. The pain of exile must not deter us from the route of conviction and principle. Trying to engineer our way back into prominence or government without conviction would mean surrendering to an exile longer and more justified than we have ever known.

The conviction that we can build a society without building more government and that there is a special balance between freedom and responsibility is worthy of our continued loyalty. The conviction that the achievements and successes of Canadian society are those of its people and not its governments remains worthy of our undoubted support. The conviction that less power at the centre, less spending, less taxation, less intervention, and less bureaucracy will liberate rather than disadvantage Canadians is worthy of being upheld. The belief in the nation and its defence against those who would put it in danger and the belief in a social order where freedom is the product of responsibility are convictions we must not desert.

The challenge is also one of never apologizing for what Conservatives have tried to do when in office, especially the difficult but necessary changes that ensured a modern and competitive economic framework for Canadians. None who have led us has been perfect. Some have been more successful than others. But they, and what we stood for with and for them, can only be marginalized if we fail to carry on the battle for a Conservative tomorrow.

Being frank with other Canadians and with other Conservatives about our perspectives and about the critical fibres of any new banner we may weave is as good a way as any to embrace the Conservative challenge. It will be joined in small towns, corporate boardrooms, classrooms, farm kitchens, and on the factory floor. It must be as much at home in the union hall as it is in the accountant's office or co-op meeting.

Conservatism is a liberating framework for a more balanced, less bureaucratic, and more productive tomorrow. It is a framework for success and freedom. It is the bulwark of community and stability.

Our challenge is not only to keep the proverbial torch held high but to make sure it conveys substantially more light than heat on issues that matter. Anything else would be beneath the Tory mission and the genuine promise of the Conservative challenge. The party's mission has never mattered more and the opportunity has never been greater. We must not and will not yield. The battle cry remains: No surrender.

EPILOGUE

IT IS PRECISELY BECAUSE OF THE POST-REFERENDUM politics we face that I remain convinced that a dynamic and progressive Conservative Party is a necessary national instrument.

The near-death experience of the close defeat of the separatists in Quebec in October of 1995 and the continuing expansion of trade with our free-trade partners indicate that the large choices made by Conservatives when last in national office were the right choices. Without Charlottetown, Bouchard would have won an easy victory. Boils were lanced and bridges were built. The courage to do what was right may have been separated from partisan benefit by a disastrous leadership change. But, most important, the nation was preserved and economic opportunities were sustained and broadened.

Each Conservative leader I have had the privilege of serving reflected both the great strengths and weaknesses of the party, each in unique measure. Yet it is perhaps from Bill Davis and David MacDonald that I gleaned the best lessons on the issue of style in public life. I remember as if it were yesterday crossing Ottawa's Wellington Street with David in 1971 and noticing patches on both knees of his suit. I asked whether it was time to get a new one. His reply: with two residences, four kids, and an MP's salary of $12,000, suits weren't a priority. "Besides," he offered matter-of-factly, "lots of people in the riding of Egmont, P.E.I., don't have suits." His honest, no-nonsense disinterest in the trappings of power always struck me as the only way to sustain the legitimacy of those temporarily entrusted with elected power.

I believe it was during the 1988 general election campaign that the Mulroney campaign bus stopped at Bill Davis's residence on Main Street in Brampton, only to find him mowing the lawn. There was nothing contrived about this. Bill Davis could be found mowing the lawn, eating with the family at Pizza Hut or Wendy's, or out smelt fishing in the early spring with the locals at Honey Harbour. He never lost touch with who he was and where he had come from.

Nor was there was anything contrived or phony about Brian Mulroney. The upwardly mobile Quebec business and political elite, in whose ranks he had earned a spot through dint of hard work and success, were not self–conscious about living well, dressing well, and appearing to enjoy both. To have adopted the somewhat more tweedy and dishevelled modesty of Ottawa would have been to raise phoniness to an art form. For the vital issues of free trade and constitutional reconciliation, the voting population outside of civil-service Ottawa meant more than Ottawa-contrived, down-market, and subsidized pretences.

All the attributes the party needed for victory Mulroney cleverly and wilfully propelled to historic successes. Not since Sir John A. have Conservatives done better; and Macdonald's contemporary and historical reputation has had its share of ups and downs, although he never faced the degree of vilification so focused on Mulroney.

As Kim Campbell found out, intuitive partisan instincts *do* matter. Their absence, and the absence of a history in the party essential to their sustenance, is, in the crucible of a campaign, utterly lethal.

Despite unreasonable criticism from some on the far right who believe that conviction is only of value if it squeezes out all moderation, Jean Charest is well placed to advance the Conservative Party from its present diminished parliamentary status to a position of major force for good in the public life and politics of our country. The courage and clarity of his referendum performance against the forces of fragmentation, xenophobia, and despair in Quebec speak eloquently to the compelling voice for a new politics of clear-minded choices Canadians have the right to expect.

As a happy warrior now fully engaged in the triple priorities of family, business, and academe, the determination to do what I can, as but one volunteer, for nation and party has not dimmed. Democracy does not work when its beneficiaries, the people, opt out or disengage. However much some in media circles may agonize with a pervasive cynicism about men and women in public life, none among us taxpayers or voters can afford to yield to that message of despair. Yielding in that fashion only turns the abdicators into victims, victims of the very democracy in which they lose interest. It is true that the processes of Parliament, local riding associations, and party policy debates lack the quick fixes and easy gratification of a TV remote control. But then the things that matter in life—love, caring, kindness, volunteering, community, faith, trust—are of more enduring value.

Canada is the greatest country in the world. And the Conservative Party is one of its great truly national instruments for self-government. And what October 30, 1995, clearly demonstrated was that we can no longer take self-government for granted. The departure of Quebec would massively diminish the quality of life and standard of living of all Canadians—and make the likelihood of a new confederation less than assured. We would face a period of deconstruction in Canada that could well see the collapse of central government and the rise of regional groupings in a loose currency union, more like the commonwealth of independent states that replaced, ever so ineffectively, the U.S.S.R. Certainly we could not expect anything remotely as cohesive as the present Confederation, the new Europe, or the American union to the south.

And, as we drew back from Canada to four Puerto Rican–style commonwealths, our noses planted firmly against the outside of the American picture window, we would, all of us, lose any meaningful element of self-government. Americans would dictate terms—for B.C. to ship lumber and gas, for Alberta to ship oil and gas, for the Prairies to ship agricultural goods, for Ontario and Quebec to ship cars, auto parts, steel. The urge to Manifest Destiny would be immense among an America with a stagnant domestic policy and even more dim social-policy prospects. And if sovereigntists in Quebec delude themselves into believing that America will respect their linguistic, cultural, and legal distinctiveness outside the Canadian rubric, they are in for the worst fall of all. Non-tariff linguistic and regulatory barriers, monopolistic statist support of Quebec stock prices on domestic and international exchanges, and a separate currency will all fall away—along with the cultural-industry exemption of the free trade accord. The price for U.S. support for an independent Quebec's entry into NAFTA will be the de facto homogenization and harmonization of Quebec rules and regulation with those of the U.S. marketplace.

But the will to self-government that has kept us an independent country, the will to set aside British colonialism, French dirigiste condescension aimed at Quebec, American republicanism and expansionism, and the remnants of French and British aristocratic pretence have shaped and moulded our particular Canadian democracy. The price of Quebec independence is the end of our own. Those who in Quebec aspire to independence will experience it for less than a millisecond in the political history of North America. This is not the alarmist excess of someone who would accommodate whatever sovereigntists in Quebec might conjure, but my clear-eyed analysis of the real costs of any failure to accommodate the reasonable mainstream across the nation.

A dynamic process of reconfederation will address the re-engineering of our national institutions of self-government in an image of Canada that reflects present reality, undeniable history, and our prospects as diverse founding peoples in one country.

Federal Liberals are in many ways spent by internal ideological rifts, disengaged and thoughtless policy, and a prime minister who may mean well but faces too much of a conflict between the exigencies of today and the stands he took on Meech and Charlottetown to provide overall leadership. To serve, he will have to change. The prime minister will have to work with the PLQ in Quebec, Jean Charest, and opposition leaders in the provinces to engage in the realistic needs of self-government—and why in Quebec those same needs must reflect the cultural, civil, and linguistic codes that must protect the only majority French-speaking jurisdiction in all of North America.

This is not about rights that are special. It is not about collective versus individual rights. It is about accepting the reality that a French-speaking founding province of Confederation has to be recognized as more than a cultural presence. It must be recognized as one of the founding connections upon which Canada is built—and we must govern in a way that reflects that simple fact. Denying that reality is the surest way to lose it once and for all.

A Conservative Party can help build consensus. As the party of Confederation itself, we can speak to dynamic reconfederation. A national conservative leader who can rally this process, shepherd it and invigorate it, is precisely what the doctor ordered. And, in Jean Charest, it is precisely what we have.

Hillcroft

Kingston, December 1995

INDEX